Emma Kennedy is an actress and writer who appeared in many award-winning comedy shows including *Goodness Gracious Me* and *The Smoking Room*. In 2003 won the Comedy Lounge Best Actress Award for her role in Bill Shakespeare's *Italian Job* and in 2005 won the British Television Advertising Craft Award for Best Actress. She has been writing for TV and radio for over a decade and has won Sony Awards for the *Sunday Format* and *The Now Show*. Her first book was *How to Bring Up Your Parents* and new website is www.emmakennedy.net.

For Midge, who kept me going

The Tent, The Bucket and Me

My Family's Disastrous Attempts to go Camping in the 70s

EMMA KENNEDY

EBURY
PRESS

11 13 15 17 19 18 16 14 12

Published in 2009 by Ebury Press, an imprint of Ebury Publishing
A Random House Group Company

The Random House Group Limited Reg. No. 954009

Addresses for companies within the Random House Group can be found at
www.randomhouse.co.uk

A CIP catalogue record for this book is available from the British Library

The Random House Group Limited supports the Forest Stewardship
Council (FSC), the leading international forest certification organisation.
All our titles that are printed on Greenpeace-approved FSC-certified paper
carry the FSC logo. Our paper procurement policy can be found at
www.rbooks.co.uk/environment

Mixed Sources
Product group from well-managed
forests and other controlled sources
www.fsc.org Cert no. TT-COC-2139
FSC © 1996 Forest Stewardship Council

Printed in the UK by CPI Mackays, Chatham, ME5 8TD

ISBN 9780091926786

To buy books by your favourite authors and register for offers visit
www.rbooks.co.uk

Contents

Introduction

The idea for this book came about when my mother asked me, about two years ago, whether I would like to go on holiday with her and my dad. I refused immediately, swearing that I 'would never go on holiday with them again'. That might seem harsh, but my experience of holidays as a child in the seventies was so dogged with ill luck, it beggars belief. It put me off camping for life.

As we laughed about the dreadful things that happened to us, it struck me that I wanted to write these stories down. And so I began the long process of interviewing my parents about our family holidays. I was amazed by how much we were collectively able to remember: my father had an extraordinary memory for tiny details, my mother for conversations, and the more we talked about our experiences, the more we were able to recall.

'Are you having to make anything up?' That's the question I have been asked repeatedly since starting this book.

My reply has always been the same: 'Sadly not. In fact, I wish I had.'

Everything you are about to read happened. Some names and place names have been changed (because my mother made me), but that's it. I hope you enjoy the book. And that all your holidays are nothing like ours.

Emma Kennedy

The Prologue
in which the universe throws down the gauntlet

I was conceived amidst the smell of damp canvas on stony ground. My life had clattered into the universe on a honeymoon between two people who had no business being married. My parents consummated their happy day on a campsite in Corby. I was unplanned. My life had begun in a tent.

If we were living in Ancient Greece the Fates would have thrown their arms up in horror. Was my destiny to be forever entwined with guy ropes, thick, rusty zips and a pervading aroma of mildew? Or would I, like the heroes before me, be able to surmount the dreadful cards I'd been dealt? If I embarked on an eternal holiday-based struggle, then one day, if the Gods gave me the thumbs up, I might reach the heady peaks of staying in a caravan with a toilet that actually flushed. Imagine that. But I had a long way to go before I reached those blessed shores. My tent trials were only just beginning.

The wedding of my parents had caused something of a stir in the small Welsh mining village of Treherbert. Sitting at the top of the Rhondda valley, the village was typical of the area. Mining was its beating heart, and small, tight terraces squashed themselves into knots at the base of the mountains. Wales's major industry was on its last legs but that was the furthest thing from anyone's mind on a sunny day in August 1966. England had just won the World Cup and one of Treherbert's favourite sons had returned to get married and show off his new bride. It should have been a day of joyous celebrations. But instead, the happy couple was greeted with incredulous stares. The bride was dressed in black. And no one knew why.

'Is it because she's English?' my aunt Gwennie had asked, in a whisper.

'Is it true she's a feminist?' mumbled a neighbour, standing on a flagstone step to get a better look, a suggestion that was beaten down with a flurry of hand gestures and urgent shushing.

The small crowd gathered outside my grandmother's house couldn't believe their eyes. They'd already thrown confetti at the wrong person, my mother's younger sister Phyllis, who had come dressed in white and was now standing, flicking tiny bits of paper off herself, and looking mortified. My mother, who only thirty minutes previously had been declaring that she wasn't going to get married, was wearing a huge, black Spanish mantilla and looking the perfect picture of misery.

'Why can't you be normal!' Phyllis had wailed in an upstairs bedroom. 'This is SO embarrassing!'

'Phyllis!' snapped my mother, Brenda, who was in no mood for platitudes. 'I am NOT getting dressed in white! I will not bow to the patriarchal expectations of society. I am wearing black in solidarity for all women's suffering at the hands of men.'

'Then why are you even GETTING married?' cried her sister.

'All right then,' declared my mother suddenly. 'You're right. I'm not going through with it! That's it! Wedding's off!'

'But I've got dressed now,' whined her sister. 'And Margaret Evans told me if you didn't marry Tony then she would. And she sleeps with firemen.'

'Fuck her then,' replied my mother. And that was that.

My mother stood, dressed in her black outfit, to a deafening silence that was only broken when my father's

brother-in-law Roy came out to do the Scramble, a valley
tradition where pennies are thrown into the street for children
to collect. As the children scurried around her, jostling for
coins, my mother began the short walk to the Welsh Baptist
chapel where she would be wed, cheered on by nothing but
audible gasps. She had refused flowers and had no one to walk
her up the aisle. She was nothing if not determined.

My father, on the other hand, had been quietly looking
forward to his big day, even if the ring he'd got for his fiancée
had been thrown down a cobbled street only three days
previously. He'd chased after it of course because it had cost
him three pounds, but he also knew that within five minutes
his wife-to-be, volatile at the best of times, would have
changed her mind back again. Tony was a simple fellow, the
sixth child in a family of seven. He had grown up in squashed
proximity with his siblings, sharing a bed with three of his
brothers and, because he was the artistic one, spending most
of his mornings having to draw lines up his sisters' legs to
replicate stockings. As the youngest boy, he had been saved
from having to work down the pit and was the only member
of his family to have gone to college and left the valley. He
was the one who got away. But now he was back. And it
wasn't quite the triumphant return he'd been hoping for.

Not a single member of my father's family mentioned the
bride in black, a sure sign that everyone was appalled. Not
only that, but with my grandfather the minister at the chapel
where they were getting married, the fact that the bride was
dressed for a funeral was a source of deep embarrassment. In
a last-minute attempt to bring a sense of normality to the
proceedings, my grandfather slipped the organist a couple of
bob and told him to 'Play anything', even though my mother
had been quite adamant that there should be no music.
She walked up the aisle, on her own, to Handel's Scipio,
black mantilla billowing around her. The congregation was

stunned. My father just smiled. The sooner this was over with, the better.

Contrary to appearances, my parents were very much in love. They had met eleven months previously at a school in Bedfordshire. My mother, who looked like a Spanish version of Julie Christie, had trained to be an English teacher. When she walked into the staffroom for the first time, my father's eyes popped out on stalks at first sight and he turned to his friend Mike, the head of PE, and literally said 'She's mine.' But there was a slight problem: my mother was engaged. To someone else. And she hated Welsh accents. So my father, being a shy sort of fellow, didn't make his move straight away. Instead, he confided in another female teacher, Grace, told her that he quite liked the look of the new English teacher, sat back and waited for the gossip to trickle in her direction.

'So Brenda,' said Grace, over a Tupperware box filled with home-made egg sandwiches, 'what do you think of Tony? Do you like him?'

'Hmm,' replied my mother with a shrug. 'He's all right.'

'Tony!' declared Grace, running up to him in a corridor. 'I've got a tree in my back garden that needs cutting down. You wouldn't come over on Sunday and give Joe a hand with it, would you? I'd be ever so grateful.'

'Sure,' said my father. 'I'll bring over a few beers.'

'Brenda!' shouted Grace, five minutes later. 'If you're not doing anything this Sunday...do you want to come round to ours? Tony's coming over to help Joe cut down the tree in the back. We'll have some beers. Yes?'

'Lovely,' said my mother.

The trap was set and the sequence of events that would lead to my birth had been thrown into motion. My entire existence was down to a dead tree and a six-pack of beer. You can make of that what you will.

The weather that Sunday was unusually pleasant and as my father pulled off his shirt and hurled an axe over his head, my mother couldn't help but stare. Despite all her best efforts, watching Tony ripping up a tree from its roots was quietly thrilling. Her fiancé, a bookish fellow called Malcolm, was not given to displays of masculinity and as the sweat trickled down my father's chest and his light blue eyes sparkled, my mother realised, with a degree of horror, that she fancied him rotten. One arm tickle and a considerable snog in the front seat of a blue Morris Minor later and my mother knew she was in trouble.

'Malcolm's got halitosis,' declared Phyllis, putting her cards of preference firmly on the table. 'Plus Tony brought Mummy a sack of onions. And coal. Don't forget the coal.'

Four months down the line, Brenda still hadn't made her mind up whether it was going to be Tony or Malcolm. She would spend the week with Tony and the weekend with Malcolm. How she got away with it was anyone's guess. But at Christmas, at home with her mother and sister, with time to think things through, she knew she had to make a decision. Torn between her fiancé and the man she couldn't keep her hands off, she turned to her sister for help. Phyllis, blunt as ever, was in no doubt: Tony was the better prospect. 'Does Malcolm's breath REALLY smell?' asked Brenda, chewing her bottom lip.

'It bloody STINKS,' nodded Phyllis. 'And he's got a wonky eye.'

And so on Boxing Day, wrapped up against the bitter wind, my mother walked through the snow to send my father a telegram. 'PLEASE COME', it read. They were engaged the following day.

My arrival came nine months and six days after the wedding. The timing was so near the knuckle that my father's eldest brother Gwyn had taken him to one side and asked if the wedding had been a necessity but, despite all the suspicions to the contrary, my conception was above board and shipshape. My parents had been forced to take their honeymoon in the unromantic surroundings of Corby, a steel town in Northamptonshire, because they were both about to start work at one of the local comprehensives. With two weeks to go before term started, they needed to find somewhere to live and my dad, ever brimful with bright ideas, had suggested that they buy a tent and camp while searching for a council house. The tent in which I was conceived was a flash affair. Flush with a little extra cash from family and friends, my father had got overexcited and fallen victim to the tent shop salesman's easy charms. So, instead of buying a small, two-man ridge tent, Tony had come away the proud owner of a continental frame tent. 'Just come in from France,' the salesman had said with a wink.

'Look at that!' my dad had said later, beaming. 'It's got a SEPARATE bedroom compartment!'

'And we can stand up in it!' squealed Brenda, because even she was impressed.

They had spent their wedding night in a hotel in Cardiff but a deafening military tattoo at the nearby castle had put any thoughts of romance on the back burner. As the windows rattled and the bed shook, my just-married parents sat, propped up in bed with cotton wool stuffed in their ears. The thought of leaving the next day to spend their honeymoon in Corby wasn't quite the sharp thrill it might have been but necessity dictated the circumstances and, besides, they were going camping. It would be fun. Wouldn't it?

The just-married couple had driven to the pretty village of Rockingham on the outskirts of Corby, where honey-coloured stone cottages crept up a steep hillside towards a castle perched at the top. There was one pub in the village, the Sondes Arms, and it was here, pints in hand, that my parents decided they would be bold: rather than drive about searching for a campsite, they would put up their tent in the first field they could find.

An unseasonable, bitter wind was blowing through Rockingham that night but my parents, flushed with the just-married glow, didn't mind one bit and, finding a field that didn't have cows in it, my father set about the slightly arduous task of getting the tent erected. Having had a practice run in the back garden of his still unmarried digs, my dad was confident that he knew what he was doing, but the practice run had been done in broad daylight – and with two mates helping him. Now he had to put up the tent on his own, in a pitch-black field and with his new wife staring on in the moonlight. As my dad grappled around on the grass trying to work out what went where and whether he could find the pegs, my mother laid out the honeymoon feast that had been provided courtesy of a plastic bag from my grandmother. In it there was one small loaf of bread, a large lump of cheddar cheese and six Welsh cakes that had been thrown in at the last minute by my father's sister-in-law Peggy. As they sat, shivering in a three-quarters-finished tent, with chunks of bread in their hands and taking bites out of the block of cheese because they'd forgotten to bring a knife, there was an air of innocent abandon. A new dawn was coming and it was closer than they thought. 'Are you sure we don't need the inner tent?' my mother had asked, casting a look about her.

'Absolutely,' said my father, putting an arm round her. 'The tent is totally fine without it.'

What Dad omitted to tell her was that he had also forgotten to waterproof the tent and that night, as their just-married passions reached a climax and my first spark of life burst into the universe, my mother looked up at my father and said, 'Why am I lying in a pool of water?'

It was an omen of things to come.

Chapter One

The Bucket

It's 1970. I'm three years old, I've got a pudding bowl of white-blonde hair and we're about to go on our first family holiday. Matters have been moving apace in our family unit and, having realised that Corby wasn't quite the green and pleasant land they'd been hoping for, my parents have upped sticks and moved to that bastion of New Town glory, Stevenage. We're living on an estate that's set around a square. It's all part of the brand-new world of modern urban thinking. In the middle of the square there's a scrub of roses where the boy next door, who my mother always whispers, 'has come from Tower Hamlets', likes to take regular shits. I have two very early memories of this house: one is of my mother banging on our front room window, shaking her fist and shouting, 'Stop shitting!' and the other is of a large blue bottle that used to sit in the corner of the dining room. I liked sticking my finger in it.

Our holiday destination was Solva, a small coastal village set in the St David's peninsula in West Wales. Not only would my paternal grandmother be coming with us, we would be travelling in a grey Wolseley, a powerful and cramped little motor whose only saving grace was that it had twin carburettors. Sadly, the twin carburettors were to have the same effect on my father's brain as the knowledge that the tent he had bought had come all the way from mainland Europe. Intoxicated by their very presence, my father, at point of purchase, had failed to notice that the chrome writing on the boot was the same colour as the car: it had been resprayed and what lurked beneath the immediate sheen was a host of mechanical woes. By the time we came to our first family holiday, the car was on its last legs. Bits were falling off by degrees and every time a door was opened or shut, there would be a tinkling accompaniment of rust rattling its way loose. 'Are you sure this is going to make it to Wales?' my mother had asked, arms folded.

'Yeeeesssss!' my father had wailed, as if that was THE most obvious thing in the world.

My unplanned arrival had had a cataclysmic effect on my parents' summers. Rendered instantly impecunious, my mother could only sit back and stare as her single, childless chums jetted off to exotic Greek islands or, even better, as far as my mother was concerned, to the South of France, a place that mustered wafting, elysian daydreams. Not for her a fortnight in the baking sun or long cocktails into the night: with thoughts of what could have been crashing round like dodgems, my mother was a grumbling pool of resentment before the bags were even packed.

'WHY do we have to go to Wales?' asked my mother, sitting on the edge of her bed and throwing her arms in the air. 'You know what the weather's like. It'll be shit.' My father, who was busy ticking things off his checklist, was in no mood to listen.

'We've gone through this a thousand times,' he replied, on hands and knees, as he retrieved a large water carrier from the back of a cupboard in their bedroom. 'We've got to go. I need to see the family. And Mam needs a holiday.'

'Tony,' began my mother, her hazel eyes ablaze. 'Taking your seventy-year-old, diabetic mother camping is hardly going to be a holiday. She's got a heart condition. It's ridiculous!'

But the die was cast. We were going camping. And we were taking a recently bereaved pensioner with us. What could possibly go wrong?

The car was packed to bursting. Like a swollen corpse, it threatened to erupt at any moment. Dad had used a sheet of chicken wire as a makeshift roof rack with everything we possessed teetering into a precarious peak. My parents didn't have much but, like refugees, everything we did have was piled on top of the car. There was a tent, tent poles, a camping stove, a ground sheet, two saucepans, a kettle, a bag of cutlery, tea towels, proper towels, a washing-up bowl, a folding table, five folding chairs (one extra in case of breakages and/or an unexpected guest), a water carrier, a windbreak, Wellingtons, one battered brown leather suitcase bloated with a month's worth of clothes even though we were only going for a week, a green holdall filled with indiscriminate sundries and, on top of everything, like a malevolent fairy, one triumphant pink, plastic bucket (with lid). Being three, I was allowed two items, space permitting, and had chosen to take a one-eyed teddy called Timmy and a scrawny, chewed-up, man-like rodent in tartan trousers and velvet jacket: his name, Mr Mouse.

The Wolseley's interior was a trim façade. Like the respray, the attractive wooden fascia of the dashboard and plump grey seats belied the cancer that raged within. My father was particularly proud of the steering wheel that he had fitted with a black leather cover, the laced-on splendour adding a requisite splash of glamour to complement the twin carburettors. To prove he meant business, he also wore a pair of black leather driving gloves complete with string backs, whatever the weather. He had even managed to convince my mother, who didn't drive, that they were essential to road safety because they ensured a 'more complete grip of the wheel'. My mother, a nervous passenger at the best of times, treated the driving gloves with the reverence of St Christopher. 'You're not wearing your driving gloves!' she would cry, however short the journey, as if their absence ensured a helter-skelter slide to Hell, and so on they would be pulled, imbuing our car with a talismanic glow. For years I thought that you weren't allowed to drive a car unless you were wearing gloves but then, as I crashed into my teenage years and realised that other people's parents were able to happily go from A to B without them, they formed a tiny part of the chisel that would chip away at my parents' omniscience.

In 1970, there were no such things as seat belts or child harnesses and I would spend hours standing on the back seat staring out the window, my mother alongside me holding on to the back of my pants. The world that flitted by was wondrous: cows in fields, a fort in the distance, a white horse carved into a hillside, everything was a bright, new experience, flashing and fleeting. I was fascinated with everything and never wanted to sleep for fear of missing any passing sensory treat: hedgerows were exhilarating, cobbled streets inconceivable and castles were straight from the books I was read at night. To my parents, the six-hour journey to Wales was as painful as a slow twist of the arm but for me, it was a fizzy treat.

There was no doubt about it; we were excited. Even my mother, who couldn't have hated the idea of camping in Wales with her mother-in-law more if she tried, couldn't contain the frisson that went hand in hand with our first family holiday. My dad, bursting with something primeval and masculine, clutched the steering wheel with the confidence of a hunter-gatherer and sang songs loudly, as if he was at a rugby match. I didn't know it yet, but every holiday we went on would be accompanied by that year's family song, a tune from the charts that we would all belt out with a sense of gay abandon. This year it would be 'Wand'rin' Star' sung by Lee Marvin from the film *Paint Your Wagon*. For some indefinable reason, my father was convinced that he could do a brilliant cowboy accent. He couldn't. Instead, we were treated to a strange Welsh/American hybrid that was so peculiar it was almost chilling. But with no radio in the car we had to make our own entertainment. My mother, whose singing voice was like the sound of a cold recorder, took it upon herself to treat us to a marathon of Simon and Garfunkel songs. Listening to her howling rendition of 'Bridge Over Troubled Water' was the very definition of enthusiasm over talent. But it didn't matter that my parents sounded awful. There was a sense of adventure in the air and it smelled wonderful.

The motorway revolution that began in the 1960s had not yet been completed in 1970 and, due to my mother's insistence that we plan our routes according to the needs of her flimsy bladder, I must have travelled through every market town from East to West, accruing an impressive knowledge of local public amenities as we went. There was the pub in Cheltenham with a toilet with no door, the tea room in Gloucester where you had to buy a scone before you were allowed to wee, the second-hand book shop in Ross on Wye whose ladies' room smelled of burnt paper and the hotel in Stow on the Wold where, if you kept the concierge busy asking about this and also that, my mother could creep off and use the Arthurian-themed lavatories that held their toilet rolls on mini Excaliburs. For my mother, going on holiday was a travel round the great bowls of Britain. It was a mystery that such a tiny woman could generate such massive amounts of urine, but my abiding memory of my mother and everywhere we went was of someone who was forever busting: if she hadn't just been then she wanted to go, if she had just been then she wanted to know where she could go next. She staked out her journeys in sheets of toilet paper, fluttering like flags to mark her way, and everywhere she stopped would get a full critical appraisal once she was done. 'Lovely soap!' she might say, or 'I was unable to sit on the seat because it was made of wood and everyone knows you can catch syphilis off those.' And then she would turn to me and say, 'Remember that, Emma! You must NEVER sit on a wooden toilet seat! NEVER!'

Five hours into our holiday and we'd reached Hirwaun, the village where you turn left to go up and then down into the Rhondda valley. We were all sung out for the time being and Mum had just had a urinary pit stop at a garage outside Cwmbran. It was the last chance she had to relieve herself before we got to my grandmother's house in Treherbert, and knowing that there was nowhere to go to the toilet between here and there was creating an electric tension in the car. The atmosphere was bristling. 'Are you sure this is the only way to get there?' asked my mother, anxiety rising. 'I mean, what if I need to go again?'

'Brenda,' explained my father for the third time. 'You've only just been. This is the only road into the Rhondda. There is no other way. If you want to go again, then you'll have to go in a bush.'

Travelling the road up from Hirwaun to the head of the valley was the most magical moment of my life to date. Coming from a council estate in a town carved from concrete where that little patch of roses was my only rub with nature, seeing what lay before me was a vast nirvana. The Neath valley sprawled away in a roll of green and there, my first glimpse of mountains, the Seven Sisters and the Brecon Beacons smouldered in the distance. The vast expanse of countryside that slipped away to the horizon was inconceivable. It was my first experience of the possibilities of space and all I could do was stand, hands on the back of the seat in front of me, and gawp with my mouth open. This sudden, undulating landscape was so fundamental and different from anything I had previously experienced that I found myself startled. I could not believe that such places were possible. 'Those are mountains, Emma,' explained my mother, pointing. 'Tony! Let's stop a while so Emma can see the view properly.'

Pulling into the designated car parking area had seemed such a pleasant idea. Perhaps it was the slow climb to the top of the valley, as the road nipped and tucked its way round the sheer granite walls? Perhaps it was the constant gear changing as my father, grinding up or grinding down, negotiated the blind twists and turns? Perhaps it was my mother screaming with fear, certain that we were only one bend away from certain oblivion? Who knows. Whatever it was, as we pulled into the scenic parking spot, the Wolseley, shattered and broken from the stuttering ascent, let out a strangled rattle and shuddered to a halt. Something below us fell off. 'What was that?' asked my mother, cocking her head to one side. 'I can smell petrol.'

My father, sensing that a wet blanket had just been thrown over our holiday, made an optimistic twist of the ignition key. The Wolseley let out a pained and juddering grind, like a wind-up toy that's been thrown into a blender, and then, as if to tell us that enough was enough, emitted a thin whine that petered out to a perfect, dead stop. Silence.

'Mountains!' I said, pointing and smiling because, even if we were now stuck in the middle of nowhere, at least the view was impressive. My father turned the key again. Nothing. My mother, sensing that this might be her fault for making us stop, did what most women do in similar circumstances: she blamed my father.

'Tony!' she yelled, giving his shoulder a poke with a finger. 'Why didn't you take the car to the garage before we left? Why didn't you do that? What are we going to do now?'

My father said nothing. A dread quiet had come over him. With my mother whipping herself into a proud peak of hysteria in the back, Tony, still in silence, opened up his door. Tinkle, tinkle, went the rust, flicking him the Vs. Treading slowly, as if he was approaching an undetonated bomb, my dad walked to the back of the car, veering away from it in an attempt to put this whole sorry mess into some sort of perspective. It didn't look good. The exhaust was hanging off but that didn't explain the smell of petrol. Backtracking to the front of the car, Tony unhooked the bonnet and lifted it so that he was out of view.

'Mountains!' I said again to my mother, smiling. Her head was slumped into the palm of her hand. I was only three, but even I knew that probably meant trouble.

'OK,' said my father, appearing suddenly at the side window. 'I know what the problem is. The petrol feed pipe has come loose. I need to screw it back on to the carburettor. And the exhaust is hanging off. But I think I can hold that back in place with one of the luggage hooks.' My mother looked up at him with the slow menace of someone who wished they weren't right all the time, but there it was.

'Shouldn't we try and call someone?' she said, frowning. 'Are you sure you know what you're doing?'

'But I'd have to walk back to Hirwaun,' said my father, gesturing back down the valley. 'I'd be gone for hours. Don't worry about it. I'll have this fixed. In fact, it won't take that long.'

'But, what if ...' began my mother.

'Brenda,' said my father, his hand out. 'I can do this. Let me get on with it.'

Solemn and nervous moments come to us all, and as Tony trudged to the boot to retrieve his toolbox, he had a small, explosive epiphany. If he did not manage to tie up the exhaust and screw back the petrol feed pipe then his matrimonial life was as good as over. Patching the car up and limping it to Solva was all that was required. Professional assistance could be arranged later but for now, it was make-do and mend. We were half an hour from Treherbert and then it would be two hours on to Solva. If he didn't turn the engine off outside his mother's house and reneged on an earlier promise to eat his sister-in-law's Welsh cakes then he might just get away with this. Tony was breaking into the sweat of possibilities. All, he reasoned with himself, would be fine.

Having taken one of the less necessary elastic hooks from the luggage rack, my dad made a loop around the exhaust and pulled it flush against the undercarriage. He attached the hooks to either side of the car, stood back and looked at it. The exhaust was off the floor, which was an improvement. Whether it was tight enough was debatable but to my mother's untrained eye, the arrangement would appear convincing.

'Exhaust's done,' said my dad, tapping on the window and giving us a thumbs up. My mother said nothing.

Even though my experience of the mystery of mothers was a short one, something primeval told me that a mother who's gone silent is as dangerous as a coiled snake. In the same way that dogs can sense danger in the wind, I too was aware that all was not as it might be. I waved Mr Mouse in her direction. She turned and looked at me. 'Come on,' said my mother with a sigh. 'Let's have a walk about. Don't worry. We'll all be fine. Let's go and have a look at the mountains. And we can have a wee while we're at it. Do you need a wee?' I shook my head. 'Well let's try and go anyway,' she added, as if clinging to what she knew would somehow sprinkle our predicament with certainty.

As we got out, my mother fixed Tony with one of her special stares. 'We are going for a walk,' she said, with a defiant toss of her dark brown hair.

'Well don't go too far,' said my dad, head still under the bonnet. 'This won't take long.'

There's something wonderful about holding your mother's hand in times of trouble. It's a panacea for all manner of ills and as we stumbled down the tufted hillside, my little fist wrapped in hers, nothing seemed to matter. 'Tread carefully,' warned Brenda, picking her route with precision. 'There are holes everywhere. And poo. We don't want that on our shoes, do we?'

'Who did the poo?' I asked, because this was fascinating.

'I think it's sheep's poo,' explained my mother. 'And rabbits. They look like currants, don't they? No! Don't pick it up. Put it down, please. No. Not in your pocket. On the floor.'

The coarse landscape was a toy box of opportunities: springy, chewed-down turf and a playground of lichen-covered rocks. I wanted to run about but my mother's hand had me good and tethered. We had climbed down far enough to be out of sight of the car and as I gazed about at the crumbled slate and rough-housed hillocks, I was saturated with wildness. Down to our left there was a larger rock, deposited who knows how, adding to the strewn complexion of the hillside. I tugged at my mother's hand. 'Let's go there,' I said, pointing.

'Actually, that's not a bad idea,' said my mother, giving a quick 360-degree sweep. 'We can have a wee behind that. Come on then. Don't run.'

But I was longing to run on. Twisting my hand away from hers, I careered towards the rock with joyful abandon.

The boulder was massive to my three-year-old eyes and I quickly decided that the first thing I was going to do was run round it, very fast, at least three times. As I crashed towards it, I could hear my mother behind me shouting 'Emma! Be careful!' But I was oblivious to her concern. I was on a steep, sloping hill and the momentum was electric. As the rock loomed up before me, I knew I wanted to negotiate its first corner but gravity had taken over and my legs were rushing away from me. The rock was sitting on a hidden ledge, and as I bounced uncontrollably towards it, I realised that rather than making a neat turn to begin my carousel-like run, I was heading for a drop. 'Emma!' screamed my mother behind me. But it was too late. And over I went.

The fall was something of a startle. It wasn't the height of the drop because, luckily, that was nothing more than superficial, but it was what was waiting for me as I came to rest that was to cause the distress. As most children do, I had bounced a bit, and in the jumble of the fall I was momentarily disorientated. Finding myself at a stop and lying on my tummy, I put my hands out in front of me and pushed myself up, bottom first, until I was standing. And then I saw it. Lying, splayed before me, a rancid, stinking and maggot-infested sheep. 'Aaaaaaaaaaaaaaaaaaaaaaagh!' I screamed, frozen to the spot. The sheep's tongue was hanging out and its belly had burst open. 'Aaaaaaaaaaaaaaaaaaaaaaaaaagh!' I screamed, again, staring at the exposed ribs, the legs pointing skywards, flies in the eye sockets. Brain overflowing with horror, I was trapped in a tractor beam of death.

'Emma!' I heard my mother shout above me. 'Oh thank God! Oh! OH! Get away from that! Oh! That's awful! Come to me! Come to me! Oh! No! Don't look at it! Oh!'

I reached up to take my mother's hands, still staring over my shoulder at the decomposing carcass, my mother's wails ringing in my ears. Dragging me up to the rim of the ledge, my mother clasped me to her. 'Oh,' she said, relief pouring out of her. 'I thought you'd fallen off a cliff. Are you all right?'

'Sheep,' I said in a whisper, pointing down.

'I know,' nodded my mother quickly. 'Let's not look at that any more. It's just come here to die. That's all. Naughty sheep. You didn't touch it, did you?' I shook my head.

'Come on,' said my mother, picking me up. 'Let's go back and see Daddy. Come to Wales, he said. It'll be lovely, he said. We can break down and it'll be full of dead sheep. What more do you want in a holiday?'

'Did you have a wee?' asked Tony, closing the bonnet, the bottom of his flares flapping in the wind.

'No,' said my mother in a firm tone. 'We did not have a wee. Emma almost fell off the cliff and we saw a rotting sheep.'

'Well, I think I've fixed the fuel pipe,' said my dad, choosing to ignore anything my mother might want to tell him. 'Get back in the car and I'll give it a go.'

We slumped ourselves into the back seat. Tinkle, tinkle, tinkle, went the rust. 'OK,' said my father, pulling on his driving gloves. 'Let's go!'

The key twisted in the ignition but there was nothing, not even the whirr of something giving it its best shot. I caught my father's eyes in the rear view mirror. He had the look of someone startled by an unexpected slap. He turned the key frantically, each time with more ferocity, but still nothing. Another silence descended. My father's brain was in overdrive. How could this be? He had reattached the fuel pipe. But why was the engine not turning over? And then it came to him. 'Starter motor!' he declared, leaping out of his seat. 'Quick!' he added, turning to face my mother. 'Pass me the hammer under the back seat!'

My mother held his gaze for a dangerous length of time, the sort of time in which worlds are created and destroyed. Saying nothing, she reached down and found the hammer. Snatching it from her, my father got down on his hands and knees and, with one furvent blow, gave the starter motor an almighty thwack. Jumping back into the car, he turned the ignition once more. *Phuur, phuuuuurr, phurrrr,* wailed the engine.

'COME ON!' shouted my dad, bouncing up and down.

Phuurr, phuttt, phuurrr, phurrrr, phurrrrrrrrrrrrrrr, it moaned and suddenly, as if the breath of God Himself had wafted through its pistons, the car was up and running.

'I TOLD you I could do it!' shouted my father, in defiant triumph. 'Yes! YES!'

Thirty minutes later and we were pulling into Scott Street, the home of my grandmother. In order to prevent another breakdown, it was imperative that my dad kept the car moving. Bubbling over with nervous energy and looking a little wild-eyed, he threw a sharp look over his shoulder. 'Right, Brenda,' he began. 'We can't stop. I'll slow right down. You jump out. Go and get Mam. I'll drive round the block. Then you'll both get in.'

My mother blinked. 'You want me to ask your seventy-year-old mother to jump into a moving car?' she asked.

'It'll be a crawl. At best! Come on!'

'This is ridiculous,' muttered my mother, opening her door on to the moving road beneath her.

'Put both your feet out before you jump!' advised my father, shouting. 'Both feet!' Brenda, checking that there was nothing coming in either direction, hooked her feet on to the edge of the frame and, with a few deep breaths, launched herself out of the side door with the urgency of a parachute jumper. I stood up on the back seat and watched as she bobbed away and skidded to a halt, clutching herself on the chest with relief. Realising that her passenger door was now wide open and I was only inches from it, my mother burst into a frantic sprint, caught up with the car and slammed the door at a stretch. I watched as she grew smaller in the back window, her panting frame heaving its way towards my grandmother's house.

'All right Tony!' I heard a voice shouting from behind me. It was a man in coal-stained overalls standing on the pavement and waving.

'All right Dai!' shouted my father, winding down his window. 'I can't stop! Starter motor's playing up! How's your mother?'

'Oh, she died!' Dai shouted back, with a nod.

'Sorry to hear it!' yelled back my dad.

'Don't worry!' yelled Dai, fading away as we turned the corner. 'It was nothing serious.' My father shrugged a little and gave a sigh.

There was a heavy and sweet smell of baking in the air in Treherbert and I would have given anything to stop and search out the source. The terraced houses were a maddening jigsaw of similarities: women in aprons, arms folded, standing in doorways shouting gossip across the street, children of my age sitting at their feet, sucking on scones. And behind them, a mountain, bearing down on everything, so close it felt as if the wind could blow it down and swallow the streets. This wasn't like where I lived: there was no one shitting in the bushes. It was a strange sensation to be creeping past everyday valley life – the scrubbing of doorsteps, the kicking of a ball, a group of young lads flicking marbles against a wall – all of it seemed familiar yet a million years away from the disparate, suspicious New Town living I was used to. A woman was beating a carpet over a washing line, another man stood chatting with three fish on a hook hanging over his shoulder and everyone, without exception, was saying hello as we trickled past. A car in the valley, even if it was one on the verge of breaking down, was still, it would seem, a major event.

We completed our slow tour around the block and were coming back to where we needed to be. Dad adjusted the car to as slow a creep as he dared. Ahead of us I could see my mum, holding a suitcase, and my grandmother, who was trying to pull on a coat. My dad leant over to the passenger door opposite him and flicked it open. 'Throw in the suitcase!' he shouted. My mother, who was wearing a scowl so intense it could have turned any living thing to stone, was happy to oblige. Any chance she had to throw something heavy in the direction of my father, she was going to take it. 'Careful!' he shouted, as the suitcase clattered on to his knees. 'Now get Mam in! Get Mam in!'

A small crowd of neighbours had dripped out of their houses, intrigued that the 'bride in black' was back and this time she was trying to get a seventy-year-old widow to leap into a moving vehicle. This wasn't how they did things in the valleys, that was for sure. 'Mam!' yelled Tony, gesturing wildly with his hand. 'Get in! You can do it!'

My grandmother, who wasn't fast at the best of times, was skip-walking next to the open door but clearly couldn't quite muster up the courage to commit to a jump, so my mother, who was hard on her heels, took matters into her own hands and gave her a shove. 'Oooh!' screamed a neighbour, holding her head in her hands.

My grandmother, falling into the car, was now flailing face down and was in grave danger of being impaled on the gear stick. My mother, thinking quickly, ran alongside the car, lifted up my grandmother's legs, swung them inside and then, realising that her charge had been dispatched, however uncomfortably, slammed the front door with a flourish. She then ran round to the other side of the car, opened the door and leapt in whilst fixing the onlookers with a strained smile and giving what can only be described as a sarcastic wave. 'Just drive,' she hissed as she threw herself into the back seat.

And for once, Dad did what he was told.

'Did I tell you about Ann?' said my grandmother. We had been driving for almost an hour and as far as I could tell, she was yet to pause for breath. She didn't need a reply. 'Well,' she continued, sucking her cheeks. 'You know she's been helping out with the district nurse? So they go down to Jones the butcher. And he lives with his mam. Anyway, they've gone in and he says, "I think there's something wrong with her. I haven't had a peep out of her since last Tuesday." So Ann goes in to have a look at her. And there she is, sitting in a chair, stone cold dead. So Ann turns to Jones the butcher and says, "I'm sorry to have to tell you that your mother's dead and what's more, she's covered in ants." And do you know what he said to that? He looked at her and said, "Oh, we get them this time of year!" Can you imagine that? "We get them this time of year!" Not bothered that his mother's dead in a chair and covered in ants! Just "We get them this time of year." I mean. That's not normal is it?'

'Solva!' suddenly screamed my mother, pointing wildly at a road sign. 'Oh we're here! We're here! Oh thank God!'

As we passed the boundary into Solva, a fat, juicy drop of rain exploded on to the windscreen. Dark clouds had been gathering and, although it was only five o'clock in the afternoon, a dread gloom had descended. A wind, sweeping in from the Irish Sea, was prowling over the cliff tops and as we drove, one windscreen wiper valiantly clearing bucketfuls of water with every sweep, my mother slumped her forehead against the window. 'Is there any chance,' she mumbled, 'that a passing ambulance might pick me up and take me somewhere for a lie down?'

'Weather's terrible,' announced my grandmother, stating the obvious. 'How are you going to get a tent up in this, Tony?'

The campsite where we were staying was little more than a field sloping off towards a cliff edge. On one side, there were a few caravans on bricks, permanent fixtures, ever hopeful that someone might want to breathe life into their damp, musty frames.

'Where's everyone else?' asked my grandmother, noticing the startling lack of holidaymakers. 'Are we the only people here?' The rain was now lashing down in sheets. My dad, who had left the engine running for obvious reasons, had made a dash for a wooden hut that looked as if it might have someone in it. It didn't. It was locked. Leaping over already forming puddles, he ran over to the caravans and peered in. Looking back towards the car, he threw us all a shrug.

'Great,' muttered my mother. 'No one's here. That's all we need.' Dad jumped back into the car, rain dripping down his face.

'I can't find anyone,' he said, wiping the wet from his eyes. 'I guess we should just pick a spot and get the tent up. If the owner comes down I can sort things out with him then.'

'Where are you going to put it up?' asked my mother, staring down the field towards the sea. 'We're very exposed. Can we try and pitch near the caravans? At least they'll give us a bit of protection.'

'Oh you can't do that,' chipped in my grandmother. 'You're not allowed to put tents with caravans. Gwennie told me.'

'But no one's here,' complained my mother. 'Who's going to be bothered?'

'Best not,' said Dad, agreeing with Mam. 'The owner could come back and tell us to move. I don't want to have to put it up and then take it down again.' My mother bit her bottom lip, closed her eyes and threw her head to the back of her seat. I stood up and stared at her and understood that this is what you look like when you wish you were in Greece but instead you're on holiday in damp circumstances with your mother-in-law.

The car bounced and slurred its way across the field. 'Over there!' Mam yelled, pointing. 'Go over there by that fence. We can tie the tent to it so we won't get blown away!' My grandmother, thinking she had been hilarious, laughed uproariously. 'Blown away!' she repeated and shook her head because the very idea was ludicrous.

'I'm going to turn the engine off now,' said Tony, with the solemnity of a family member agreeing to switch off a life-support machine. The Wolseley gasped into the abyss. Whether it would live again was anyone's guess. The rain clattered in our ears, pounding on the roof with such intensity it was as if we were being beaten into the ground.

'This is terrible,' said my dad, craning to look up at the sky through the windscreen. 'I don't know whether to wait or just get on with it.'

'Just get on with it,' ordered my mother in a heartbeat. 'I've been sitting in this car for eight hours.'

'Hmm,' nodded Tony. 'I think you're right. At least then we'll be able to set everything up. Get some tea on. Right. Well. Wish me luck.'

Putting a tent up is complicated at the best of times, and watching my father battle with poles, pegs and flapping canvas whilst being hosed down by the onslaught of rain was a bit like watching an episode of 'It's a Knockout' where contestants are blown over by water cannons. My grandmother, deciding that we all needed our minds taken off the fact that this was our holiday, kept us going with sorry wartime tales.

'Then there was the time,' she said, tapping a finger on her knee, 'when the Germans bombed the munitions factories in Cardiff. And one of the bombers went off course, saw a spark or a light or something, and dropped his bombs on the valley. Twelve people killed. Terrible, it was. And because everyone was so sad with it, they decided to have the funerals all on the same day. Now, the only vehicle available to carry all twelve coffins was the Corona pop lorry. All stacked up, they were, in the back. But the thing was, when the pop van brought the coffins up the valley, people didn't know whether to laugh or cry. You know why?'

Silence.

'Because the slogan for Corona pop, which was written in massive letters on the tailboards, was "Cheaper by the Dozen"! Terrible. Cheaper by the Dozen. Just terrible. Because there was twelve of them, see. Which is a dozen. Imagine not noticing a thing like that?'

'I saw a dead sheep today, Grandma,' I said out of the blue.

'You never did?' said my grandmother, with alarming urgency. 'Ooooh that's not good. They say it's bad luck to see a dead sheep on a day of travel. Not good. Not good at all.'

As my grandmother, who was prone to the supernatural, tutted on about how a dead sheep portends nothing but doom I began to believe that the storm might be my fault. Had my random encounter with a rotting carcass precipitated our family into a spiral of disaster? Were the Holiday Gods throwing down their first thorn? I clung to my mother, who had assumed the limp, lifeless form of someone who, at that moment, would be more than happy to pass into spirit. 'Let's not talk about the dead sheep any more,' she mumbled, clutching her forehead. 'It was just a dead sheep.'

Meanwhile, against all the odds, Dad had got the tent up. As feats go, it was up there with scaling Everest. His face, dripping with rain, appeared at the window. My mother, sensing his presence, rubbed a hole in the condensation so we could get a better look at him. Nothing, not even seaweed, could have looked wetter. 'Come on then!' he shouted through the wind. 'Let's get in.'

The dash to the tent felt dangerous, even though it was no more than a few feet. The rain was whipping down and each drop landed with a sting. 'This is like when it snowed in 1947!' shouted Mam, running towards the tent. 'Snowed right up to the bedroom windows. Although that was snow. Not rain.'

'Jesus!' exclaimed my mother, shaking the water off. 'It's torrential. Are you sure we're safe?' My dad looked out through the tent door at the screaming weather.

'It can't stay like this for long,' he said, with a hopeful nod. 'It'll be blue skies in half an hour if we just wait for a bit. And then when it stops I can get the stove up and get the tea on. And then we can go for a nice walk. Maybe go down to the beach?' He turned and looked at us with a smile.

'You must be mad,' said Mam, all matter of fact. Then, throwing me a look, 'This'll last for days. She saw a dead sheep.' Everyone turned and stared at me and somewhere, in the distance, there was a low rumble of thunder.

Storm or no storm, this was an occasion for me to savour. It was my first time inside a tent, a tent that was going to shape my foreseeable summers. Everything was already damp or completely wet. I was standing in a small puddle of water and a metallic smell of rain permeated the interior. The walls were a bright, synthetic orange and the door, which was undone and tied to one side, was a plastic, crayon-coloured blue. There was a bedroom compartment, accessed through a fat zip, with a flimsy cotton divide giving the illusion of not one, but two sleeping quarters. To me, it was exciting and exotic and the war-like drumming of the rain on every inch of canvas made the experience all the more intense.

'I need a wee,' said my mother, with a sigh, 'and a cup of tea.'

'Can't put the stove up in this,' said Dad, with a shake of his head. 'Wouldn't get it lit for starters. I suppose if you're desperate I could get it going in here. Might be all right if it's near the door.'

'But what about the fumes, Tony? The fumes?' wailed my mother, throwing an arm around to simulate gaseous emissions. 'Or do you want to poison us all on top of everything else? And what if the tent catches fire? What will we do then?'

'Oh diawl,' chipped in Mam, 'wouldn't worry about that. Rain would put it out. This rain could extinguish the fires of Hell!' She was standing staring down towards the cliff edge, clutching on to her handbag. 'And the wind's picking up. Look at that tree. It's practically bent over on itself. This is bad, Tony. Very, very baaaaad.'

'Here you are,' said my dad, handing my mother the pink, plastic bucket.

'What's this?' said Brenda, staring at it.

'Toilet,' muttered Dad, who then unfolded four chairs and placed them in a line.

'You want me to piss in this whilst you all sit there and watch?' asked Brenda. 'What am I? The evening's entertainment?'

'Well we'll all go and stand in the bedroom compartment and look the other way. That's what we'll do. Come on, Mam, Em, let's go. We'll let Mummy have a wee. Come on.'

'I need to go as well,' announced Mam, as we trooped off to the other side of the tent.

'Right,' said Dad, 'then you can go second. And I may as well, so I'll go third. Do you want to have a go?' He looked down at me, with eyes like plugholes. I nodded. 'Good,' he declared, as if this was going very well. 'Well that's that sorted.'

I was quite determined to take my turn on my own so when my mother asked me if I could manage, I was adamant that I could. The pink bucket, now sloshing with three layers of urine, was perched in the darkest corner of the tent. I had made sure that everyone was not only in the bedroom compartment but zipped in as well. This was a solo flight and I would complete my ablutions unassisted. My parents sensing, in the absence of any other sort of holiday-based fun, that this was an opportunity to humour me, were happy to play along. 'Don't LOOK Daddy!' I shouted, as I negotiated my path towards the bucket.

'We've all got our eyes closed!' he shouted back. 'Haven't we? No one's looking!'

'No one's looking!' piped up my mum.

I'd never pissed in a bucket before, so as I took down my tights and pants I had a quick, negotiating peek. Clearly I could just sit on it, like a toilet. So I did. But my three-year-old body was smaller than the bucket's circumference and the next thing I knew, I was concertinaed, knees thrown up and squashed against my chest and I was sinking, slowly, towards two generations of excretions. I let out a small yelp, the sort of yelp that cubs stuck down wells might make. 'Oh Christ!' I heard my mother yell. I was still clinging to the idea that this was something I could deal with. So as I heard the compartment zip being frantically ripped upwards, I made a surge using both my arms and legs. It was a terrible error. The bucket, teetering on uneven ground, rode with my body weight and tipped itself over to one side. Warm liquid flooded up under my cardigan and gushed down my arm.

I was literally covered in piss.

'Oh God, Emma, no!' yelled my father as he yanked me out of the bucket. My mother, incredulous that this day could get any worse, just stood and stared with a hand over her mouth.

'Don't worry,' announced my grandmother. 'Urine is an antiseptic!' As if that would sweeten the pill. 'Or is that just your own?'

'What are we going to do?' wailed my father. 'We've got no water to wash her!' My mother, thinking quickly, came to an obvious conclusion.

'We'll have to use the rain. She'll have to go out and stand in the rain. That's all we can do. Take her clothes off. Emma, you're going to have to run round the car as quickly as you can. And the rain will wash you clean. And I want you to rub yourself as hard as you can as you're going. Yes? And then you'll run back here and we'll get you dry. Have we got a towel? Tony! Have we got a towel?'

My father, who was undressing me as I stood, my arms out and stiff with horror, nodded towards a green bag. 'In there. There's some clothes as well. Get those out.'

'There's pee all over the floor,' Mam proffered, pointing. 'All under there. And over there.'

'Right,' said Brenda, taking hold of my hand and walking me towards the tent door. 'Let's pretend that the rain is a great, big bath. And you're going to run into it and then you're going to run right back. Do you understand?'

I was cold and naked. I looked out into the sheet of freezing wet. The Wolseley was so battered with rain that it was disappearing into its own halo of spray, grass was turning to mud and brooks of water were bubbling down and away. The last thing I wanted to do was run out into it, but whatever this short, sharp shock was going to offer, it was still better than being covered with the sticky by-products of my family's kidneys. So out I dashed.

The rain was like ice. With a slap of cold, my breath caught in the back of my throat. Slimy mud was squeezing up through my toes and fat, thrashing raindrops were washing salt into my eyes. I slid round the front of the Wolseley, putting my hand out to stop myself from slipping away. Over the waterfall of noise and wind I could hear my mother shouting at me to scrub myself. So as I ran, mud exploding up my legs, I clung on to myself and rubbed. Emerging from behind the car, I dashed for the open door of the tent. My dad was holding a large towel like a safety net, and as I ran in, he caught me and scooped me up. The combined instant warmth of the towel and being held close to my father was a blessing.

'Well,' said my Welsh grandmother, as she pulled a jumper over my head and my mother rubbed my legs. 'It could have been worse. I could have had a poo.'

Three hours later and the weather still raged. It had turned dark and the wind was so ferocious that the tent frame was complaining with the strain. The canvas sides were buffeting back and forth and my grandmother, who still hadn't let go of her handbag, was terrified. With only the light of one small torch to comfort us, we took it in turns to eat pickled onions out of a jar, the only food we could eat without cooking. 'This is the grimmest meal I've ever had,' said my mother, chewing.

'I'm not being funny,' began Mam, 'but this isn't just a storm. It's something more evil. I can feel it.'

'And why is no one here, Tony?' complained Brenda. 'Why? It's like everyone knows something except us. You

don't think everyone's been warned away or something?
What are we going to do?'

My father, who up till now had managed to put a brave
face on things, had to concede that things were not as they
should be. 'I know,' he said with a quiet nod. 'That's been
bothering me. Look, I've been thinking. What about if I try
and break into one of the caravans? I don't know about you,
but I'll feel a bit safer.'

'Can you do that?' asked Brenda, eyes widening with
hope. 'What if you damage it?'

'Blow that,' said my grandmother, standing up. 'I'm
eating pickled onions, the tent's about to tip over and
I'm sitting in a pool of piss. Let's get the Hell out.'

Unzipping the tent door, the storm hit us straight on.
The wind was now so fierce that it was almost impossible to
walk. Picking me up, my mother held me close, folding me
into the crook of her shoulder. I looked back and watched
the tent, now open to the elements, billow out as the wind
raged through it, delivering body blows. I gasped as it
swayed violently to the left, then right, putting up one last
fight before crumpling to the floor. It was as if the wind had
assumed a monstrous form, strode into our camp and torn
the tent at the neck. Mam was immediately behind us.
Handbag flapping in the air and holding on to her hat, she
was unable to move forward. Instead she spread her legs and
dug in, waiting for the gusts to pass. The ground beneath
her was now so sodden and precarious that she seemed to be
sinking into it. I looked forward to see my father jimmying
open the large back window of one of the caravans. Pushing
himself up with his arms, he slid inside and disappeared from
view, only to reappear moments later at the caravan door.
He was shouting and gesturing for us to come but the wind
was now so strong that he was completely inaudible. I again

looked back at my grandmother, and watched in horror as she tried to pull one of her legs out of the swallowing mud. She took one brave step forward but lost her footing, fell over and then slid, at some speed, towards the cliff edge, screaming as she went. I looked back at my father, who had now leapt from the caravan and was running to my grandmother. But he fell over as well and slid on his stomach, scrabbling at the grass. Whether divine intervention or the presence of my father's driving gloves was to thank, there was no way of knowing. But somehow, against all the odds, they managed to collide, cling on to each other and come to a dreadful, muddy stop. My mother, meanwhile, had done nothing but scream without stopping from the tent door to the caravan. Unaware of the slippery chain of events unfolding behind us, she threw me into the caravan, jumped in after me and shouted, 'Where's your father?' I ran to the back window and pointed out. Through the murk we could just make them out, two blackened figures sliding and falling back up towards us. The door of the caravan flung open. Mam's startled, mud-covered face appeared from behind it.

'*Yffach wyllt!*' she panted. 'Remind me never to come on holiday again!'

In anyone's book this was a bad state of affairs. We were drenched, frozen and hungry. The caravan, which we had hoped would be an oasis of calm, was instead a stinking hole. There was mould on the walls, a strange, troubling yet indefinable smell, like bad eggs spliced with fish guts, and worst of all, wind was piping up through the kitchen sink plughole with a haunting, devil-made screech. The pipe-based wailing was the final straw for my grandmother, who, as well as looking like she'd just been dragged up from the bottom of a lake, was now slumped, like a Guy tossed on to a bonfire, on a bench seat next to the window. 'This,' she declared, raising a finger into the air, 'this is more than an act of God! Someone has brought this upon us!'

'Well,' said my mother, walking towards the tiny toilet in the centre of the caravan. 'It's got nothing to do with ME!'

'Here, Mam,' said Tony, wiping mud off his face with a tea towel. 'You didn't bring any of that ouija board nonsense with you, did you?'

'There is seaweed in the toilet!' screamed my mother, reappearing. 'Seaweed! That's it! The sea has risen over the cliff! Oh God, Tony! We're going to be swept away! Swept away!' Bursting into tears, she threw herself across a brown plastic work surface and wailed into her inside elbow.

'Of course the sea hasn't come over the cliff,' soothed my father. 'Don't be daft! It'll just be a bit of seaweed. In the toilet. Maybe it isn't even seaweed. Maybe it's spinach.'

My mother's sobs racked on.

'Well check it!' she wailed. 'Check and see if it *is* spinach!'

My dad, with a sigh, poked his head into the caravan toilet. 'Oh,' he said, as if it was properly interesting. 'It *is* seaweed.'

And off my mother went again.

'But that doesn't mean it's come up from the sea!' encouraged Tony, giving my mother a pat on the back. 'Come on, now. There's no way the sea can rise over the cliff. Is there, Mam?'

'Well, it can if it's a tidal wave,' she mumbled from under her hat.

'But it's NOT a tidal wave, is it?' battled on my dad. 'Anyway, it looks like very old, dry seaweed. That's not fresh seaweed.'

'Do you promise?' cried my mother, looking up at him.

'Yes. It's definitely not just been put there by the sea. I can promise you that. We are perfectly safe.'

And as he said those fateful words, the back window, which he had climbed through to give us shelter, blew in.

'Aaaaaaaaaaaaaaaaaaaaaaaaaaaaaaaaaaaah!' we all screamed, because there hadn't been enough screaming on this holiday, not by a long chalk.

Wind howled through the caravan, punching everything in its path. My mother, who had been bent over by the sink, was now clinging on to its edge, hair streaming back from her face. Mam was on her knees on the floor, and Tony was grabbing a foam bench seat and fighting to get to the window, which was now hanging on by a single hinge. I was pinned against the toilet door, splayed by the weather. Everyone's voices had been swallowed up by the wind and although I could see that everyone was shouting, nothing could be heard above the jet-engine din. Tony, drenched and desperate, battled with the window, but the wind had the better of him. Brenda, realising that this might be an all-hands-to-the-pump situation, careered forwards, just as Mam, throwing down her handbag because it was that serious, surged to grab at the window. The force of three adults clattering to one end of the caravan was catastrophic: everything lurched forwards and, with a tree-cracking shudder, the front end of the caravan came off its bricks. Everyone was thrown to the floor.

'Get out!' Tony cried, pushing Mam up to a standing position. 'Get out! Everyone get out!'

Grabbing hold of my arm, Brenda hooked her free hand around a cupboard unit and hauled me towards the door. The caravan was creaking with such menace that blind terror took hold. There was no doubt in any of our minds: get out of the caravan or die.

Pulling me hard behind her, Mum shoved at the caravan door. 'Hold on to me tight!' she yelled, looping an arm around my waist. The caravan was now at such a severe angle that the drop looked terrifying. We leapt into the rain, rolling on to the floor as we landed. Dad jumped out after us, turned and held out his hands towards Mam, poised in the door-frame and gripping either side to stop the inevitable slide back to the front of the caravan.

'Jump, Mam! Jump!' yelled my father, gesturing wildly. And with one heaving leap, Mam launched herself into the air and towards my father, who had his arms out and was ready to catch her.

The caravan groaned; a deep crunch shattered out from its underbelly. With one terrifying yaw, the rear creaked up to the vertical, flipped over and then rolled, end over end, crashing down the field, metallic smashes punching through the howling wind. Then with one sliding finale, the caravan fell off the edge of the cliff.

'We're in Hell!' wailed Mam, as she watched it go. 'Hell!'

By now, everyone was in tears. I don't know how much families are supposed to endure in a lifetime but we'd managed to condense most of our allotted misery into twenty-four hours. We were back in the car, tent collapsed to the right of us, caravan destroyed to the left. We weren't to know it, but we were in the eye of a force-ten gale, whipped up out over the Irish Sea and sent smashing into the Welsh coast without a single thought for life, property or holidays. The reason no one was at the campsite was because everyone else knew it was coming. They'd packed up and battened down the hatches. But not us. We had driven straight into it and set up deckchairs. And no, the Wolseley didn't make it back. We drove home the next day in the back of an AA lorry.

My grandmother never came on holiday with us again.

The Holiday Gods had thrown me their first curveball. Game on.

Chapter Two

On the Verge

'Please tell me you're joking,' said Brenda, turning to stare at my father. Her hands were in fists that were dripping off her hips.

'No. I'm not joking. I think we should go back to Wales,' said my dad, who was now taking things so seriously he'd grown a beard. 'Because we didn't get to see anything last time. And this way, we can stop off, see all the family and then go on to the Gower. And Phyllis can come, too. With her boyfriend. It'll be nice.'

A determination to send some demons packing, combined with what we all suspected was a wilful act of madness, had set our summer in stone: we would be returning to the scene of the crime.

The grand social experiment of New Town utopia was in its early bloom on our council estate in Stevenage. The egalitarian dream was to house young doctors next to young factory workers, to place engineers shoulder to shoulder with cleaners, and our estate, the rectangle that was the sum total of my world, was no exception. It was a jam jar of political destiny. Post-war government had concocted a vision whereby classless communities would meet on equal terms, cohabit and enjoy common cultural and recreational amenities. It was an artificial construction, with designated zones dictating work and play. There was nothing organic about Stevenage: its concrete corners barked what to do and when.

For my young, idealistic parents, this new social order was the shape of things to come. For me, I was just interested in playing in the communal rectangle in front of our house. There were two rules my mother forced me to adhere to. First, I was only allowed to play within the confines of the rectangle, and second, under no circumstances whatsoever was I to wander into the concrete underpass that led off to the shops, a place where evil, chips and sweets lurked like malevolent goblins. Because this was a fledgling estate, all of the families who lived on it were about the same age, creating a wondrous pool of playmates. Nowadays, it would be unthinkable to leave a four-year-old to her own devices, but back in 1971, being tossed out the front door after breakfast and not coming back till lunch was perfectly normal. I would run up to my dressing-up box, pick out that day's outfit and off I would scamper, climbing into my little red pedal car to do endless circuits of the paved circumference. I didn't have a care in the world. What I did have, however, was a constant compulsion to inform my mother of everything that was happening. My mother, the English teacher, always had books to prepare or marking to do and would valiantly try and get on with things. But she would be interrupted by me ringing the doorbell every ten minutes with an on-the-spot update. 'Susan Fletcher has hurt her knee,' I would announce, hand on hips. Or, 'We were playing 50-50 and Simon Hall said he was it but then Paul Harwood said he wanted to be it and then they were both it and Simon Hall pushed Paul Harwood in the bushes and now Paul Harwood's gone home and Simon Hall says he's stupid.' Or, and this one was a daily occurrence, 'He's done a poo in the roses again.'

Shitting Boy was my mother's *bête noire*. Secretly, she wanted to tell me I wasn't allowed to play with him but, because his family had been shipped out from the dark ghettos of a London slum, her liberal sensibilities were prepared to overlook his social shortcomings in the hope that our middle-class aspirations would rub some manners into him via osmosis. In reality, he was a little bastard, and no amount of well-meaning lenience was going to change him any time soon. But my mother, ever the nurturer of lost causes, was always ready to bite the bullet and welcome him in with semi-open arms.

The day before we were to return to Wales, Shitting Boy had cornered me in the rectangle. He was three years older than me and had a tangle of lanky brown hair. He seemed to have olive skin, but it could have been dirt, and the faint smell of chip fat used to waft off him as if he'd been rolled in greasy paper. He was skinny, with legs like Twiglets, and in the summer months he always wore a tatty T-shirt and foot-ball shorts. I wasn't quite sure what I thought of him. I knew he was naughty, which felt dangerous, and was aware that he regularly stood in the concrete underpass while I would stand, rooted to the spot with my mouth open, before running off to tell my mother. But then again, he was totally different to anyone else on our estate. He was an *amuse bouche*, a finger pointing into the unknown, and for that he elicited my curiosity.

'Like my bike?' he asked, as I stared at him from my pedal car. He was sitting astride a magnificent, bright orange Mark One Raleigh Chopper. I'd never seen anything like it. The majesty of the high, drooping handlebars, the knife-thin saddle and that gear stick all combined in my mind to create one of the most impressive things I'd ever seen. I nodded. I thought it was brilliant. As if to double underline my fascina-tion, Shitting Boy pushed down on the pedals and rode off. He was a little bit unsteady but he tore around our rectangle with a speed I could only dream about. Screeching to a halt in front of me, Shitting Boy sat back, leaning into the back rest of the saddle, one black plimsoll on the floor. He looked cool, and he knew it.

And then we heard the yelling. 'Oi!' came a voice from the underpass. 'Oi, you!' I looked over my shoulder to see an angry, burly-looking man striding towards us. Holding his hand was a small, ginger-haired boy who was crying and pointing.

'There he is,' sobbed the boy. 'That's him.'

Shitting Boy, sensing that the game was up, kicked down on the pedals to sprint off. The Chopper, a precarious ride at the best of times, wobbled away and, unable to control it, Shitting Boy was thrown to the floor as the bike veered off in a loop and clattered to a stylish rest in front of me. A large adult arm entered the frame and picked Shitting Boy up off the floor. 'Is this him?' asked the man, looking down at his tear-stained boy. The lad nodded and ran to pick up his bike, which he swiftly sat on, as if to reclaim his property. The man turned back to Shitting Boy. 'Try and steal my boy's bike again,' he said, pressing a finger into Shitting Boy's chest, 'and I'll rip your arms out. Understand?' And then, because it was still only 1971 and no one gave a damn, he gave Shitting Boy a proper, old-fashioned wallop. Bug-eyed at the entire incident, I got out of my pedal car. 'Where are you going?' asked the man, throwing me a look.

'To tell my mum,' I said, pointing in the direction of my front door, because this was easily the most exciting thing to have happened since Becky Martin's skipping rope broke.

'Well take him with you,' said the man, shoving Shitting Boy in my direction. 'And tell your mum he's a very bad boy.' As I ran towards my house, my brain whirred with the urgency of it all. By the time I had my finger on the door-bell, I was actually jumping up and down. 'There was a bike and a man and a boy,' I rattled, as the door opened, still jumping. 'And then he fell off it and the man came and the bike was on the floor and the boy took it and the man smacked him...'

'All right,' said Shitting Boy, who had sidled up behind me.

'Oh, hello,' said my mother, folding her arms and throwing him a glance.

'...And the bike was orange and had bended arms and he rode it round,' I clattered on, pointing over in the direction of where it had all happened.

'That's nice,' said my mother, not paying an awful lot of attention. 'Are you going upstairs to play? Come in then. Do you want a drink? I've got lemonade. Do you want lemonade?'

'Yeah, all right,' said Shitting Boy, pushing me in through the door. 'Where's your room then? Upstairs?'

'...And they came out of the pass to get it and...yes.' And up we went. I felt like Bonnie and Clyde.

My bedroom was an oasis of mess. The arrangement that I had come to with my parents was that, as long as I respected every other room in the house, I could do what I wanted in mine. I was allowed to draw on the walls, I was allowed to paint the floor, I was allowed to leave every book, doll and lump of Lego I possessed strewn across the bright yellow carpet in a sea of activity. It was an Aladdin's cave of organised chaos, a cacophony of toys that would leave other children gasping. One of my more uptight friends, a small boy called James, actually used to burst into tears on a regular basis whenever he came over to play. He couldn't cope with the idea that nothing had to be put away. The lack of boundaries made him anxious. I, however, adored it.

Shitting Boy, being three years older than me, took immediate charge of playing and began practising knots by tying me to my bunk bed and then throwing bits of Lego at me. Tiring of that, he then decided that he'd like to conduct further grubby experiments. There was a small desk in my bedroom and he pushed me over towards it. 'Now we're going to play a game,' he told me, positioning me so I was facing the desk with my back to him. 'You're going to bend over the desk. And then I'm going to pull down your pants.' It was at this point that I felt a chat coming on.

'Why do you want to take off my pants?' I asked him. 'Why am I on the desk?'

'I need to check something,' he told me. 'I need to see if I can put a pencil in your bottom.' Being four, I wasn't quite sure what this was all about. I'd seen a pencil being put in one of my dad's pencil sharpeners. Was that it?

'Are you sharpening the pencil?' I asked. 'Can you sharpen pencils in bottoms?'

'Something like that,' he said, putting a hand on the small of my back. I felt myself being pressed forwards on to the desk. There was then a sharp tug at the top of my pants. He was pulling my pants down. I fell silent. I couldn't quite work out what it was that was bothering me. All I knew was that something strange was happening and I was pretty certain that my mother wouldn't be pleased about it. What happened next is still open to conjecture. Something was shoved up my arsehole. It might have been a pencil. It might not. We will never know.

'Are you sharpening the pencil now?' I asked, trying to look over my shoulder.

'You need to be very quiet for a minute,' said Shitting Boy. 'I'm just checking something.'

'Emma!' called out my mum, footsteps coming up the stairs. 'Are you up there?' Whatever was in my anus was swiftly removed and I was pulled up from the desk by the back of my jumper. I stood, pulling my pants up, bemused and slightly baffled. The door to my room opened and in walked my mother, two glasses of lemonade in her hands. Taking in the scene with one sweeping glance, she looked down at me and then shot a deadly look in the direction of Shitting Boy. 'What's going on?' she growled, stepping towards us.

'He's been sharpening pencils,' I blurted, eager to fill the silence. Shitting Boy shrugged and leaned against a wall with his arms folded. Brenda, using her patented Mother's Sixth Sense, wafted an arm towards the door.

'I think you should go home now,' she said with low menace. 'We have to get ready for our holiday.' If she had known the full truth of what had just been taking place there is no doubt that my mother's liberal leanings would have been tested to breaking point.

'Do I get to have the lemonade first?' asked Shitting Boy, flicking his hair out of his eyes with a toss of his head. My mother fixed him with a penetrating stare that might have gone on for days.

'No,' she said, unblinking. And off he scuffed. Unable to fully explain what had just happened, I decided the best thing to do was to stand very still. My mother's eyes were darting over me like an X-ray. 'Is there anything you want to tell me, Emma?' she said, leaning over me a little. I shook my head. I may have only been four, but I wasn't stupid: unleashing the wrath of my mother was on a par with launching a nuclear bomb, something that my aunt Phyllis's boyfriend Steve would discover in just under forty-eight hours.

I was looking forward to going on holiday with my aunt Phyllis, not because she always plaited my hair or let me watch her putting on her make-up, but because I thought she was Cilla Black. 'My aunt is Cilla Black!' I would happily tell play-mates and they would stare at me, slightly incredulous. I wasn't lying, because I completely believed it. Looking back, the only evidence I had that my aunt was the seminal Liverpudlian entertainer was that they had vaguely similar hair. That was it. She wasn't even from Liverpool. She was from Basingstoke. But the slim and passing resemblance was good enough for me. As far as I was concerned, whenever my aunt was out of sight she was Cilla Black, and nothing would convince me otherwise.

At the time of our holiday, Phyllis was nineteen and going out with a young man called Steve whom she'd met on the dodgems at a local funfair two years previously. Steve worked in a laboratory that made retreads, whatever they were, and was a mod with a pug nose, hazel eyes and a mop of spiky, short brown hair. I'd met him a couple of times but I'd also met Phyllis's other secret boyfriend, Paul, who, for reasons of subterfuge and because I had flapping lips, was only ever referred to in my presence as Mr X. He had shoulder-length hair and looked like the lead singer of the Bay City Rollers. It was the first time I'd encountered a fashionable man. My father had no interest in clothes whatsoever and was an unimaginative jeans-and-jumper kind of guy. But Mr X, with his wild, untamed hair, yellow flares and purple platform boots, was a visual sensation. He was a peacock of a man and I adored him. Because I was too young to appreciate the subtle difficulties surrounding having two boyfriends at once, I was curious as to whether Mr X would be joining us. 'Is Mr X coming on holiday?' I asked my mother, as she stood stuffing clothes into a suitcase.

'No,' she explained with a smile. 'Mr X isn't coming on holiday with us. It's just Phyllis and Steve.'

This, of course, was a bitter disappointment not least because Steve had such an impenetrable Hampshire accent that he might as well have been talking in a foreign language. 'What did he say?' I would ask every time he opened his mouth and then look at him, with my nose scrunched up as tight as it would go.

'Now you're not going to mention Mr X in front of Steve, are you?' asked my mother, turning to look at me. 'Remember how we explained about that? Mr X is a secret.'

'But what if he comes too?' I asked, running my finger along the edge of my mother's dressing table. 'I can say his name then, can't I?'

'Well, yes, if Mr X is there then you can say his name,' explained my mother. 'But he won't be there. He's not coming on holiday with us. And when Mr X isn't there, we don't say his name. Steve wouldn't be very happy if we talked about Mr X all the time. So it's best to just not say his name at all.'

My mother was playing with fire. Nothing captured my interest more than something that made no sense. 'Why does Steve not like Mr X?' I asked, throwing myself down on the carpet and staring up. 'I like Mr X. I like Mr X more than I like Steve. Why doesn't he like him? Why can't I say his name?'

Brenda, sensing that she was heading down a dead end, picked up a T-shirt and folded it with military determination. 'Never mind about Mr X,' she muttered. 'Let's just forget about him. It doesn't matter whether Steve likes him or not. Anyway, we're going on holiday tomorrow, aren't we? And we're going to see Mam and Gwennie and Roy. And Gary and Margaret. And Adrian. And John. And Peggy. And little Gary. And Paul. And Gwyn. And Ann. And Beverley. And Jean. And Arthur. So that's nice, isn't it? And we'll see them. And we can go up the mountain because you'll like that. And then we'll go camping. In the tent. And we'll see Phyllis. And Steve.'

'But not Mr X?' I asked, rolling about a bit.

'No,' said my mother, through teeth that were approaching gritted. 'Not Mr X.'

A fact that I found intensely interesting.

Our new car was a white MG 1100 saloon. It had red plastic seats and went like the clappers, roaring with a proper old-fashioned vroom that people who like driving can only dream about. Tony, determined not to repeat the débâcle of our previous trip, had not only had the car serviced but had invested in a proper roof rack and, to keep me quiet, my mother had given me a Milly Molly Mandy book to bury my nose in. It was almost as if we knew what we were doing. The plan, travelwise, was to drive down to Phyllis's house in Basingstoke and then journey on to Wales in a convoy. As we pulled up outside my aunt's house, Steve was putting a suitcase into the boot of his blue Ford Anglia. 'Oiiiroiii!' he said with a wave.

'What did he say?' I asked, throwing a look over at my mother.

'Never mind,' she said. 'Now remember what we said about you know who.'

My dad, because he was a proper man, strolled over to Steve's car with his hands in his pockets. Steve's car had large, fat wheels which Dad felt compelled to kick with the side of his shoe. 'Special wheels, are they?' asked Dad, leaning over to take a better look.

'Gorrum orf fellah up Haaaatch,' said Steve with a nod.

'What?' I asked again, looking up again at my mother, who chose to ignore me.

'An oi got a nuu steerin whoil,' Steve continued. 'Ave a look. Bootiful. An a goir stick an all. An ave a look at thaaaaat. Fellah at worrrk dun it.'

Dad was peering in through the driver's door window.

He gestured over to me. 'Emma! Come and look at this!' he said, as if I was going to be interested. 'Come and see what Steve's done to his steering wheel.' I stood on tiptoes and looked in. 'Can you see there,' continued my dad, pointing. 'He's taken the boss from the centre of the steering wheel and he's replaced it with a watch. Isn't that amazing? It's a proper watch. And it works. How did you do that, Steve?'

Steve joined us in the window frame. 'Oi took it uht, got the waaatch, stuck it insiiide. Can kip it wound up an all. Juss woind it there.'

'Is Mr X coming?' I asked abruptly, because I'd just about had enough of this strange babble. My mother, emitting a sudden and involuntary high-pitched whine, swept me up quicker than a whirlwind and carried me promptly into the house as my father, ever the dependable sweeper-upper, shrugged his shoulders and claimed not to have the first idea what I was talking about.

Two minutes later and my aunt Phyllis was sitting with her hand over her mouth. 'We'll just have to pretend Mr X is her imaginary friend or something,' said my mother, throwing her arms into the air and pacing. I was sitting on the edge of my aunt's bed, having been perched there so the relevant grown-ups could stare at me and work out what to do. My aunt was in the middle of doing her make-up and was halfway through applying the heavy black eyeliner that gave her that trademark smoky look. One eye was fully made up, with false eyelashes applied, while the other was untouched, giving her an odd, pirate patch appearance. The horror of my blabbering mouth had rained down a blanket of terror and Phyllis was clearly not amused.

'Oh God!' she whined. 'I knew this would happen! Thank God we called him Mr X! Can you imagine?'

'It's not funny, Phyllis!' chided my mother. 'This is what

happens when you play with fire. I can't spend the next week on tenterhooks that she's going to tell him everything. It doesn't bear thinking about.'

'You won't tell Steve about Mr X, will you?' said Phyllis, leaning towards me. 'In fact, if you promise me that you won't mention Mr X again then I'll put your hair in pigtails. Would you like that?' I nodded. 'And,' continued my aunt, 'for every day you don't mention Mr X, I'll buy you a bag of sweets. Deal?'

In short, I was being bribed to keep my mouth shut.

As far as I was concerned, travelling in convoy was hilarious. I couldn't get enough of watching my aunt and Steve in the car behind. If I wasn't waving, then I was pulling stupid faces. If I wasn't sticking my tongue out, I was holding up my Milly Molly Mandy book and anything else I could lay my hands on: Mr Mouse, a hat or a packet of crisps, it didn't matter. I was convinced that whatever I could find and hold up would be nothing short of fascinating. My dad, who was an avid tennis fan, had, at the same time, slipped into a driving reverie and was saying the name of that year's Wimbledon ladies' champion, 'Evonne Goolagong', to himself as if it were a travelling mantra: 'Evonne...Goolagong. E-vonne. Goo-la-gong' and so forth. My mother, whose nerves were already partially frayed by the Mr X incident and shredding further with every passing minute, was near to breaking point.

'OK!' she snapped, crushing her eyes closed. 'That's it. Emma, sit down. Tony, I swear to God, if you say "Evonne Goolagong" one more time I'm going to commit a murder.'

'I can't help it,' explained my dad. 'I've got Evonne Goolagong" on the brain. Do you think it really is her name? Or they just made it up? Do tennis players have stage names? Like actors? Evonne Goolagong. It's not right, is it?'

'Evonne Goolagong!' I shouted with a grin. 'Evonne Goolagong!' And then, because this felt like something to share, I stood up again, stared out the back window at my aunt and Steve and yelled, 'Evonne Goolagong!' repeatedly while bouncing on the seat. As my mother, exasperated and frazzled, tugged at the back of my tights and told me to sit down, my father was busy negotiating the large roundabout we had found ourselves at. We were turning right, to take us on to the A40 that bypassed Oxford, but as we pulled out, a sudden phalanx of cars filed round, preventing Steve from following us. As my dad drove off and away, Steve, not realising that we'd taken the right-hand exit, happily carried straight on, speeding blindly into the centre of Oxford.

It was quite a while before any of us noticed. In fact, it was me, creeping up to sneak a look out the back window, who was the first to raise the alarm. 'Where are they?' I asked, staring out into the face of a strange man with a moustache. He waved at me. I didn't wave back. My mother twisted herself round and squinted.

'They're not there, Tony,' she said, with something approaching panic in her voice. 'Where are they? Tony! Where have they gone?'

'They'll be a couple of cars back,' said my dad, peering into his rear view mirror. 'I'll slow down a bit. Let some people overtake.' But they weren't a few cars back. They were stuck in a slow-moving one-way system, trapped in Oxford town centre and having a blazing row. With every turn of the wheel, we were being catapulted further away from them. The dreaded reality of what had happened struck my mother.

'What are we going to do?' she whispered, clutching my father by the shoulder. 'Shall we stop? Can we stop? Can we wait? Can we go back and look for them? Do they know where they're going?'

'Well they know we're going to Wales,' answered my father, shaking his head. 'But we can't go back. They could be anywhere. And we can't stop. There's nowhere to stop. I suppose I could stop when we get to Wales. We could wait for them at the border. But what if they get there first? You know how fast he drives.'

'Is this your fault?' asked my mother, sitting forward to give my father a proper glare. 'Did you do something wrong?'

'No!' squealed Tony, his blue eyes flashing. 'I just went round the roundabout. That's where he must have gone wrong. It's his fault. Not mine. If he'd been looking at the signs, he would have turned right.' And then, sensing that he was getting himself off a considerable hook, my dad shot my mother a look over his shoulder and added 'Bloody idiot', because when in doubt, it's very important to pass the buck of blame to anyone who's not there to defend themselves.

'What was Steve thinking?' wailed my mother, throwing an arm into the air. 'Why wasn't he looking properly?' My father, who's no fool, threw in a couple of murmurs in agreement.

'He was probably looking at that watch in his steering wheel,' said my dad, as if to underline the moment. 'Or something. Well, let's look on the bright side. At least he knows we're going to Wales. He'll realise what he's done, turn back and turn the right way up the A40. That's what he'll do. That's what I would do.'

'I bet Aunty wished Mr X was on our holiday now,' I said, to throw my tuppence worth into the pot, at which my mother looked at me, fixed me with a gaze and then sunk her forehead into the palm of her hand.

This was all going terribly well.

There was one small crumb of comfort: Steve knew the name of the campsite. If the worst came to the worst they could head there under their own steam. Our paths could still collide. But we had Welsh family to deal with first: Phyllis and Steve would have to wait.

We would be staying overnight at Mam's and as we arrived back at the terraced street we had passed so fleetingly a year before, a large coal wagon was making deliveries. Huge slabs of coal were being dumped on the pavement in front of people's front doors and the street was a clatter of activity: the delivery men, covered from head to toe in black dust, were banging on doors; lads of all shapes and sizes were breaking up the table-sized blocks of coal into manageable pieces and from the top of the street to the bottom, women were standing on their flagstone steps and hollering out orders. Mam was no exception. Being in her seventies, she wasn't expected to break her own coal or take it through to the cellar so a young man from the coal wagon was heaving her allotted ton through the house. 'Don't you get any coal on my suite!' she was yelling after him as he struggled past her with a lump the size of a sink. As fast as the coal was being squirrelled away, so the paving stones were being drowned in soapy water as the women scrubbed away the dust, leaving a filthy grey slurry to cascade down the road.

As ever, our arrival was causing as much fuss as the coal. 'That Emma, is it?' shouted a woman from the house opposite. She was tall and fat, wrapped in a flowery apron, with the sleeves of her jumper rolled up to her elbows. She had squinty eyes and was wearing a bobble hat. Standing next to her, with a bucket to collect the smaller pieces of coal, was her husband, who, in contrast, was as thin as a pole and tiny. My dad turned to acknowledge her.

'Yes!' he shouted back, holding my arm out as if presenting a prize cow. 'This is Emma. Say hello to Vangie, Emma. That's it.'

'Come up from England then?' asked Vangie, leaning against her doorframe.

'Never you mind where they've come from, Vangie Bull!' shouted my grandmother back. 'Always got your nose in everyone's business!'

'All right, Brenda?' persisted Vangie. 'Not wearing black today then?' My mother, preoccupied with thoughts of her sister, mustered up a weak smile and shook her head. It wasn't the quiet arrival she'd been hoping for.

My grandmother, incensed at her neighbour's nosiness, pushed us rather forcefully in through the front door. 'Vangie Bull, Come Push Come Pull!' she moaned, waving a thumb over her shoulder. 'That woman would know if someone was pregnant if they were still a virgin! She's unbelievable. Where's your sister, Brenda?'

'We don't know, Mam,' explained Dad. 'We lost them at Oxford. And they don't know where you live. We'll have to keep our fingers crossed that they make their way to the campsite.'

'You're mad going camping again,' muttered Mam, grabbing a loaf of bread and shoving it under her armpit. 'Bloody mad. Now then. Bit of bread and butter?'

My grandmother's house was very basic. With seven children to raise, a surfeit of money had never been in the offing. And with nothing but a small pension to live on, Mam was still getting by with an outside toilet and no bathroom. The toilet, which grumbled at the bottom of the long, thin garden like a tethered bear, may as well have come with its own screaming woman, it was so terrifying. To look at, it was reminiscent of the tiny, confined Hell holes you find in horror films, and I had the sense that my mother, as we walked towards it, needed me just as much as I needed her. The toilet frame was wooden and the door, clinging to three blackened hinges, was partially rotted away at the bottom and down one side panel, giving it a battered, beaten-down appearance. As my mother creaked the door open, a smell of oil dripped through the air, wafting from the old brass lamp hanging next to the cistern to stop the water freezing during winter. The toilet was unlike anything I'd ever seen. There was no bowl to speak of. Instead, there was an old seat and riser: a rectangular box of heavy oak with a hole cut into its middle. A roll of toilet paper sat to the right of the hole and to the left was a pile of newspapers and magazines, reading material for the long, contemplative silences that went hand in hand with a trip to the 'lav'. As I stared at the hole, I was reminded not only of my mother's terrible warning about the cataclysmic consequences of wooden toilet seats but also of my mishap with that bucket twelve months previously. There was no way I was sitting down on it. Imagine if I fell down that! I wouldn't be found for days. So instead, as my mother stood outside, with the door slightly ajar to let more light in, I decided that the best thing to do was to stand on the riser, aim for the hole and hope for a miracle. As I stood, feet placed on either side of the hole, I pulled down my tights and pants as best I could. Sadly, my best was not quite good enough and as I started peeing, I found my pants and tights were rapidly becoming warm and very wet. Unaware that just standing upright and weeing was a disaster, I shifted slightly to adjust my aim. Even though I was now missing my pants, I was instead hitting the back of the riser, sending a plume of pee spray splattering everywhere. I had hosed the place with piss. It was everywhere, all over the newspapers, all over the toilet paper and most of it in my left shoe. I was in Wales and covered in urine. Again.

'Oh, Emma, no,' whined my mother as she surveyed the devastated scene. 'What were you doing?'

I was still standing on the riser but with a look of wretched despair. I needed a bath but my grandmother didn't have a bath: what she had instead was a large tin tub dragged up from the cellar, placed in front of the black, iron fireplace and filled with bucket after bucket of warm water. Basic it may have been, but as I sat, covered in suds in my grandmother's front room, I found the experience exhilarating. To this day, it is the best bath I've ever had.

Having said that, there was one aspect of my bath that wasn't very enjoyable, and that was the constant stream of visitors into Mam's front room. In Treherbert, no one shut their front door. Neither did anyone knock on the door as they came in: banging on a front door was a sign that someone had died and so, as news spread that the Bride in Black was in residence, the steady trickle of neighbours began. Bopa Jackson was first into the sitting room. In her seventies, hair tied tight into a bun, she was a small, slight woman, but with a voice that belied her size. 'Hello, Tony!' she boomed, as she wandered in, like a fly might flit in through an open window. 'How you keeping? All right? I'm fine. Had a bad knee. But other than that…That Emma? Enjoying your bath? Hello, Brenda. What's that you're wearing? Smock, is it? That what they wear in London, is it? Very nice.'

Bopa was a particular favourite of my father's. As a child, he would run errands for her at thruppence a go. Not only that, but every Sunday Tony would scamper across to Bopa's house, where she always kept the last fat spoonful of rice pudding waiting for him. As kind as she was, she was also renowned for her temper. Woe betide the child who made the paving stones in front of her house dirty. When Dinky cars came to the valley, the children would spend hours marking out roadways on the pavement with chalk. But if you did it in front of Bopa Jackson's doorway, you not only had your

roadway scrubbed away with a stiff brush, you also had
your lump of chalk thrown in with the washing water where
you could only watch as it melted away to nothing. Fast on
Bopa's heels was Katie, a short, stout barrel of a woman who
lived next door. She would bang on the wall of the kitchen to
signal her imminent arrival and then appear, still wiping her
hands on the bottom of her apron, to see if a pot was brewing or if there was any news from the street.

'In the bath, are we?' noted Katie, nodding in my direction. I stared up and nodded. In normal circumstances I
would have entered into an extended and overly complicated
explanation of the chain of events which had led to me sitting
in a tin tub in broad daylight, but the fact of the matter was,
I was a bit embarrassed.

'Messed herself in the lav,' explained my grandmother,
looking down at me. 'Thought you had to stand up on it.
Never heard of such a thing.'

'Stand up on it?' wailed Katie, letting out a hoot. 'No! We
don't stand up on toilets in Wales. Is that what you do in
England?'

'Mummy said you can't sit on wooden toilets,' I began,
pointing in my mother's direction. 'Or bad things happen.'
Everyone turned and looked at her. Brenda, sensing an
unwanted awkwardness, threw in a sudden and perfectly
performed laugh.

'Ha ha ha ha,' she splurted, throwing in a solid shake of
the head for good measure. 'I didn't say that. What I said was
that you had to be careful about splinters. Generally. Not just
from toilet seats. From wood. Anything made from wood.'

'No you didn't,' I said, staring.

'I was once in the lav,' chipped in Bopa, saving the day,
'and a rat ran out between my legs. Bold as brass. Up it came.
From the sewer. Screamed the place down, I did.'

'Vangie Bull's getting an indoor toilet,' added Katie, settling herself into the sofa. 'That's what she says, anyway. Her husband's aunt died. Turns out she had all this money, and they're getting some of it. But I heard you can apply for a grant. And get indoor toilets, bathrooms, all sorts. A woman up at Blaencwm told me. She knows someone from Blaenrhondda who's been given a proper bathroom suite. They got a bidet. All it does is wash your bum. That's all it does. Proper posh, like.'

'What's wrong with a flannel?' asked Bopa, hands on her knees. 'Bidets. Load of nonsense.'

'Anyway,' said Katie, giving my mother a nudge. 'I come round to ask if Emma would like to light the lamps with Danny this evening? He's my husband. Does the gas lights in the street. I'll tell him to pop in when he's doing Scott Street, shall I? I bet she's never seen the lamps being lit. All electric where you are, ain't it?'

'Oh, that'd be brilliant,' smiled my mother, relieved to have got past the social hiccup. 'She'd love that. Wouldn't you?'

I didn't reply. I was still staring, having learnt a valuable lesson: my mother was a liar.

My dad was the youngest boy in a family of seven. He had three brothers: Gwyn, Gary and John, and three sisters: Marion, Gwennie and Jean. The eldest sister, Marion, had emigrated to America after receiving a ticket in the post from her GI boyfriend, Gus, whom she had met at the end of the war while working in an armaments factory in Salisbury. They had written to each other every week for twelve years before Gus had enough money to send for her. Every Christmas they would be sent a large parcel from America, which my dad would look forward to with wide-eyed excitement. It would be packed with all manner of mind-boggling treats:

tinned food, chocolates, comics and, on one occasion, a startling blue silk tie that had a woman in nothing more than a bikini emblazoned down its centre.

They were a close and loving family, even if they had all gone their separate ways, and there was genuine delight at seeing their youngest brother home and back in the fold. Within hours of our arrival, they had filed in, one by one, until the whole family, bar Marion who couldn't be there, was crammed into Mam's front room. Being an only child and living in Stevenage, where we were two hours from the nearest relative, I was filled with a glowing warmth from being surrounded by family. I was enraptured by my Welsh aunts and uncles and thought them fabulous. The loudest and most entertaining was my dad's eldest brother, Gwyn. He was a member of the Selsig Operatic Society and would burst into song mid-sentence, filling the room with syrupy baritone sounds that made my chest rumble. He was funny too, and as I sat, cuddled into my aunt Gwennie, who had the kindest face you could ever be blessed with, he had the family howling with laughter.

'Remember Dafydd? Number 34?' Gwyn began, nudging my dad on the knee. 'Skinny thing, all bones. Couldn't beat a gnat. Well, he got married, see. And he finds out his wife's having an affair. So he goes to have it out with the fellah. But he can't fight him. A gust of wind would have him over. So he waits and waits until the fellah, who's a plumber, goes down into the side culvert at the bottom of Scott Street.'

'You know, it's like a big well. Got to use a ladder to get in and out of it,' explained my uncle John with a twinkle.

'So the fellah's gone down into the culvert,' continued Gwyn, 'and up comes Dafydd, stands over him, says, "You been sleeping with my wife", whips out his cock and pisses all over him!'

'Terrible!' shouted Jean, who was handing round some sticky slices of Teishen Lap.

'Pissed all over him!' shouted Gwyn, thumping his thigh and laughing. 'Still. He had it coming. Tupping someone else's wife. Not right. Not right at all.'

'No,' they all mumbled in agreement.

'So you're going camping tomorrow, are you?' asked Gary, who had brought some of his homemade wine for everyone to drink. 'I hope we don't have a repeat of last year? Mam not going with you then?'

'No fear,' muttered Mam, folding her arms. 'Never again.'

'We're going up the Gower. To Port Eynon,' nodded my dad. 'Brenda's sister's supposed to be with us. But we've lost her.'

'Roy and I went camping couple of weeks ago,' said Gwennie in her soft lilt. 'Drove down to Spain. But it was so hot, Brenda, we just lay in the tent all day. Couldn't go out. Exhausting, it was.'

'No chance of it being too hot in Port Eynon,' chipped in Gwyn. 'I hope you've packed jumpers.'

'Hey, have you seen John's motorbike?' butted in Gary. 'He's got a sidecar! Let Emma have a go in it! She'll love it!' An outbreak of enthusiastic agreement exploded in the room and I was bustled out to the front of the house, where my uncle John's Vincent 1,000cc motorbike was parked. I'd never seen a sidecar before and, as I was placed inside, it felt like being put into the cockpit of a Spitfire. Goggles were pulled down over my eyes and Gwennie tightened the strap at the back of my head so that they wouldn't fall down.

My uncle John was the good-looking one in the family. He had a head of tight black curls and a cheeky smile that made all possibilities endless. Being the closest in age to my dad, John was the brother with whom Tony had got up to most of his adolescent high jinks. They had broken windows together, chased girls together and had once even almost drowned together in an ill-thought-out dash into an angry sea hell-bent on carrying them to a watery grave. As with all proper handshakes with death, the brothers' near miss had not only forged a special bond between them, but had also left them with a determination to embrace life. As I looked up at my uncle, goggles on and grinning, there was an infectious sense of fun: we were going for a ride on his motorbike and it was going to be brilliant. As John thumped his foot down on the starter pedal, the thick rasp of the engine kicked in, shaking my body with fat vibrations. Everyone was standing on the pavement, laughing and waving. Everyone, that is, except my mother, who just stood looking pale and tortured in that way mothers do when they know that sometimes they have to stand back and let their children have an experience.

We thundered through Treherbert, screaming up the straight roads and bouncing round corners. Although we couldn't have been going more than thirty miles an hour, being so near the floor and exposed to the elements, it felt a lot faster. As first rubs with speed go, it was electrifying, and I found myself gripping the walls of the sidecar with white-knuckled intensity. We weaved our way through the terraced streets and reached the uphill climb to the top of the mountain. Houses gave way to sheds that, in turn, gave way to desolate lumps of rock, lingering among the ferns. Sheep and ponies stopped what they were doing to stare at us as we hurtled past, and with every twist of the road, I felt a jolt of fear that I could fly off the edge of the mountain at any moment. Wind was battering through my hair and even though it was a sunny day, the sting of a cold Welsh wind was at my cheeks. I was vaguely aware of my uncle shouting things as we passed a trout farm or an abandoned car but I couldn't

hear him, so fierce was the roar from the exhaust. At the head
of the pass my uncle slowed a little so that I could take in the
glory of the view. We had reached the Big Stone, an enormous
obelisk of rock that seemed propped up out of nowhere.
Below us flew away the magnificent river valley of the
Rhondda, towns and villages climbing as far up the mountain-
sides as they dared, and in front of us two incredible peaks:
ahead of us the Graig Y Ddelw mountain and to our right the
Pen Pych, a striking, flat-topped summit. Neither mountain
had any trees and, in 1971, before the Forestry Commission
planted the area with pines, they were still open spaces, where
anyone could wander as they pleased. Off in the distance I
could see a group of boys cascading down the mountainside,
sticks in hands, ferns in pockets. But it wasn't just the natural
beauty of my father's homeland that caught my attention. As
we drove on, I could just make out the pit head, a giant wheel
rising up from the horizon. The mountain was being disem-
bowelled before my very eyes. In the midst of the green
ramble, the dark mechanics of the pit stuck out like a black
menace. Low, moody buildings surrounded the pit tower, coal
trucks waited on gloomy rail tracks and men and pit ponies
stood, blackened with dust, almost shocked that such a dirty
industry could have found itself in such an idyllic location.

Wales was a constant contrast of beauty and hardship and
as we made our quicksilver descent back into the valley, my
delight at the speed, the sights and the smells was tempered
with a sense of the brutal. There was a raw honesty to the
mountain, one that commanded respect. This was the land of
my father, my heritage, and as we clattered back up Scott
Street where my family was all standing in the street waiting
for me, I felt a terrible sadness that these riches weren't mine
on a daily basis.

*

'Do you think Phyllis is all right?' asked my mother later, as we sat eating Gwennie's homemade pickled onions. They were so sweet and juicy that I couldn't keep my hand out of the jar.

'Look,' began my dad, holding out one hopeful hand. 'If Steve has got any sense he'll have made his way to the campsite. They'll be there now. They'll have got their tent up. They'll be fine. A man who can put a watch in the middle of his steering wheel can find a campsite. Trust me.'

My mother chewed her lip a little and nodded. 'And I suppose there's nothing we can do about it tonight,' added Brenda. 'And you're right. They'll be at the campsite. They will. Emma, don't eat all those pickled onions. They'll give you terrible wind.'

The pickled onions I'd eaten before had always come with that acrid, sharp twist but these were so delicate and bursting with flavour they were like sweets. The jar, which I had had my fist in for the past fifteen minutes, was taken away and the top screwed back on, but I felt such a terrible longing I just sat and stared at them bobbing away and uneaten. 'Don't stare at the onions,' whispered my mother, giving me a pat on the knee, a phrase that I don't think has ever been said to me since.

Thankfully, a visitor was on hand to distract me. It was Danny, who lived next door, the husband of Katie who had been round earlier to ask if I'd like to accompany him as he lit the gas lamps in Scott Street. Danny was a tall, thin man, very fit, and with a face that glowed with the health of a man who is out in all weather. He was wearing heavy, brown boots and a battered leather jerkin that had all manner of half-stuffed pockets. With the natural, wiry energy of a man who had a job to do, he stood in the doorway of Mam's sitting room and spoke very fast, words shooting out of him like bullets. 'How do?' he began, fidgeting on his feet. 'Come to see if Emma wants to come up the street, see the lamps lit, got to get on, mind. Still got Tynewydd, Blaencwm, Blaenrhondda to get to, got a mantle needs fixing at the bottom end, you can watch me do that an' all. Hello, Tony, Brenda. Glad to see you well. You coming?'

Danny, who had to light all the gas lamps in four villages, would walk miles every day. He only needed two things: an eight-foot ladder that he carried over one shoulder and a long wooden pole with a hook on the end that operated a small lever at the top of the lamps. 'Now the lamp', he explained, as we stood beneath the first of Scott Street's two lamps, 'is operated by a small switch. When we switch it on, the gas comes out and then we have a light. So shall we have a go at turning it on?' I nodded. Putting a hand on my shoulder, he manoeuvred me in front of him so that I was facing the lamp. 'So let's see if you can get the hook on the lever,' he said, as I stood between his legs, staring up. He had one hand on the pole steadying it while I had both hands on the bottom, gripping it tight. I didn't know what I was trying to latch on to but Danny's guiding hand flicked the hook on to the top of the switch. 'Now pull it down,' he instructed. I gave the pole a tug. A small fizz sounded from above and, as if by magic, the gas mantle, a small, white ball made of mesh net, filled with a wondrous glow. Suddenly, there was light. It was like being asked to turn on the Christmas lights on Regent Street.

As we waved off Danny, who was already scampering up the street to bring light to the rest of the valley, my dad noticed that the cockle cart, which came round once a week, had appeared at the bottom end of the street behind us. It was being pushed by a woman whose voice was being carried up towards us. 'Cockles!' she was shouting. 'Cock-les!'

The cockle cart was a metallic, lead-coloured box on a trolley that had four, pram-like wheels. The cockle woman, or 'cockleooman' as everyone called her, was a tiny, ancient, shrivelled-up thing who couldn't have been taller than four foot five inches. She was bent over like a broken shoe and, to me, seemed incredibly scruffy, in a long, dirty waterproof and a brown flat cap with a fat brim. Her hands were red and gnarled and looked rough to the touch. She had a pint glass in one hand and as the women of the street came up with their pans and buckets, she lifted the two lids on top of the trolley to reveal hundreds, if not thousands, of cockles in their shells. Thrusting the pint glass in, she would fill whatever receptacle was presented to her, all the while shouting, 'Cockles! Five pence a pint!'

My dad lifted me up so I could look into the trolley at the cockles. 'What you do,' he explained, 'is take the cockles home and then you put them in a bucket with some fresh water. And then you leave them like that for a day. And that gets rid of all the salt water that's in them. And they sit in the bucket, bubbling away. Sometimes they open up and you can see the cockle cleaning itself. Just bubbling away. And then, when all the salt water has gone, you throw them all into a big, hot pan and they open up and cook. Fresh cockles. Delicious.'

'Is that you, Tony?' said a voice from behind us. I turned round but was puzzled to see that no one was there. 'Tony!' the voice called out. 'Down here!' Following the sound of the voice, I looked down. There was a woman staring up at me from a tiny, barred window that seemed to sink below street level. I tugged on my dad's arm. This was startling. There was a woman shouting at us and she appeared to live underneath the pavement.

'Auntie Lal!' shouted my dad with a wave, as if this was nothing out of the ordinary.

'Get me some cockles, would you?' yelled back Lal, who had now opened the window and was holding out a ten-pence piece between the bars. 'Just two pints, mind.'

I was rooted to the spot. What a day I'd had. I'd covered myself in urine, I'd had a wash in a tin bath, I'd had my first go in a sidecar, I'd lit a street lamp and now my father was conversing with a woman who lived in a hole underground. 'Why is she down there?' I asked, turning and looking up at my father.

'Oh, she lives in the cellar,' answered my dad, as if that was the most normal thing in the world. 'That's Auntie Lal. She loves Shakespeare. Two pints, please.' The cockle woman pulled out a bag and filled it with cockle shells, all clattering against each other, like pebbles being dragged on the shoreline.

'Let's give them to Auntie Lal,' said my dad, handing me the bag. Lal's face was still at the window. She had piercing blue eyes that blazed out of a round, well-filled face and her hair was tied up into a lazy knot.

'Oh thank you, Tony!' she shouted up, as we passed the bag down to her. 'This your Emma, is it? Doesn't she look like Bec? My goodness. Same eyes. You getting some cockles?'

'Not today, no,' said my dad, shaking his head. 'We won't have time to clean them before we leave. We're off camping tomorrow.'

'Camping, is it?' said Lal, raising her eyebrows. 'Didn't you go camping last year? All ended very bad, didn't it?'

'It did a bit,' said my dad with a nod. 'That won't happen this year, mind. Nothing will go wrong this year.'

'Ooh, don't speak too soon,' tutted Lal, eyebrows knitting together. 'Never tempt fate, Tony! Look what happened to Hamlet!'

But it was too late. We had tempted fate. And fate was very tempted indeed.

*

I had slept like a log but was woken by the vague sense of raised voices and a distant clattering that seemed to be coming from outside. 'Shoo!' I could hear. 'Shoo! Away with you!'

'Bin day,' said my dad with a morning yawn. 'Bloody sheep. They come down off the mountain and have a go at the bins.' The plan was to have breakfast and get going. My mother, despite everyone's reassurances, had had a restless night fretting about her sister and was anxious to be on our way as soon as possible.

'When I know she's all right I'll be fine,' said my mother, getting dressed. 'It's just the not knowing. I can't bear that.'

As a treat, I was being given a boiled egg and soldiers for my breakfast and had scampered down the stairs to take my place at the table. My grandmother, who seemed to have been up for hours laying fires and cleaning, was watching my toast as it cooked under the grill. 'Would you like some nice Welsh butter?' she asked, slipping the hot toast on to a plate. I nodded and picked up a spoon, ready to knock the top off my egg. It was at this point that I noticed something moving by the kitchen door. I looked over and was so shocked that I could only emit a small, startled squeak. My grandmother glanced over her shoulder. There were two sheep standing staring at her. 'Oh!' she yelled, running at them with a tea towel. 'Out you go! Out you go!' The sheep, who were clearly used to wandering into people's houses, didn't seem to be in any sort of rush to leave. Instead, realising the game was up, they turned around and trotted off, only to be met with an ear-piercing scream from my mother who happened to be coming down the stairs just as they were coming out of the sitting room.

'Aaaaaaaaaaaaaaaaaaaaaaah!' came the wail. 'There's sheep! Sheep in the house!'

'Every week!' shouted my grandmother. 'Every week!'

'Yeah,' said my dad, wandering in with a shrug. 'They do that all the time. Ooh. You got an egg, Em? Lovely.'

I had had a wonderful time visiting my Welsh relatives and as we were seen off by what seemed to be half the street I stood on the back seat of the car, facing out and waving until they had all evaporated into the horizon. 'Well,' said my mother, clapping her hands together. 'That was lovely. Still. Onwards and upwards. We're going camping!'

'Hooray!' cheered my dad, who then burst into a solid rendition of 'Take Me Home, Country Roads', which, because it was the holiday song, we all joined in with. He then followed on with a rousing interpretation of the Welsh national anthem but because neither my mother nor I was able to speak Welsh, we just sat and listened. As my father was belting out the high notes my mother shot me a glance and rolled her eyes. Sometimes, it would seem, Welsh men just had to be indulged.

We had been driving for about an hour by the time we reached Swansea. My dad, who wanted to take a more scenic route, had decided that he would take the coastal road so we could drive past the sea. There was a large dock area packed with cranes and containers where the coal that came from the mountains sat, waiting to be shipped out of South Wales. Swansea Bay itself was a flat area and picturesque. It was typical of the open seafronts perched on prime coastland but was unusually empty of holidaymakers, most of whom would have chosen to travel on to the Gower where the beaches and sea water were more pleasant. Being next to the port, Swansea Bay had suffered from its proximity to heavy industry and the sea water, which would normally be so inviting, presented a muddy prospect, blackened by the regular oil spillages that left emulsified and fluffy suds slithering across the surface. The odd cockle shack stood out, the only things that paid lip service to a summer trade, but even these were functional affairs: fresh cockles and Bara Law, or lava bread, a thick black mud of a meal that would be wrapped in greaseproof paper and carried wearily home. We stopped briefly so that my dad could pick some up, and as he showed it to me all I could think was that he had taken leave of his senses and wanted to eat an astringent-smelling, loose horse manure for supper. A supper, I was pretty sure, he'd be eating on his own.

We had just passed the golf course on our right when we saw it. About a hundred yards ahead of us there seemed to be the sort of commotion that goes hand in hand with a road traffic accident. Cars were stopped helter-skelter in the road and people were out of their vehicles and standing about with their arms folded. 'Oh,' said Tony, with that all-seeing eye of his. 'Accident. Not much of a tailback though. We'll be through this in a few minutes.' But as we drew nearer, there was something horribly familiar about one car that was up on the pavement. Not only that, but there was something disgustingly recognisable about the man standing picking glass out of his windscreen. 'Jesus Christ!' shouted my dad. 'It's Steve! It's bloody Steve!'

Steve and Phyllis had had a crash. And there was no sign of Phyllis.

A dreaded silence descended as if time had stopped dead in its tracks and there was a sense, for a brief moment, that we were suspended in water looking out at a muffled world. Shock bristled through the car and, although I couldn't quite grasp the full implications of what I was seeing, I was overwhelmed with an instant feeling of anxiety. My mother, letting out a small, fearful moan, was first out of the car. 'Steve!' she shouted, both hands out. 'What's happened? Where's Phyllis? Where's my sister?'

Steve, who looked more terrified than relieved to see his girlfriend's sister bearing down on him, stopped what he was doing and, in something of a daze, said, 'They took her up hospitaaal. In amb'lunce. She's gorrt cut on the head.'

'What did he say?' I said, staring up at my dad. Things did not look good. One side of the windscreen had been completely smashed and it was obvious that someone had gone through it. Broken glass was scattered across the top of the bonnet and a rather ominous pool of blood had gathered on the grass verge by the passenger door that was hanging open. Steve, grey and shaken, was holding a large piece of broken windscreen in his hand and looked as if he didn't quite know whether to keep it or throw it to the floor. My mother, who was glaring at the car with a touch of the gorgon, was clearly about to explode. I looked at her. I looked at Steve. 'Is he going to be in trouble now?' I asked Dad, who had one hand on my shoulder.

'If I find out,' my mother began with a hiss, 'that this was your fault, then I will make it my life's mission, my LIFE'S mission, to track you down and cut your balls off.'

'Ooh,' said Dad, leading me to the back of the car. 'You wait here. I'll just try and calm things down a bit.'

A small crowd had started to gather, drawn not only by the accident, but by the entertainment that was being played out. My mother, in full swing, was creeping ever closer to Steve and pointing a lot, and while I couldn't quite make out what it was she was saying to him I had no doubt that whatever it was would have sent chills like a nuclear winter through the hearts of anyone within hearing distance. The onlookers were rapt.

'You know the girl that was hurt, do you?' asked a woman standing next to me, as my mother blazed on. I nodded.

'It's my aunt,' I said. 'Cilla Black.'

'Cilla Black?' said the woman, suddenly staring at me. 'Cilla Black? Did you hear that?' She looked at the people around her. 'Cilla Black's been in a car crash! Right here! In Swansea!'

'No!' came a wail from the back. 'Not Cilla Black!'

'Oh that's a shame,' said a man, shaking his head. 'I like her.'

My father, who was now physically dragging my mother away from Steve, gestured over to me to get back into our car. 'Come on, Em!' he yelled. 'We're going up the hospital! Get in!'

'Oh, what if she's brain damaged!' wailed my mother, bursting into tears. 'She might be a vegetable! And she's only just passed her typing exams! And what if she's got a clot? On the brain? She might die! Or be blind! It's that bloody watch in his stupid steering wheel! I bet he was looking at it! Oh, what are we going to do? What?'

'Brenda!' snapped my father, as we sped away. 'Calm down! There's no point in dwelling on anything until we know what the situation is and then...'

'Look out!' screamed my mother, as my father narrowly missed a collision with a milk van. 'Oh, that's all we need! My sister's probably dead. And now you're going to kill us as well!'

I was keeping quiet. My mother was in hysterics and my father was sweating profusely. There was a palpable tension in the car and as we screamed into the car park of the Swansea Hospital Accident and Emergency department, my heart was thumping in my chest. My aunt had been in a car crash and she was hurt. Suddenly, the seriousness of the situation hit me.

'Come on, Em,' said my dad, picking me up as we ran towards the entrance. 'Don't cry. Phyllis'll be fine.'

'Don't say that yet!' yelled my mother, who was properly sprinting. 'She might have an eye hanging out!'

'Is it because I wasn't waving and they got lost?' I whimpered, holding on to my dad's shirt collar.

'No,' said my dad, 'it's not your fault. It's because Steve's a fucking cock.'

'My sister!' screamed my mother, waving her arms in the air as we clattered into reception. 'She's been in a car crash! Where is she? Where is she?'

'Daddy,' I said, staring down. 'There's blood on the floor.'

'Yes. Don't look at that,' said my dad. 'It probably doesn't belong to anyone we know.'

'My sister!' wailed my mother again. 'Has anyone seen my sister?'

A thumping tub of a nurse waddled into view. She had a face like a just punched mule and looked as if she could strangle sharks. 'We'll have no shouting here,' she said in a deep, nasal accent. 'Calm yourself. Now then, who are you looking for?'

'It's my sister,' sobbed Brenda. 'She's been in a car crash. She's called Phyllis.'

'Oh no,' we heard a small voice behind a screen whimper. 'It's my sister. Oh please don't let her in.' It was my aunt. She was alive.

'Phyllis!' wailed my mother, pushing her way past the nurse to get to her. 'Oh Jesus and Mary! What have they done? Where does it hurt? Do you know who I am?'

'Oh shut up, Brenda,' said Phyllis, who had two big dressings on her face, one over her left eyebrow and the other on her left cheekbone. 'Some holiday this is.'

'You all right?' asked my dad, putting me down. I went straight to the chair next to my aunt's examination table and promptly squeezed my hand into hers. Holding someone's hand was what you did when they were ill, I knew that for a fact.

'I've had stitches and I feel a bit worn out,' said Phyllis with a shrug. 'But other than that I'm fine. Please don't make a scene. This is bad enough as it is without you embarrassing me as well.'

'What happened?' asked Brenda, taking Phyllis's other hand. 'Was it Steve? I'll kill him. KILL him.' My dad shot my mother a long, hard glare. She ignored it.

'I don't know. I wasn't facing the right way. My hair had gone frizzy and I wanted to flatten it. And I had a pair of pants in my handbag. So I reached back to get them and I was putting the pants on my head to flatten my hair and then the next thing I know I've hit the windscreen. And then loads of people came and someone took me out of the car and lay me on the floor. And then the ambulance came and that was that.'

'So when the ambulance came,' said Tony, with something approaching a small smirk, 'you were lying on the floor with a pair of pants on your head?'

'Yes!' screamed Phyllis, with a hoot. 'Oh, don't make me laugh. It hurts. Where's Steve?'

'He's still with the car,' said Dad, throwing a thumb over his shoulder. 'He's in a bit of a state, to be honest.'

'He's got to wait for the breakdown truck to come,' explained Phyllis. 'Poor thing. He loves that car.'

'Never mind the car, Phyllis!' interjected my mother. 'You could have been killed.'

'Well I haven't been. So don't go on,' replied my aunt with a sigh. 'Anyway, they've said I can go. They've arranged for an ambulance to take me to the campsite. Listen, Tony, you should probably go back to where Steve is, wait with him and then bring him on. He won't be able to get there otherwise. Brenda and Em can come with me in the ambulance.'

I'd never been in an ambulance, but rather than feeling excited, I decided to take my mother's lead and assume a reverential hush. Phyllis had been lain down on a stretcher while my mother and I sat in two seats, one facing forwards and the other, just behind the driver's seat, facing backwards. The driver, a wiry man with greased-down hair, was full of chat and good humour, which my mother, still in something of a state, wasn't quite in the mood for.

'So let me get this straight,' he said, glancing back over his shoulder at us. 'You came on holiday to Wales last year and had to go home and you've come again this year and now you've got to go home again? Well! There's always next year! Third time lucky and all that.'

My mother rolled her eyes. 'Over my dead body,' she mumbled. 'I'm never coming on holiday to Wales again.'

It was a first for the Port Eynon campsite: they'd never had anyone arrive in an ambulance before and as we bumped towards my aunt's pitched tent, we created a small buzz of interest. Not that we were going to be staying, of course: Phyllis's injuries and the towing away of Steve's car meant that it now fell to us to get her back to Basingstoke. Our holiday was all but over. The ambulance driver, struck with a small twinge of guilt that he had made light of our predicament, took down my aunt's tent as we sat in the back of the ambulance and watched on. 'There you are then,' he said, as he folded up the ground sheet and placed it on top of the packed-up equipment. 'I hope you all get home safe. Oh, and have these,' he added, passing us half a bag of barley sugars. 'For the little one.'

The three of us sat on the folded ground sheet and waited for my dad to arrive with Steve. We were all sucking on our sweets and not saying much – other than my mother, who needed to explain to every passer-by what had happened. 'Jesus,' she moaned, as the seventh person had wandered over. 'It's like being the resident freak show.'

By the time my dad arrived, we were all fed up and ready to get going. Packing a second tent, as well as my aunt and Steve, into our already crammed car was a challenge and we found ourselves crowbarred into an extreme squeeze. I was in the back, squashed between my mother and my aunt. Seeing as things had fallen into a catastrophic silence, I felt now was probably the best time to throw in my twopennies' worth. I turned to my aunt. 'I bet you wish Mr X had come now,' I said, popping another barley sugar into my mouth.

Everyone turned and stared. 'Who's Mr X?' asked Steve, turning round to look at me.

'Auntie's secret boyfriend,' I said, beaming.

My aunt, fixing me with a glare, said nothing, but with one sharp tug took the bag of barley sugars and chucked them out the window. We drove the rest of the way home in silence. We had been in touching distance of a proper family holiday. Our tent hadn't even left the boot.

Chapter Three

The Whitsun of Discontent

In 1972, I was interested in only one thing: the Wendy house at my local nursery. I had been at nursery school for a year, and had been solely responsible for what had been a small, voluntary organisation being given proper funding by the local education authority. They had needed one more child to become eligible for government money and I was it, the last child to come knocking. The nursery was tucked away behind a tired-looking row of shops in a Methodist church that seemed to have been built by the Stevenage planners just to dot that i and cross that t. It was a modern, oblong building with a low, peaked roof and through its impossibly sticky double doors there was a large, open space that, from Monday to Friday, was the hub of my social existence. Finger painting and potato prints were my new *raison d'être*: if I didn't take a picture home with me for the daily parental show-and-tell then life wasn't worth living.

As the late newcomer to the nursery I had missed out on the crucial pecking order that had been established prior to my arrival. The Wendy house, which was to become my consuming obsession, was the domain of Julie, a fat little girl who, because she always wore nylon, was forever giving people small electric shocks. A rumour went round that she was a wizard and her ability to pass on pinching, sharp snaps was just a taster of her formidable powers. To cut a long story short, I thought Julie could kill me and so I would stand, staring over at the Wendy house, and longing for the day that Julie would get out of it so I could get in.

The Wendy house was beautiful. Unlike its more common gaudy fabric cousins, this one was made of wood and had a proper window with shutters that opened out. Cups hung on hooks on the walls and a small shelf had been built to accommodate a teapot for those intimate and imaginary parties over which Julie reigned supreme and from which I was excluded. I had never known such longing as the constant dull ache that went hand in hand with that Wendy house. I could keep myself occupied with the dolls' house and its pipe cleaner-made family of five and I always had my finger paints, but it was never enough. There was a hole in my life and it was Wendy-house-shaped.

'Mummy,' I said one day as the pain kicked in, 'I wish I could go in the Wendy house.'

'Well why can't you?' she asked, sticking yet another of my paintings up on my bedroom wall.

'Because Julie's got electric in her hands and she hates me.'

'What do you mean she's "got electric in her hands"?' asked my mother, turning to throw me a quizzical look.

'When you touch her, it hurts sometimes. Like you've been stung by a wasp.'

'Oh, you mean a little electric shock? That's not electric in her hands. That's called static. If I pull a pair of nylon pants out of the airing cupboard then I can get a little shock sometimes. Julie can't do that on purpose. Anyway, what's that got to do with the Wendy house?'

'Julie sits in it all day. And she won't let me in it. And I want to go in it.'

'OK,' said my mother, pulling me on to her knee. 'Well

here's what you do. Tomorrow, when you go in, before you do anything else, get into the Wendy house, pack the entrance with toys so no one can get in and when anyone tries to get in then you tell them they can only get in if they know the secret. And if they don't know the secret and you like them then you can tell them the secret by whispering it in their ear. If you don't like them then you can just say "I'm not telling you". How's that?'

'"I'm not telling you"?' I repeated.

'Yes. You can either say "I'm not telling you" and then they can't come in. Or you can say "Come here and I'll whisper it in your ear" and then they can come in. It'll be a new system for the Wendy house. Julie will have to like it or lump it.'

This was very daring and I liked it. 'So what is the secret?' I asked, because as I understood it, that part of the new system was crucial.

'Well you can just make it up,' explained my mother. 'It can be whatever you want it to be. But make sure it's a secret.'

I thought about this for a moment. 'Can the secret be that Nathan Gregory rubs his willy through a hole in his pocket?'

'How do you know that?' asked my mother, giving me a sharp stare.

'Because he showed me,' I said, as if that was perfectly normal.

'Don't let boys show you their willies in pockets, Emma,' explained my mother. 'This is what men do. This is how it starts. Put your foot down now and you'll have a career. No. Pick a slightly nicer secret, please.'

'I like Curlywurly,' I said, hopeful that would hit the spot.

'Well that's not technically a secret,' said my mother, frowning a little. 'But it'll do. So that's what you whisper to anyone you want to come into the Wendy house. Got it?'

I nodded enthusiastically. Tomorrow felt like it was going to be the first day of the rest of my life.

I had woken early and, as was the tradition in our house, I had joined my dad for breakfast. Dad had a limited range of breakfast on offer. There was always toast, occasionally Sugar Puffs or Cornflakes and sometimes, on very special days, a dubious reconstituted meat product called a breakfast slice, which was like a poor man's bacon and almost certainly carcinogenic. I was never aware of my mother at breakfast; she just didn't appear. Instead, she would remain hugged to her bed for as long as possible. My father, who was the only responsible adult in the house, would have to shout up the stairs every morning to get my mother to work and, because of her, we were forever on the knife edge of running late. That morning I definitely didn't want to be late so I helped out and joined in the upstairs hollering to get Brenda up and out. 'Muuuuum!' I shouted. 'Get up now! I need to get to the Wendy house!' There was a reluctant muffle. I could only live in hope.

As always, my mother's total inability to get herself moving meant we were up against it. I had decided to hurry things along by just getting into the car and sitting there. But it had little effect. As my parents bundled themselves in ten minutes later, the usual mutual morning snipe was in full flow: 'Every day, Brenda! Look at the time!' squealed my dad.

'Oh stop moaning!' my mother would reply. 'Honestly! If you spent less time having a go at me I'd be ready sooner!'

None of this mattered one jot as far as I was concerned. I had tunnel vision: it was Wendy house or bust. We pulled up outside the nursery with moments to spare. I could see Julie, standing next to her mother's car, in a coat that made her look like a hairy pompom. I had to think fast. Running in through those tricky double doors, I made a beeline for the Wendy house. My luck was in. Julie was still outside and her gang, the favoured few, were hanging back, not daring to set foot inside the Wendy house without their leader's say-so. Remembering what my mother had told me, I scanned the room for some toys to block up the doorway. I needed to barricade myself in, but with what? There were a few baskets of dressing-up clothes and a box of cars and trains but nothing was the right size or shape. And then it struck me.

Every afternoon at my nursery, after all the children had gone home, a new set of children would arrive. These children were all special needs children, most of them severely disabled. My dad, who was an art teacher, had taken it upon himself to design special chairs for the children with cerebral palsy who were unable to sit in anything other than their own wheelchairs. Using the massive, solid cardboard tubes that came from the paper mill where Dad got his art supplies, he would cut the tubes down to three feet in length. Then, after carving out a section from the front to make a basic chair shape, he would use the compressed wooden spools from the end of the cardboard tubes to make a base and a seat. He would then upholster the seat with some foam and any left-over material he could lay his hands on and cover the whole thing in brightly coloured felt. The result was a chair that, because it was curved, not only held the cerebral palsy children firm and upright, but was virtually impossible to knock over. They were brilliant. The chairs that my dad had made were dotted round the edges of the room. One of them was directly next to the Wendy house. If I could slide it over to the door and get myself inside, then I could pull the open part of the chair into the Wendy house with me and block up the entrance. It was a plan of genius.

I didn't have a moment to lose. Julie had taken off her fluffball coat and was wandering into the nursery room with the confidence of a prizefighter. With Julie distracted by the immediate attentions of her gang of three who had all skipped over to do homage and receive their instructions for the day, I seized my opportunity. Grabbing the chair by its back, I heaved it over to the Wendy house. Positioning it so that the seat section was facing inwards, I crept through the gap. I was inside. Allowing myself a brief moment of ecstatic whimpering, I then pulled the chair towards me and the door was as impassable as a bridge made of feathers. Now all I had to do was sit and wait.

There are few moments in anyone's life when achievement and bliss coincide, and sitting inside the Wendy house, the mistress of all I surveyed, I was bursting with happiness. I had done it. Now all I had to do was hang on to it.

'Why is that chair there?' I heard Julie's voice moaning. It was my cue to appear. Thrusting open the shutters to the Wendy house window, I stuck my head out.

'You can't come in unless you know the secret,' I said, unflinching in my determination.

'What?' said Julie, hands travelling to her considerable hips.

'If you don't know the secret you can't get into the Wendy house,' I repeated. 'Those are the rules.'

'I don't know what it is,' said Helen, a scrawny, brown-haired girl given to outbreaks of eczema. 'I don't know what the secret is. Do you?'

Julie, who was staring at me incredulously, shot Helen a look and then pinched her, suddenly, on the arm.

'Ow!' cried out Helen, grabbing the stricken spot and rubbing it.

'There is no secret,' said Julie, turning back to stare at me. 'She's making it up.'

'There is too a secret,' I said, nodding my head. 'And if you don't know it then bad luck.'

'Well what is it, then?' asked Julie, tossing her chin upwards with defiant anger.

'I'm not telling you,' I said, making a mental note that I couldn't wait to tell my mother.

The four of them gasped. No one had ever spoken to Julie like that before. Helen, who was nervous at the best of times, was so terrified that she'd covered her eyes with both her hands and was now looking at me through gaps in her fingers. By now a small crowd was gathering. A tiny lad called Christopher who always smelt of Brussels sprouts wandered up to the window. 'What you doing?' he asked, throwing a few bits of Meccano in through the window.

'You can't come in unless you know the secret,' I said, because I was in charge now.

'What is it?' he asked, picking his nose.

'Come here and I'll whisper it to you.' I beckoned him towards me with my hand. Christopher leant in and, cupping my mouth to his ear, I whispered, 'I like Curlywurly.'

There was another horrified gasp from the girls. They couldn't believe it. Christopher, now in possession of the terrifying and powerful secret that I was a fan of a chocolate-based caramel bar that could be purchased in any reputable sweet shop for three pence, sauntered towards the chair and shifted it to one side. 'I know what the secret is,' he said, glancing back over his shoulder before squeezing himself into the Wendy house to join me. It was too much for Julie, who, overcome with a combination of fear and rage, wet herself on the spot. As she was led away, sobbing, my triumph was complete. There was a new queen in town. And it was me.

My conquering moment, however, was short-lived. The nursery teacher, having cleaned up fat Julie, had ascertained during the course of those ministrations that something was afoot over at the Wendy house. Wandering over, she moved the chair blocking the doorway to one side and bent down to look in. 'Emma,' she said, giving me a look. 'What's all this about everyone needing a secret to get into the Wendy house?' I froze and put down the teapot.

'You can't get in if you don't know the secret,' explained Christopher. 'I know what it is, though.'

'Well we don't need a secret to play in the Wendy house, do we?' asked the teacher. 'Everyone can play in the Wendy house. Emma, you come with me, please. Let's find you something else to do.'

As fast as the coup had happened, so it was ended. I was put on papier mâché duties for the rest of the day.

My assault on the Wendy house had taken place on the last day of term. It was the Whitsun holidays and our plans were to take us north, first to visit friends of my mother in Newcastle and then on to the rambling delights of Northumberland. My mother, who still clung to the hope that one day we might get to go somewhere where there was a fighting chance that the sun might be shining was, as ever, reticent. 'I think it would be lovely to go to Northumberland,' Tony had said with an enthusiastic nod.

'Why?' said my mother, throwing her arms into the air.

'Because we can show Emma Hadrian's Wall. And tell her about the Romans,' said Dad, thinking quickly.

'Then why don't we just go to Rome?' asked my mother in a flat monotone that wasn't a million miles from despair.

'Because they've got rabid dogs in Rome,' said Tony, who may have been making that up. 'And you need injections.'

Still flushed from my day of thrills, I had been boring my mother witless with a blow-by-blow account of Wendy-gate. I had also been able to produce a small disembodied head that I had made from covering a small balloon with papier mâché. 'It's Daddy,' I had said, holding it aloft.

'I wish it was,' my mother had mumbled before wandering off to do some half-hearted packing.

With Mum upstairs and Dad outside seeing to the car, I found myself left to my own devices. As an only child, this wasn't remotely alarming. I was more than used to quietly getting on with things, whether it was having a lengthy and intense conversation with Mr Mouse or playing Kerplunk (which I loved). It didn't matter; I was brilliant at keeping myself amused. Because I had enjoyed making the papier mâché head of my father, I decided there and then that the best thing for me to do would be to make a matching head of my mother. That, I thought, would be a lovely thing to do. Picking up a newspaper that was in the kitchen, I shut myself into the downstairs toilet which, for the purposes of this experiment, would now become my papier mâché laboratory. Taking the newspaper, as my nursery teacher had taught me earlier, I sat on the floor ripping it into pieces until I was surrounded by a vast mound of lumpy confetti. I was vaguely aware that I now needed a balloon and some glue but quite where I was going to get those from I wasn't entirely sure. I knew the paper had to be wet before it could be turned into papier mâché and so, as a stopgap, I took all the ripped-up pieces, shoved them into the sink and turned the tap on. Leaving the water running, I then decided to turn my attentions to finding a balloon. So off I wandered, in the direction of my room.

Strolling into my homemade clutter of chaos was never going to be straightforward. As I meandered into my room, there was a loose sense of purpose hanging by its fingertips, but with distractions all around me it was only a matter of time before I quite forgot what I'd come upstairs for and, instead, remembered that I hadn't finished colouring in that picture of a lion that I'd been doing yesterday. Before I knew it, I had cleared a space on the carpet and was lying, belly down, pen in hand, and humming. Downstairs, forgotten and unseen, the tap was still running, the torn-up pieces of newspaper slowly and surely plugging everything up.

It must have been an hour before anyone went into the downstairs hall: I was still colouring, my mother was packing and my dad, having finished with the car, was in the kitchen making supper. He was making my favourite, moussaka, a dinner I adored: its combination of cheesy sauce and secret lumps of mince was, to me, the most wondrous supper imaginable. I liked it so much that my dad had to keep it a secret until it was served because if I got the merest whiff that moussaka was on the menu then I would stand, staring into the oven as it cooked, and ask if it was done yet on a loop. I could hear my mother in the next room. She had just let out an enormous sigh, the sort of sigh that says, 'Well THAT's done but what's the point?' One day she would get to go abroad. But not yet. I was busy working on the hindquarters of my lion picture and was trying to decide whether I should use red for the tail or stick with orange. My mother, popping her head round my door to see what I was up to, was satisfied that I was gainfully employed and asked a quick, 'Are you doing a drawing?' Then, after receiving an affirmative grunt, she turned to go downstairs. And that's when the screaming started. The downstairs hall was ankle deep in water.

'Tony!' she yelled. 'Tony! Water! Where's the water coming from? Tony!'

There are times in everyone's lives when they realise, with the most freezing of chills, that they may have done something terrible. As I heard my mother, and then my father, screaming, 'Bloody hell! What's this?' and 'Christ!

Christ! Christ!' a heavy and sickening dread crept up my spine. I had left the tap running downstairs. And now the house was flooded. Something told me the two things might be connected.

'Emma!' came the yell from downstairs. 'Come here now!'

With the tread of a guilty man walking to the gallows, I came out from my room. My mother was standing on the stairs, just above the water, and my father was standing in the doorway of the downstairs toilet, water lapping round his feet, his hands filled with mushy paper. 'What's this?' he asked, holding my experiment aloft.

'I was making papier mâché,' I whispered, 'to make a head of Mummy. You have to rip paper up. And make it wet.'

'Well!' announced my mother, hands on hips. 'At least we're getting this year's disaster out of the way early!'

But of course we weren't. We hadn't even started.

The journey up the endless A1 to Newcastle was surprisingly dull. The landscape was bland and monotonous and there was nothing of particular interest to look out for. Dad, as ever, kept us going with regular renditions of that year's holiday song: Alice Cooper's 'School's Out', which my mother, unusually, sang along to with immense enthusiasm. She particularly liked the bit about school being out 'for EVER!' which she wouldn't just sing along to at the top of her voice but would follow up with a punch to the air and an occasional 'Oooh, just imagine, Tony. Wouldn't that be LOVELY?' Other than that, the only thing to spice up an otherwise boring trip was the presence of the special treat sausage sandwiches that had been bought from the greasy spoon café in the Glebe shopping centre that morning. They had been sitting, wrapped in greaseproof paper and wafting their olfactory delights in our direction, ever since. We had stopped, somewhere just north of Melton Mowbray, 'You know, where they make the pork pies?' my father had told us over and over, and parked up in a lay-by where we had unwrapped the sausage sandwiches with an almost religious devotion. We then sat, grinning like loons, sinking our teeth into doorstops of buttered white bread filled with crisp skinned herby bangers smothered in brown sauce. It was to be the highlight of the holiday. But we didn't know that then.

We were heading into unknown waters and the bleak moors of Northumberland. It was another adventure. My mother, for whom the North was somewhere you only went to in an emergency, like the imminent death of a much-loved relative, had her suspicions that our holiday was going to be another calamity. But surely, she had reasoned with herself, we couldn't have three shit holidays in a row? And besides, even though the prospect of a holiday up North was a swell of disappointment, at least she'd be visiting her friend from university and that, and only that, was sweetening the pill. No, she had decided, everything this year was going to be fine.

We were going to stay with my mother's friend Jenny, who had been something of a partner in crime during my mother's younger, more excessive years. After university, the two had gone their separate ways: Mum had come South to start teaching and Jenny had gone North to marry a man called Tim, a bookish fellow who smoked a pipe and was so serious about it that he kept the tobacco in a ceramic jar. They were an odd-looking couple: Jenny was tall with bird-like features, whereas Tim was a stout, solid man whose face might have looked cherubic if not for the compulsory early-1970s man-beard that rubber stamped his academic status. My mother didn't care much for Tim but that was because he was forever staring at her tits. But then, in 1972, that's what all men did. They still do, of course, but in those days they didn't have to pretend that they weren't.

Britain, two years into the decade that promised new horizons and opportunities, was struggling. We had begun the year under a cloud of social unrest and as we drove into Newcastle, it was a stark reminder that extreme poverty was rife. Slum clearance was in full stride and we drove past street after street of boarded-up houses, condemned communities broken up by local councils and forced into the new concrete high-rise estates. Acres of land had been flattened: only the pavements remained, arterial reminders of what had been, and street lamps stood abandoned in scrubland, once full of houses where families had lived next to each other for generations. This was the regeneration of the North, a scattering to the winds. I don't think I'd ever seen anywhere lonelier.

Jenny and Tim lived in a Victorian terrace that, because it had nice bay windows, had been saved from the developer's Blitzkrieg. Their house was the last in the row, a delightful red-bricked curiosity with a small garden in front and steps up to the front door. 'This is nice,' said my mother, as we stared up at it. And it was, from the outside. When lives are on the cusp of crumbling the first thing to be thrown out the window is a sense of order, and as we walked into the house there was an unnerving atmosphere of impending doom. The interior was a total tip: plastic bags filled with lager tins, real ale bottles, clothes, books and newspapers were everywhere. The carpet was covered in clumps of wispy detritus and dirty dust mice that clogged up the corners while ashtrays, full to bursting, were balanced on every available surface. Jenny, who had the look of someone past caring, was distracted and drawn. 'How was the journey?' she asked, as she led us into the kitchen.

'Not too bad,' said Tony, putting his hand on to a work

surface and straight into a small pool of marmalade. 'Oooh, I've just...never mind.'

We had been travelling for six hours and, that delicious sausage sandwich aside, we'd had nothing to eat or drink. In normal circumstances it would have been reasonable to expect a cup of tea or a glass of squash followed up with something solid like an evening meal. But Jenny, who was more interested in staring out the window than seeing to her guests, just stood and made two slices of toast, spread them with Stork margarine and then ate them as we gazed on. We had clearly entered into some sort of domestic Hell.

'Something's not right,' whispered my mother when Jenny left the room to answer the phone. 'Let's suggest we go to the pub or something. Then we can get something to eat.' My father nodded silently.

'Tim's on his way,' said Jenny, coming back into the kitchen. 'I don't know what he's been doing. Or where he's been...'

An awkward silence filled the room. My father, never one for appreciating the subtler requirements of the female species, cleared his throat. 'Malcolm MacDonald's been a great signing for Newcastle, hasn't he?' he said with a nod. 'Lots of goals this season.'

No one knew what he was talking about, so we all ignored him. 'Is everything all right, Jenny?' asked my mother, moving in to take her hand. 'Is there anything you want to tell me?' Jenny, looking down at my mother's hand in hers, went very quiet and then, with a significant heave of the shoulders, started crying like a wounded animal.

'Ooooh,' said my dad, bundling me out of the room. 'Let's go for a little walk. Leave Mummy and Jenny to have a chat.'

'Why is Jenny crying?' I asked as we left the house. 'Is she upset?'

'I expect so,' said my dad, zipping up his jacket with purpose. 'I think we should try and find a fish and chip shop. Don't you?'

'Fish and chips!' I yelled, throwing my arms in the air. 'Fish and chips!'

Fish and chips were always worthy of a victory dance as far as I was concerned. We weren't allowed them at home because my mother thought they destroyed our middle-class aspirations, but whenever we were away from home, the fish and chips by-law did not apply. When we were away from home we could fill our boots with fish and chips. Sometimes, we could even have scampi, which, to me, was as glamorous a meal as you could get. But in Stevenage, fish and chips were forbidden. Even so, Dad and I, who loved fish and chips, would sometimes sneak down to the local shop, buy a bag of thick, salty, vinegar-soaked chips and then stand in the forbidden concrete underpass and eat them before returning home. We would giggle and nudge each other because we couldn't believe how naughty we were being and the chips were all the tastier for their illicit pleasures.

Because we didn't quite know where we were, Dad decided we would have a quick drive round to see if we could find some shops, but we had barely got to the end of the street before we came to a screeching halt. Tony, winding down his window, shouted, 'Tim!' and waved in the direction of a man with a pipe in his mouth. The man plodded over to us and thrust a hairy arm in through the window to shake my father by the hand.

'That Emma?' he asked, pointing his pipe at me. 'Haven't you grown? Where are you going?'

'Going to find some fish and chips,' explained Dad.

'Fish and chips!' I cheered, waving my hands in the air.

'Brenda's with Jenny. They're having a chat,' added my

dad, whispering the last bit in man code. Tim stood upright and gave that matter a small think.

'Tell you what,' began Tim, 'if you're going to the chip shop, you wouldn't mind dropping me off on the way, would you? Just got to drop something off with a colleague. Then we can, you know, pick up the chips and come back. It's not far out of the way. It won't take long.'

It was rare that I ever found myself in adult male company and, as Dad and Tim chatted in the front of the car, I quickly ascertained that I didn't have the first clue what they were talking about. According to them, Best was off form, SuperMac was a godsend and there was a new club opened in Newcastle where you could see something called *Deep Throat* at lunchtimes but for some reason it was probably best not to mention that in front of the wives. Tim, who had continued puffing on his pipe in the car even though all the windows were wound up, was not someone I felt instantly drawn to. There was something slightly unsavoury about him, like a damp rag that you'd find hidden behind a toilet.

'If you just take this next left and park up by the second house on the right,' he said, gesturing with his smoking pipe, 'that'll be grand. I won't be long.'

We had pulled up outside a large 1950s-style semi. There was a low wall at the front and behind it was a well-kept lawn that stretched about twenty-five metres to the front of the house. There was a large tree to the left and, where we were parked, we could see straight into the lounge. A woman with voluminous curly blonde hair had answered the door, and as Tim disappeared inside, I asked who she was. 'Someone Tim works with, I think,' said Dad, who was staring in the direction of the lounge. Following his eye line, I turned to look as well. Tim and the woman were now standing in the lounge talking but, as we watched, the woman put her arms round

Tim's neck and right before our very eyes, they started kissing. 'Jesus Christ,' said my dad, gripping the steering wheel. 'Jesus, Jesus Christ. What the hell is going on here?'

'They're kissing, Daddy,' I said, by way of explanation.

'Oh Jesus,' said my dad again, putting a hand to his forehead. 'Jesus. Oh Jesus. Don't look, Emma. Oh Jesus. Jesus. Jesus Christ.'

My father, terrified that he had found himself implicated in a marital indiscretion, stared into the lounge with incredulity and slumped his forehead on to the steering wheel. A small indefinable moan seeped out from the corner of his mouth.

'Why is he kissing that lady?' I asked, still staring. 'Is that his job?' But my father didn't answer. He was still emitting involuntary whimpers. Tim, meanwhile, had finished his kissing and was now caressing the woman's face. Because my father had his head down, I felt duty bound to provide a running commentary. 'He's stopped kissing now. They're talking now. Oh. They are kissing again. They've stopped again. I can't see them now. The front door is opening. He's coming, Daddy. He's coming back to the car now.'

Tim, far from being bashful or coy, was beaming from ear to ear. 'Ahhhh,' he said, as he leapt into the car. 'That's better! Now then. Chips!'

My dad, who had previously been full of manly chat, was now projecting the silent demeanour of a man shocked to his core. Tim blathered on as if nothing untoward had taken place, as my father, head bowed, was ignoring him as best he could. Whichever way you cut it, this was a sticky business and my dad, who was physically incapable of keeping anything from my mother, knew that he was going to have to squeal like a canary as soon as we got back. I, on the other hand, was just thinking about the chips. And tartare sauce. But mostly just about the chips.

'Fish and chips! Fish and chips!' I sang as we walked back in through the front door, arms full of our paper-wrapped supper. Mum and Jenny were still in the kitchen, but on hearing us arrive, Mum came out into the hallway.

'Hello, Brenda!' bellowed Tim, grabbing her and pulling her to him. 'Let me feel your tits! Ha ha! Only joking! We got fish and chips. I've got some bottles of ale in the fridge. I'll crack a few open.'

'Thank you, Tim,' said my mother, pulling herself to a safe distance. 'Jenny's in the kitchen. You might want to see her.'

'Boohooing again?' asked Tim with a revolting grin. 'What is it with you women? Always bloody crying. Eh, Tony?'

My dad, who was painfully aware that my mother was watching him like a hawk, said nothing but instead stared at the top of the banister and chewed his lip. As Tim sauntered off to the kitchen, my mother threw her hands up and rolled her eyes. In our absence, the shit had clearly been hitting the fan.

'Did you have fun?' she asked, taking the tangy parcel from me.

'Yes,' I said, with a vigorous nod. 'We went to the fish and chip shop and I watched them put the fish in the oil. And there was a big jar full of eggs. And we saw Tim and a lady…'

'Yes!' interjected my father, gripping me by the shoulder. 'I just need to take Emma upstairs to wash her hands. Brenda, why don't you put the fish and chips down and then help me wash Emma's hands?'

My mother threw my father a quizzical look. 'But she can wash her own hands. She's big enough now.'

My father, rooted to the spot, widened his eyes to the size of saucers and gestured urgently up the stairs. 'Come on,' he said through gritted teeth. 'Let's all wash our hands. ALL of us.'

My mother, still not comprehending what my dad was getting at, looked at him, screwed her face up and said, 'I don't need to wash my hands. What are you on about?'

'Just get upstairs,' my dad whispered at speed and then, because my mother had still not grasped the urgency of the matter, mouthed something incomprehensible but dangerous-looking.

Bundling us both into the bathroom and locking the door, my father spun on his heels and said, 'Jesus Christ, Brenda. This is awful. You won't believe what we've just seen.'

'The jar of eggs was massive,' I said, holding my arms out. 'It was THIS big!'

'We bumped into Tim,' blurted on my dad, ignoring me, 'and he asked me to drive him round to this woman's house. And he said he had to drop something off. And I thought it was something to do with work. And he goes in. And we can see EVERYTHING from the car. And he only bloody goes inside and starts kissing her. We saw the whole thing. Emma saw it too.'

'What?' said my mother, leaning back on the sink.

'He was bloody kissing her, Brenda! I didn't know what to do. And Emma saw it. You saw it, didn't you?'

'Tim was kissing a lady. Inside the house. Can we have fish and chips now?'

'What are we going to do?' whispered Dad.

'Oh no,' said my mother, head dropping down. 'This is terrible. I've just had her sobbing ever since you left. She thinks he's having an affair. What a bastard. What a bloody bastard. Do you think I should tell her? Do you think I should do that?'

'You can't,' said Dad, shaking his head. 'We've only just got here. And what are we going to do about this one...' My dad stopped and nodded in my direction. 'You know what she's like for blurting things out.'

My mother turned, stood up and pointed a very strict finger. 'Emma,' she began, leaning over me. 'You and your father did NOT see Tim kissing another woman. Do you understand?'

'But I did see them,' I replied, not understanding one little bit. 'They kissed for ages.'

'No!' said my mother, in the voice she reserved for cataclysmic occasions. 'You did NOT see them. And if anyone else asks you about it you just say nothing. Or you'll be in a lot of trouble.'

'Lot of trouble,' said my dad in agreement. I looked at my parents. Adults, I was forced to conclude, were quite mad.

My mother, who was pacing, said again, 'I think I should tell her. Seriously. It's the right thing to do. I can't know and not tell her. I'm going to have to tell her.'

'Brenda!' squealed my father, holding her by the forearm. 'You just can't! We've only been here an hour. We can't drive for six hours, unpack and say, "Oh by the way, Tim's shagging some big-breasted woman with a tidy garden." We just can't. It's none of our business. I can't believe he did that to me! Got me to drive him round there! Cheeky bastard.'

My mother nodded. I had to take my hat off; my dad had played a blinder. By rolling out the carpet of moral outrage, his back was well and truly covered. 'All right,' said my mum, with a sigh. 'But I don't like it one bit. One bit!'

An atmosphere not unlike the Arctic presided over supper. There is nothing worse than being at someone's house when they need to have a blazing row and break some china but can't because you're there. My mother, in an attempt to get everyone thinking about something else, suggested that we all go out for a drink. So we found ourselves, ten minutes later, standing outside a large Victorian pub. The interior was beautiful: on one wall, huge floor-to-ceiling mirrors etched with scenes of merry excess – fawns holding cups aloft and scantily clad nymphs lolling on grapevines. Dark mahogany panelling hemmed in the rest of the room and plump, generous, leather easy chairs gave the saloon an inviting, comfortable finish. Inviting and comfortable, that is, if you were a man.

As we stood, surveying the room, a man in a flat cap was staring at my mother as if she'd stepped off a spaceship. 'Nah, nah, nah,' he said in a broad Geordie accent. 'No wimmin here, like. Off you go, pet. Here's men only.'

'Pardon?' said my mother, who hadn't quite caught that.

'No wimmin,' said the man again. 'Yer no allowed.'

'Not allowed?' said my mother in a high tone. '*Not allowed?* This is 1972, not 1872!'

'It's men only, Brenda,' said Tim, pulling on her elbow. 'We'll have to go.'

'Oh I'm not going anywhere,' announced my mother, pulling away and striding to the bar. 'I will have half a pint of Guinness, please. Two pints of ale. A gin and tonic. And what do you want, Emma?'

'Babycham,' I said, because I liked the little leaping deer on the bottle.

'No, you can't have that,' said Dad, shaking his head. 'That's got alcohol in it.'

'But you let me have it at home,' I said, frowning.

'Ssssh,' said Dad, because a storm was bubbling at the bar and he might have to punch someone.

'Cannae serve wimmin, pet,' said the barman, polishing a pint glass. 'Men only.'

My mother, fixing the barman with a stare that could atrophy a walrus at twenty paces, rose to her full height. 'I would like,' she repeated with a voice of steel, 'to be served some drinks. I am not a second-class citizen. And I demand to be served.'

As all the men in the bar stared at her, there was something electric and dangerous in the air. Hostility bristled all about us and my dad, sensing that we might be about to get ourselves into a bit of bother, pulled me by the shoulder and shoved me to the back of him. The barman, who was still polishing the pint glass as if it were a loaded weapon, remained resolute. 'Look, pet,' he began, leaning his considerable barrel frame forwards, 'this here is a men-only bar. If yer wanna drink, yer'll have to gah somewhere else.'

Spurred on by my mother's stand for female liberation, Jenny, who had barely said boo to a goose all evening, thrust herself forward. 'And I want a drink too!' she shouted. 'Why shouldn't we have a drink? You're all bastards!'

'Ooooh,' said my dad, squeezing me tighter to him and edging towards the door.

A small cacophony of guffaws burst out around the room. 'Yer've got a hell cat there, man!' yelled out a thin fellow sitting at the far end of the bar while another shouted out, 'Yer nat in London now, pet! Get home. Where you should be!'

Tim, sensing that matters were turning ugly, took both Jenny and Brenda by the arms. 'Come on,' he said, with a false bonhomie. 'There's no point. Not up here. They'll not serve you. Let's go. Who wants to drink here anyway?'

My mother, refusing to concede defeat, turned as they got to the door. 'You're all dinosaurs!' she yelled. 'Ignorant dinosaurs!' And with that, she slammed the saloon door behind her.

'That was a bit steep,' laughed Tim, as my mother puffed with rage.

'You,' said my mother, pointing a very sharp finger into Tim's face. 'Don't you speak to me. Or we shall all be very sorry. And as for you,' she continued, turning to my father, 'don't even think about saying anything. Come on, Jenny. Fuck the lot of them!'

I just stared at my mother in awe. She had provided a textbook display of raw female courage. I don't think I'd ever been more impressed.

In retrospect it was a terrible idea to ask Jenny and Tim to join us on the morning excursion to Hadrian's Wall. We were going to Chesterholm, to the Vindolanda Fort, where I would receive a fast-track education on the Roman invasion of Britain and witness the bare-knuckled destruction of a disintegrating marriage. For us Hadrian's Wall was a convenient stopping point to break up our drive into Northumberland, but for Jenny and Tim it was to be a simple full stop.

The weather was verging on bleak. We had got up to heavy, leaden skies and a wind whining through the rooftops. As we left Newcastle, the grumbling day worsened, and by the time we got to Chesterholm, the skies were heavy and begrudging. Not only that, but it was clear that Jenny and Tim had done nothing but argue from the moment we were out of earshot. Jenny's face was tear-stained, her eyes red and puffy. My mother, flushed with sisterly solidarity, took Jenny by the arm and marched off, telling Tim he was a 'bastard!' as she went. Tim, pipe in mouth, popped open the boot of his car, got out ten bottles of Newcastle Brown ale and then informed my father that he was going to 'drink the lot and kill himself'. It was going to be an interesting day.

Tony, who was trying to pretend that none of this was happening, decided to concentrate on me. 'Let's pretend we're Roman soldiers,' he said as we scrambled up a steep bank to walk along the wall. The landscape was startling: the wall itself, Hadrian's glorious attempt to keep back the Barbarians, slithered off as far as I could see, and off to our right an expanse of moorland rolled away to the Cheviot Hills in the distance. The weather had imbued everything with a dread foreboding, the sense of menace increased by the presence of fat, cawing crows that perched jealously on the wall's ridge and strutted on the ground before me. The wind, which was more intense out in the open, buffeted through my hair and spiked my cheeks to rosy peaks. 'So this is the wall that Emperor Hadrian built,' began my dad. 'And he was a Roman. And Britain was part of the Roman Empire.'

'Is this a Roman wall?' I asked, pointing at it.

'Yes,' said Tony. 'And Roman soldiers used to march along here shouting "*Sinister, dexter! Sinister, dexter!*" That means left, right. You know, like when soldiers are marching. *Sinister, dexter! Sinister, dexter!*' As Dad was speaking, he was striding backwards and forwards as if he were a Roman legion. I think he was enjoying it more than I was.

'Is that a Roman crow?' I asked, pointing up at a particularly fat one. 'Is that a Roman stone? Is that Roman grass?'

'It's all Roman! *Sinister, dexter! Sinister, dexter!*'

'Tony!' said a voice behind us. 'What are you doing?' It was my mother. She looked anxious.

'We're pretending to be Roman soldiers,' said Tony, smiling.

'Daddy's pretending,' I corrected. 'I'm not.'

'This is a bloody nightmare!' said my mother with a sigh. 'Jenny's in bits. I can't say anything about you know what. It's just awful. Awful. Where's Tim?'

'In the car park drinking himself into oblivion. I thought it best to leave him to it.'

'You can't let him do that!' said my mother, voice going up a notch. 'That'll just make matters worse. Go and get him and walk him round. Jenny's in the loo. I think we should all walk the whole thing off. Calm everyone down.'

My father sighed and stared off into the billowing moorland, the life dripping out of him. 'Do we have to get involved?' Tony pleaded, turning back.

'Of course we have to get involved!' gasped Brenda. 'We're already involved. Look. We'll walk along the wall. The fresh air will do everyone good and then that's it. We can go off and leave them to it.'

My father, with one desperate glance up into the air, stuck his hands into his pockets and slouched off. I had clambered up on to a low part of the wall and was pointing off into the distance for no other reason than that I could. Just on the horizon I could see two figures, an adult and a child, weaving in our direction, but I didn't give them much thought. I was distracted by the crows. Normal birds would flap off if you came anywhere near them. Not this lot. They were defiant and grouchy, hopping about with proprietorial arrogance. One of them was sitting right by my foot and cawing up at me, its thick, black beak snapping like a misanthrope. 'Come away from there,' warned my mother, waving up at me. 'Crows peck people's eyes out, given half the chance.' Alarmed, I jumped down and ran to my mother, grabbing her coat at its hem for extra safety. Jenny was now trudging her way up the sharp incline towards us, as desolate as her surroundings, her long, thin frame bending in the wind. My mother, keen to regain an atmosphere of normality, launched into a rousing historical lecture: 'Now the Romans,' she began, 'invaded Britain and they marched all the way up to here and stopped. And then, because they didn't like the Scottish, they built this wall to keep them out. So this wall is sort of like the end of the Roman Empire garden. This is where the Roman Empire came to an end.'

'Why didn't they like the Scottish?' I asked, looking up.

'They were a bit rough, I expect,' opined Mum.

'Although both Roman and Scottish men wore skirts. So you'd think they'd have plenty to talk about.'

'Don't ever get married, Emma,' said Jenny as she puffed her way up to us. 'Ugh. What horrid crows. They look like undertakers. Waiting for us all to die. Oh what's the point!' wailed Jenny, suddenly. 'We're all going to get eaten by crows or maggots or worms! So I may as well be happy now! Except I'm not! I'm miserable! And it's all that bastard's fault. He's a bastard! A bastard! I'm going to be eaten by worms and he couldn't care less!'

'But you're not going to get eaten by worms for ages,' said my mother, putting an arm round her distraught friend and throwing a desperate look over her shoulder. 'Let's think about the Romans instead. That will be far more uplifting.' My mother, increasingly exasperated, decided to battle on. 'So the Romans had amphitheatres and gladiators. And they had lots of Gods. There was a God of War. He was called Mars. And a God that just sent messages. He was called Mercury. And they had a God of Love, called Cupid. And he used to shoot arrows into people which would make them fall in love.' Jenny let out a dirty, guttural sob. 'Hmm. In fact they had a God for just about everything.'

'Did they have a God for shoes?' I asked.

'Probably,' said my mum. 'And the Gods used to play tricks on the humans. And they would sit in their house, which was a big castle at the top of Mount Olympus, and they would think up naughty things to do to people. And give them impossible tasks and throw things in their way to trip them up. Oh wait. Was Olympus the Roman Gods? Or was it the Greek Gods? I always get them mixed up.'

The temperature had dropped and a bruised purple crept across the skyline, darkening the landscape and giving off a weird, unsettling light. Dad, who had somehow managed to persuade Tim not to go down in a blaze of alcoholic glory, was heading towards us along the ridge, Tim in disgruntled tow. Jenny had settled herself against the wall, leaning into it as if it were the only thing keeping her upright, and my mother was a vision of false happiness, clapping her hands together to muster up any last scraps of enthusiasm and rattling on about how the Romans invented under-floor heating. I was staring off towards the horizon again. The adult and child had made good progress and were almost in proper view. I could now see that it was a woman and, although the child had an anorak on with the hood up, I was guessing from the way it was skipping and staying close to the woman, that it was a little girl. Someone to play with, I thought. That would be a welcome distraction.

'And the other thing the Romans loved eating,' rattled on my mother, 'was dormice. They used to roll them in poppy seeds and roast them. And sometimes eat them with swans.'

'Hello,' said the woman, as she and her daughter approached. 'Got cold all of a sudden hasn't it?'

'Yes!' said my mother, delighted to be able to chat to someone who wasn't having a nervous breakdown. 'Though I think it's sure to rain. That sky's looking very ominous.'

The child, sniffing me out like a truffle, came up and stood staring at my hair. 'I used to have long hair,' she said. 'But then I got scabs and they had to cut my hair off.'

I didn't have a response to that so instead I said, 'Let's play Romans,' and scampered off to stand in a small inlet in the wall. 'We have to pretend we're the Roman soldiers,' I explained. 'And anyone who comes here has to be sent away. Unless we know them. And watch out for the crows. Because they eat eyes.'

'Your hair is lovely,' said the girl, still staring. 'I've got a comb in my pocket. Let me comb it. Because you need to look smart when you're a Roman soldier.'

'All right then,' I said, noticing the jagged tufts of new growth hidden under her anorak hood. The girl reached into her pocket and produced a small, pink, plastic comb. Taking a length of my hair in her hand, she drew the comb through it, gently at first because it was tangled from the wind, but as the weathered knots came out, the comb cut through my hair like a knife through butter. Because we had run ahead and hidden in a small carved-out section of the wall, we were unnoticed by the adults, but as they drew level, the girl's mother let out a small cry. 'Lucy!' she said, surging towards her hand and pulling it away from my head. 'What did I say to you about not touching people's hair? You haven't been using that comb, have you?' Lucy stared down at the floor and said nothing.

'She did comb my hair,' I said, pulling up my anorak hood to prevent any further intrusions. 'With a comb.'

'Give it here, please,' said Lucy's mother, holding her hand out. Lucy, with great reluctance, handed her mother the comb, a few long strands of my blonde hair still attached to it. Taking me by the shoulder, Lucy's mother gave me a penetrating once over, patted me twice and said, 'I'm sure you'll be fine. Don't worry.' I had no idea what she was talking about, but as I gazed up at her, there was something nagging at the back of my mind: I'd seen her before.

'Oh Jesus Christ!' said a voice suddenly to our left. It was Tim.

'Uncle Tim!' shouted Lucy, scampering over to him.

'*Uncle Tim?*' said Jenny, bewildered. And then I remembered.

'Mummy!' I shouted, running to my mother. 'That's the lady Tim was kissing!'

'Oh Jesus Christ!' said Tim again, because if there was ever a time that a man needed divine intervention, it was now. My father had his head in his hands, Brenda was standing with her mouth hanging open and Jenny, in all her emaciated glory, was striding towards the woman with a raised hand. With the wind howling around them, Jenny slapped the woman full on the cheek. The woman cried out and bent down to her left, clasping her face as she stumbled. Tim, desperate and with anger raging from his eyes, scrambled to the wall, grabbed a loose and hefty rock from its top and ran at Jenny, arms aloft. My father, realising that murder was about to be committed, leapt at Tim and brought him down with a rugby tackle. We stood, dumbstruck, as the two of them rolled down the incline and came to an undignified heap at the bottom.

'What are you doing?' screamed my father. 'Are you mad? That's a bloody heritage site! You can't take rocks out of it and throw them about!'

'Never mind the fucking wall!' yelled Jenny. 'He was trying to kill me! And who's this bitch? And what the fuck is she doing here?' My mother, sensing that ugly scenes were about to cascade around us, gripped me by the hand.

'You come with me, Emma,' she said sharply. 'Let's go and sit in the car.'

As I was dragged away, I watched over my shoulder at the ascending crisis. 'He told me you were in a wheelchair!' shouted the woman, gesturing pointlessly at Jenny's legs.

'And the lesson for you to learn, Emma,' my mother muttered as we tripped over grassy clumps in our haste, 'is that men cannot be trusted.'

'Even Daddy?' I asked, because that needed to be clarified.

'No. Daddy's all right,' said my mother, but then added, 'but only just.'

Coincidence or another twist of the Holiday Gods' dagger? Miserable happenchance had brought separate lives colliding with our holiday at the epicentre. As I sat with my mother in the car and watched, Tim and the blonde woman, Lucy wailing behind her, came screaming into the parking lot. There was a lot of shouting and gesticulating and Tim had the beaten expression of a man whose life was now beyond his control. They had slammed themselves into the woman's car, where more shouting had taken place, before screeching off, no doubt, to shout a bit more in that living room at the end of the long garden. Moments later, Jenny, weeping, limp and held up by my father, was presented, like a broken kite, at my mother's window. 'Uhhhhhhh,' Jenny moaned, shuddering. 'Uhh huh huh huuuuh.' My mother got out, embraced her friend and helped her over to her own car, where they then sat, Jenny retching with misery. Dad got in the car with me.

'Bloody hell,' he said, exhausted. 'What a thing to happen. Unbelievable. Don't worry. What are the chances? Unbelievable.'

Everyone was shell-shocked. Jenny, having been emotionally patched up by my mother, made her way home resolute that her life was only temporarily shattered. Like a phoenix, she would rise again, happy in the knowledge that her soon-to-be-ex husband was now shacked up with some tart while she was free to do whatever she damn well pleased. My mother, drained and spent, slumped into the car and put a hand over her eyes. 'Just once,' she pleaded, 'just once, can we have a holiday where nothing happens?'

'Fat chance,' said my father. We drove on.

We had taken the picturesque route to Beadnell in the hope that the outstanding natural beauty of the Northumberland countryside would lift our spirits and erase the grubby memory of what had just happened. I, who had been spared the gory minutiae of the encounter, was the easiest to please and so was happy to stare out the window at the rolling hills and the stunning views across the North Sea. However, my mother, who had been at the coalface of the marital collapse, felt the need to have an in-depth debrief. 'I mean, I don't know what he was thinking of,' she said, shaking her head. 'And I don't care what you say, he ARRANGED for her to be there. I'd bet money on it.'

My father, who had turned a special shade of grey, was driving with one hand on the steering wheel while resting his head in the palm of the other. Happy to let my mother's verbal exorcism wash over him, he was able to proffer only one thing to the conversation: he just 'hoped the pubs were open'. And that was pretty much that.

Beadnell, once a thriving fishing village and blessed with an expanse of golden sands, was a beautiful little place. It was lunchtime and we had had nothing to eat and so, instead of heading straight to the campsite, Dad parked near the harbour. Two domed lime kilns dominated the seafront and a few battered trawlers rocked against the harbour wall. A fresh, salty wetness hung in the air and off to the left the beach stretched away to grassy dunes where you could get lost for hours. The weather was deteriorating and a penetrating drizzle was casting a damp, dull blanket. We were hungry and my father was in need of a stiff drink. But in 1972 you could only get a constitutional uplift within the confines of very strict licensing hours. We had arrived at five minutes past one: the window of alcoholic opportunity was slammed shut. Not only that, but everywhere else seemed to be closed too.

'I don't believe this,' said my mother, as she peered into the darkened window of the village shop. 'This is all we need. Now what are we going to do?'

'Pub,' muttered my father, staring over in its direction

with the longing of an Arthurian Knight within grasping distance of the Holy Grail.

'But it's past one,' said my mother, tapping her watch. 'We won't be served. Keep your hood up, Emma. Or your hair will get wet.'

Tony, determined to break into the pub if he had to, stood staring in through the window at the landlord. Perhaps, thought my father, by exuding the plaintive air of a man in need of beer the landlord would feel more predisposed to an emergency intervention. No such luck. Pub hours were pub hours and neither man nor tide was going to change that. My mother, having extricated my father's fingers from the pub windowsill, decided that a more upfront approach was required and tapped on the window with her forefinger. 'Crisps?' she yelled. 'Can we have some crisps? We've had no lunch.' Much to my surprise, a hand holding three bags of crisps popped out. Money was exchanged and my mother, triumphant, walked towards me and my father, bags aloft. 'Look at that!' she declared, giving them a little tap. 'Three bags! That's one each!'

We had returned to the car and sat, no one speaking, only the occasional snap of a brittle crisp breaking the sorry silence. The crisps we'd been given were the flavour-yourself kind: hard, plain potato crisps that came with a small, blue sachet of salt for you to tip into the bag and shake like hell. They were unready salted and the crisps had patches of green and brown bits on their edges, hewn from the very worst of potatoes. They were bland and revolting, snapping in the mouth with such sharp intensity it was like chewing a razorblade. As lunches go, it was bleak. 'Did he say what time the pub reopened?' asked my dad in a strained monotone, his forehead leaning against the steamed-up window.

'Five o'clock, I think,' mumbled my mother, staring into

her empty bag in the hope that it might yield an unexpected treasure.

'Suppose we should go and get the tent up then.'

'Hmm. Do you think it's drizzling in Rome?' asked Brenda, a question that was answered by nothing but the sharp turn of the ignition key.

The campsite was on the western edge of Beadnell, separated from the coastline by the village. Set on flat ground, it was open to the elements and penned in by nothing more substantial than a flimsy wire fence. There was a small brick building on the left as we entered and behind it was a basic toilet block. There were no other amenities: no shop, no pool and no form of entertainment. In all, it presented a desolate aspect. Tony, having signed us in and paid the camping fee, drove to the furthest corner of the site. 'I'm not in the mood for neighbours,' he had snapped.

The fine spray-like rain was still dusting down and so I remained, with my mother, inside the car, kneeling on the back seat and rubbing peep holes through the condensation. Having tipped a fabric sock full of disparate metal pipes on to the grass, Tony, who had been practising assembling the mainframe in our back garden like a man possessed, had the roofed section together in moments. Taking the longer legs on springs and bending their top sections into the roof, he then tipped out a heaving canvas that slumped on to the ground with sluggish malevolence. Heaving the canvas over the roof, Dad then took each corner pole, snapped the springs into place and shifted the legs into the upright. We had a tent. Flicking out a large, creamy brown ground sheet into the tent's interior, Dad then polished off our living arrangements by hanging the inner tent, our sleeping quarters for the remainder of the holiday, from hooks in the roof.

'Done,' he announced, opening the boot of the car. 'Is it five yet?'

What we didn't know was that he wasn't done. He was far from done. He'd forgotten to put down the separate, smaller ground sheet for the inner tent, which was sitting, scrunched up and forgotten, at the bottom of a bag. We would be sleeping on the grass with nothing but a flimsy piece of cotton to protect us. The Holiday Gods were howling.

Dad's efficiency meant we had more than three hours to kill before he could set foot in a pub. Itchy, distracted and in no mood for sitting around, Tony decided we would fill the pointless hours with a short drive to nearby Ross, where a gentle cake walk of sand and grass tipped us on to Ross Back Sands, a flat and wide stretch of beach. In finer weather, it would have verged on idyllic: sand slipped away as far as the eye could see, snipped to a point by a curve of coastline to the left and punctuated by Budle Bay to the right, with the magnificent outline of Bamburgh Castle dominating the skyline. On a grey day, with a drenching mist rolling in off the North Sea, however, it was far from idyllic: it was a chore, a time filler, a trudge towards a damp horizon. We had the place to ourselves, and while my parents dragged themselves forwards, I ran ahead, stopping only to pick up coloured shells and fill my pockets with pebbles. The sand, hardened in the rain, scuffed off the tops of my shoes and, intoxicated by the vastness of the wide, open space, I sprinted into the breeze, zigzagging from left to right.

My parents, still reeling from the morning's events, were preoccupied and troubled. My father was hunched into the neck of his jacket and seemed as dark as the clouds gathering over Bamburgh Castle. My mother, never able to let something go until it had been dissected down to its entrails, was worrying out loud. 'I don't think we should have let Jenny go off on her own like that,' she said, shaking her head. 'She'll be in a state. But what a thing to happen! I'm convinced he did it deliberately. He must have. Got that woman to turn up at the exact same spot of Hadrian's Wall at the exact time we were there? That's not a coincidence. And she spoke to me! Actually spoke to me. What a cheek! And to think he got you to drive him over there. Absolute disgrace.'

'And he broke off a bit of Hadrian's Wall,' mumbled my father, kicking a stone lost on the sand. 'It's not on, Brenda. That's crossing the line. What's the time?'

'We've got ages,' said my mother, glancing at her watch again with a sigh. We had walked to the end of the sand spit that fingered into the sea at Guile Point and were looking North towards Holy Island. 'Can you see that building?' asked Brenda, pointing into the sea mist. 'That's the Lindisfarne Priory. Where the monks live. Godforsaken place. Locked into the past. It's not part of the modern world at all. If you moved across to Lindisfarne, you'd be travelling back hundreds of years.'

I looked out over the flat waste of grey sky and dull, sickly sea. The distant con tours of Lindisfarne were ominous and brooding. 'We don't have to go there, do we Mummy?' I asked, feeling spooked.

'Well there's only monks there,' said my mother with a shrug. 'And ghosts. Loads of ghosts, I expect. Positively packed with them.'

'Hey, look at that!' said my dad, suddenly pointing over to our left. 'There's a truck on the causeway. It's trying to get across. He'll have to look sharp. Tide's coming in. Jesus. Water's halfway up his wheels already.'

We stood, huddled against the elements, and watched as the lorry stopped and stalled its way through the ever-rising waters, sea lapping at its axles. As it struggled against the inevitability of the tides, we found ourselves rooting for it, shouting and hollering in the hope that at least one thing that day would rise up against the odds stacked against it. Bloodymindedness, determination or blind luck: whatever it was, somehow the lorry crawled its way on to dry land and, as it did, there was a feeling that maybe we'd be all right too. Our holiday wasn't hopeless, our situation was surmountable.

'What's the time, Brenda?' asked my dad, flushed with a renewed purpose.

'Five to five,' declared my mother, and off we went, scampering over the dunes.

We stopped at every pub between Ross and Beadnell. We tried in Elwick, in Bamburgh, and in Seahouses, but every response was the same. My father would ask for a drink and the landlords would point at me, shake their heads and refuse him service. By the time we got back to Beadnell, my father, who was almost on the verge of tears, was actually contemplating tying me to a tree with a piece of string. 'We can't tie Emma up with a piece of string,' argued my mother, pointing at me. 'She's not a stray dog.'

Not only that, but we were still to find anything substantial to eat. We had managed to locate a small pot of cockles and a loaf of bread and, forced to retreat back to our corner of the campsite, we sat sucking vinegar off crusts and chewing tangy molluscs as the rain worsened around us. With the weather settling in, my parents, who had valiantly tried to make the best of a bad lot, admitted defeat. As the day darkened into the early evening, there was nothing to do but go to bed. To stretch the elastic of our evening to breaking point, my mother decided to get all of our clothes out of our suitcase and arrange them in small, convenient piles around the edges of the inner tent while my dad set about inflating the air beds that would bear us floating into the Land of Nod. Intrigued with the mechanics of bedmaking, I decided I would lend a hand and happily jumped up and down on the domed rubber pump that piped itself into the bed valves. Before long, we had two bouncing mattresses which I, about to have my first proper night's sleep in a tent, found exotic and enchanting. Lying, tucked into a sleeping bag, the smell of wet grass in my nostrils, I was in raptures. My parents were not.

They, still haunted by the events of our first, explosive holiday, lay clutching the tops of their sleeping bags, eyes darting to every sudden billow of the tent walls. The wind, while not quite howling, was certainly cantankerous, and the rain, while not quite lashing, was hefty and persistent. 'That lorry made it out of the wet,' whispered my father, 'and so shall we.'

Given the surfeit of fresh air that I'd been exposed to, the emotional nature of the day and the soporific beating of the rain, I drifted into a quick sleep that slipped so deep I was passed out till morning. As I roused, I was aware of muffled noises from the campsite, the sound of rain still beating and a strange, almost overpowering, itching in my head. Scratching at my scalp I could feel a patch of something soft and soggy to the touch. Being sleepy, I wasn't quite aware of what I was doing, but as I scratched, the wetter the patch seemed to get and the itchier it became. My parents were still asleep, exhausted by their tense vigil. Unaware that I was allowed to get out of bed without their say-so, I remained, idly scratching and listening to the steady thud of the weather. But the itching was getting worse, and with every fingertip dig, waves of irritation burnt across my scalp. It was unbearable. I was going to have to tell my mother. 'Mummy,' I said, sitting up. 'My hair is itchy.' My mother, whose mouth was hanging open, failed to stir. 'Mummy!' I said, a bit louder. 'Wake up! My head is sticky.'

My mother, opening one eye to look at me, mumbled something about it 'being fine', but by now my head was so aflame that I was desperate for her to do something about it. Getting out of my sleeping bag, I crawled over to her and presented the side of my head to her one open eye. 'Look, Mummy!' I said again. 'It's all wet and itchy.'

'What the fuck is that?' whispered my mother, recoiling. 'Tony! Wake up! Emma's got porridge in her hair.'

'Don't touch it, Emma!' said my dad, five minutes later. 'If it's itching then it's probably infected. We need to get dressed and get her to a doctor.'

'But what is it? Did you put some seaweed in your hair yesterday? Perhaps she's been bitten by something microscopic. It could be a biological hazard, Tony! Oh! It's AWFUL.'

'What the...?' my dad shouted out suddenly. He'd got out of bed and grabbed at the pile of clothes designated as his. 'Everything's soaking! Oh for fuck's sake. There's water everywhere. I don't believe this.'

'Oh God,' said my mother, leaping up to check the rest of our clothes. 'Everything's wet. How can this be? How?'

'Oh fuck,' squealed Tony. 'The fucking ground sheet! I forgot to put down the fucking ground sheet!'

'Tony,' said my mother, setting her jaw to a place that meant business, 'I've had enough. I don't know why I stay with you. I really don't. Just one nice holiday! That's all I want. Just one! I don't think that's unreasonable. I'm an attractive woman! I should be sitting on a sun lounger in the South of France! Instead I'm standing in a half-made tent, all my clothes are soaking wet and my child has picked up some sort of medieval illness. I swear to God, if Emma didn't have something very fucking weird wrong with her then I would be marching straight through the door of the nearest solicitor and asking for a divorce!'

With everything we owned saturated with rain water and the weather set in for the long haul, we had no hope of getting anything dry. More significantly, I had contracted a highly contagious disease that, while rare, was enjoying a resurgence in the North East: I had impetigo, a pus-filled, rapidly spreading itching ulcer that developed in every part of the body it touched. I had caught it from the comb at Hadrian's Wall and all my hair was going to have to be shaved off. Yet again, our family holiday had not made it into a second day. As we drove home, my mother, who had refused to speak to my father from the moment we left the doctor's surgery, announced that we would 'never go on holiday in this country again!'

Jenny came to live with us four days later.

Chapter Four

Crashed Gallic

It was big. Britain had joined the European Union and our mainland neighbours were waiting to welcome us with open arms. Brenda, determined to have it all her way for once, had put her foot down: we were going to France. The sun would shine, we would feel sand between our toes and our days would be filled with peaches and cantaloupes. Going by plane was out of the question: Arab terrorists were hijacking aircraft left, right and centre and by the summer of 1973, if you hadn't been held hostage at least once then your dinner party conversation over a fondue and a bottle of Liebfraumilch could expect to be severely curtailed. With the journey in mind, my father was dispatched to purchase a new family car, one that would happily carry us and all our camping equipment in comfort: the Kennedys were going continental.

Tony, who took any task he was given by my mother extremely seriously, had been keeping a quiet yet observant eye on the car owned by his school's new deputy head. The Champ, an ex-army vehicle not unlike a jeep, had impressed my father as the very thing that might do the trick: it looked solid, it seemed reliable and it had considerable packing space. If Tony could find something a bit like it then our cross-channel adventure would be getting the very best of starts. And so, when Tony passed a local car dealer and saw the light blue Series 2A Safari Land Rover sitting on the forecourt, the spark of a biting thrill ignited in his heart: it was love at first sight.

'You've bought a twelve-seater Land Rover?' asked my mother, baffled. 'But there's only three of us. And how are we going to afford thirteen hundred pounds? We can't afford thirteen hundred pounds. Twelve seats? That's not a car. That's a bus.'

'Brenda,' said my dad, wafting a reassuring hand through the air. 'Wait till you see it. It's perfect. You'll love it. And I've got it on hire purchase. We can use your salary to pay for it. Trust me. I know what I'm doing.'

My mother cast me a sideways glance: seeing would be believing.

The Land Rover was impressive: just standing next to it was exciting, getting into it wondrous. There were three seats in the front, a second row of three seats behind and then an open section at the back where two long seats accommodating three people on either side faced each other. On the second row there were metal handlebars in front of each seat and on the outside of the Land Rover, there were footplates underneath each door, a concept I found mind-blowing. 'You can stand on the OUTSIDE of the car?' I asked, pointing with my mouth open.

'Just sitting in this makes me feel rich,' said my mother, whose hesitance had been blown away the moment she clapped eyes on it. 'It says Tunisia, here I come. Look at us. In a Land Rover. Who'd have thought?'

'What is the car called, Mummy?' said I. 'Can we give it a name?'

'Why not?' said my mum, turning to look over her shoulder at me. 'And we should do it properly. I've got a bottle of Babycham in the fridge. Let's break it on the car. Like they do for ships. You know, for luck. But we'll have to make sure the bottle smashes. Because if it doesn't, then that's bad luck. Very bad luck.'

'Don't worry,' said Dad with a toss of his hand. 'I'll break it. No worries.'

Five minutes later and we were all standing in a line. My dad had found a bit of blue ribbon that he had tied round the neck of the Babycham bottle, a small touch that my mother found hilarious. 'Look at the ribbon!' she guffawed. 'Look at it!'

'Right then,' said my dad, grinning because he was enjoying riding a rare crest of familial popularity. 'What shall we call it? Do you think it's a boy car or a girl car?'

'Girl car!' I shouted with a small jump into the air.

'It's quite posh,' said my dad, staring at his new pride and joy. 'We could call her Tabitha.'

'I think she's the queen of cars,' said my mum, folding her arms and dropping her head to one side. 'Let's call her Bessy! Good Queen Bessy!'

'Bessy!' I yelled, because I liked it. 'Yeah!'

'OK,' said Dad. 'So you do the naming and I'll throw the bottle.'

My mother, who was always delighted to provide any sort of theatrical entertainment, stood on her tiptoes, pursed her lips and in a faux aristocratic voice said, 'I hereby name this car, this WONDERFUL car, Bessy! God bless her and all who drive about in her!'

Dad, taking that as his cue, chucked the Babycham bottle at the side of the car, towards the front. It should have hit the flank, but instead it struck the corner of the front wheel arch, bounced straight off and boomeranged back to hit me square on the forehead with a thwack. Startled by the impact, I fell backwards into my mother who caught me, took one look at my head and screamed. There was blood everywhere. 'Has she lost an eye?' wailed my mother, gripping me by the shoulders. 'Oh God! Tony! She's lost an eye!'

My dad, who was trained in first aid, seemed glued to the spot, frozen in horror by what had just happened. He looked at me, looked at the wheel arch, pointed at both for a bit and mouthed something inaudible; his moment of triumph shattered. What should have been a momentous family occasion had turned into a freeze-dried disaster. Thankfully, I had not lost an eye but the blood pouring from the cut at the top of my hairline was so extensive that it looked as if my eyeballs were a river of blood. Because I couldn't see what was going on, I had managed after the initial blow to remain quite calm but my parents, standing over me and staring into a massacre of dripping blood, were paralysed. 'What shall we do?' wailed my mother. 'She's bleeding to death, Tony! Oh God! Someone help us!'

Alarmed to hear the word 'death' in reference to myself, I stood and wondered whether I should feel more alarmed, but the truth was, apart from the dull ache at the top of my forehead, I felt fine. The fact that my flesh wound looked ten times worse than it was, was of no concern to me but for my parents, one of whom was in tears (Tony), the vision of my gore-ridden face had rendered them useless. Thank God then that my mother's wailings had roused a neighbour, who came wandering out of her back garden to see what all the fuss was about. Having quickly ascertained that both my parents were hysterical, she led me off quietly, sat me on a chair in her downstairs toilet, wiped my face clean and applied a small plaster to the superficial cut on my hairline. I was delivered back to my parents within minutes, where I was showered with kisses from my mother and a bag of black jacks and fruit salads from my father.

Everyone was relieved. We had got away with it. But we'd forgotten one thing.

The bottle had not smashed.

My father, having taken daily advice from a man called 'Dave Cox' who had been 'going to Spain for years in his caravan', had been preparing for our road trip to France for weeks. According to 'Dave Cox', food in France was a) extortionate and b) inedible, and that if my dad knew what he was doing, he would start stocking up on tinned food immediately. To not do so would be a fool's path to the bottom of a stinking pond where only misery and pain would be our hand-maidens. To this end, Tony had been methodically squir-relling away tins of Spam, corned beef, silverskin onions and piccalilli. Every now and again he would open a cupboard, stare at his hoard and nod quietly, happy in the knowledge that he had hunted and gathered enough low-grade tinned meats and pickled vegetables to keep us afloat for a month. Saving money was now a priority: we had Bessy to pay for.

My mother was preparing in different ways: flushed with the glow of a trip to the continent, Brenda had concentrated her efforts not on what we were going to eat but on what she was going to wear. French women, she had heard, were sartorially elegant, and looking down at her cotton flares and cheesecloth top, she was pretty sure that, as things stood, she was offering little or no competition. 'I've got nothing to wear,' she declared, hands on hips. 'I'm taking Emma to Biba': a phrase that my father, whose grip on the family wallet was vice-like, dreaded.

Biba, a department store in London like no other before or since, was a sensation. It was and still is the most exotic shop I have ever been in. The interior was extraordinary: black walls swallowed up the shop floor across which were dotted mirrored pillars with dark, plump banquettes lazing about their bases. Ebony peacock feathers plumed out of every corner and pencil-thin shop assistants stared out from behind their counters with expressionless, effortless style. It was like stepping into a Bob Fosse musical. We only went there a few times – the store had to close because people were just going there to stare, not to buy – but its impression was indelible: the corridor that turned, with every step, from night to day and delivered you into the children's department with its giant record player, where you could stand on the record as it turned, and the restaurant (where you could eat curried eggs and potato gratin) with its white grand piano and the man playing a violin who was so old he looked as if he was made from tissue paper. Despite our family funds being severely curtailed, my mother had decided that our first trip abroad was an occasion so special that budgets could go hang. 'No, Brenda!' my father would say, swiftly followed by a high-pitched, 'Look at the price of it!' and a frantic point of his finger. To this my mother would stop, throw him the coldest of stares and just say, 'Tony!' in a sharp slap of an exclamation that could leave no one in any doubt that if she wanted it she was going to have it. After protracted negotiations she came away with a cord jacket and a pair of striped mules. I got a pack of cards. Tony got nothing.

My mother was dressed to the nines for our inaugural voyage on a cross-channel ferry. Decked out in her recent Biba purchases, she had finished the outfit off with some large Brigitte Bardot sunglasses. She was delirious with joy: by the end of the day we would be in France. *France!* Because my hair was still growing back from the impetigo incident, there was little if no point in putting me in anything other than a pair of shorts and a striped rollneck jumper. Everyone thought I was a little boy so I might as well dress like one.

Still, we had polished the look off with a pair of rather natty flip-flops: I was feeling more European with every step. Dad, who had seen most of the holiday funds slip through his fingers and washed away on a tide called fashion, could only pack the back of Bessy with military precision and thank God for 'Dave Cox'. By sticking to our tinned diet, we might get home with a penny in our pocket.

In terms of family politics, it was important for Tony to take small triumphs where he could. The packing of Bessy, which had assumed the sacred mysteriousness of the Virgin birth, was for my father his greatest achievement to date. Having measured her internal dimensions, he had worked out, on a piece of graph paper, what would go where and on top of what: the base of the rear section would be laid with the large, blue bag that held the tent, the long orange bag that held the tent rods and the small, white bag that looked after the mallet and the pegs. One layer up, like a holiday lasagne, would be the more solid camping equipment: the stove, the gas bottle (which attached to the stove), the water carrier, the table, the chairs and the malodorous bucket. On top of that lay the suitcases (of which there were many – we were going to France after all) and on top of that were the sleeping bags, the pillows and the duvets. Last, but not least, was me. I would not be sitting in Bessy. I would be lying, tossed on top of the rest of the gear, horizontal and sunken into a perfectly arranged trough at the end of which would be provided a convenient heap of books, toys and comics, thus ensuring my total silence for the entirety of the journey. It was my father's grandest design and for every year that we had her, that same piece of graph paper would be produced and followed with great solemnity until Bessy was full to bursting.

We were sailing from Southampton to Cherbourg, a six-hour crossing that, as far as we were concerned, was going to

be as exciting as a carpet ride into outer space. The ferry port
was a slithering snake of vehicles, all creeping slowly towards
a fat man in a fluorescent jacket who was shaking everyone
down according to size. As we sat, crawling towards the fat
man, Tony was in a sweaty stew. His concern: whether or not
Bessy would pass the height requirement. If she failed, we'd
have to pay more and, to be honest, if we did have to pay
more then our holiday, according to my father, was 'fucked
from the off'. This holiday was going to have to be reined in
on the tightest of shoestrings and in 1973, when no one had
credit cards, our holiday funds were limited to the cash in my
father's pocket. 'Everyone smile nicely at the man,' whispered my father from the corner of his mouth, the smell of
fear wafting off him. My mother, thinking that just looking
glamorous might save the day, dripped herself into a devas-
tatingly relaxed sprawl, arms draped outwards and head to
one side, presenting a vision of nonchalance to which nothing bad could possibly happen.

'You're an inch over,' said the fat man. 'You'll have to pay
the surcharge.'

'But it's only an inch, officer,' pleaded my mother. 'Does
it really count?'

'I'm afraid so, madam,' said the man. 'And I'm not an
officer.'

'Oh God,' moaned my father, shoulders slumping. 'How
much is it?'

'Fifty pounds, sir,' said the man, consulting a clipboard.

'Oh God,' said my father again.

'Fifty pounds?' squealed Brenda. 'For an inch?'

'My dad,' I said suddenly, piping up from the back, 'says
if we have to pay more money we're fucked from the off.'
Everyone turned and looked at me, startled at the unexpected profanity. My mother, wide-eyed and startled, opened

her mouth to remonstrate but was stopped by the fat man, who was laughing his head off.

'Did he now?' he howled. 'Ahhh go on. Off you go. Follow the yellow line there please, sir, and park up behind the caravans. Have a nice holiday.'

As we drove off, showering thanks as we went, the fat man was still laughing and shaking his head. My mother twisted round and looked at me. 'Well done, Emma!' she grinned, eyebrows shooting up from behind her sunglasses. 'Well, well done!' But then, thinking about that for a moment, she added, 'But don't say that again. Swearing is very naughty.'

'No it bloody isn't!' yelled my father, grinning. 'You can swear as often as you like!'

I lay back into my trough, feeling pleased with myself and happy. Not only had I saved the day, but I was now allowed to swear. This holiday was starting brilliantly.

The industrial doors to the lower decks of the Townsend Thoresen *Free Enterprise* ferry were locked during the voyage, while the upper decks played host to duty-free shops, bars, lounges and restaurants. We had gone up to the outer deck to watch as we left port, a smell of salt and diesel raged in my nostrils and the deep roar of the ship's engines vibrated up through my feet. It was my first time at sea and, as I clung to the railings, I leant over to stare at the water as it chopped away from the hull. We were lucky: it was a beautiful, sunny day and the sea was a millpond. We stood and watched as England disappeared into the horizon, the sea wind fingering through our hair and, as the last sliver of land slipped into an endless expanse of blue, we turned our attentions to something far more pressing: lunch.

'Would you like to try our Scandinavian Smorgasbord?' asked the steward, gesturing towards a heaving table.

'A smorgasbord?' trilled Brenda, peering in at the banquet on offer. 'Is that where you pay and then you can eat as much as you like? I've never had one of those.'

'You can eat as much as you like?' asked Tony, eyebrows knotting in disbelief. 'That can't be right.'

'No,' said the steward. 'Your wife is right. You can go back as many times as you like. Just pay for the plate and help yourself.'

Astonished and tiptoeing, we might as well have been handed swag bags and asked to help ourselves to the Crown Jewels. We stood, plates in hands, and stared at the bank of food laid out before us. There was every conceivable cold meat layered in towers, neat rows of filleted fish, pyramids of tomatoes, shelves of sliced cucumbers and bowl after bowl of dressed salads: creamy coleslaws, potato salads sprinkled with chives, coronation chicken that was so yellow it looked radioactive, halved eggs filled with spiced mayonnaise and grapefruit hedgehogs pierced with cheese and pineapple chunks on cocktail sticks. There was so much to choose from, it was impossible to know where to start, but my mother, who always had an eye for the expensive, had set her sights on one thing.

'Oh. My. God,' she breathed, gasping. 'There's smoked salmon! Tony! They've got smoked salmon.'

No sooner had Brenda seen it but she was out of the traps and on it, shovelling it on to her plate with an air of the frantic until her plate was so heaped with smoked salmon there was little room for anything else. My father, convinced if he played this right, it was going to be the deal of the century, had piled his plate high with every meat on offer and had created a salad-based volcano that threatened to spew itself over every available surface. I had decided to take a more practical approach: I would only put on my plate anything that I knew I liked. So I just picked up the cheese and pineapple grapefruit hedgehog and put the whole thing on my plate. We had taken enough food to feed a family of ten. And this was only our first visit to the table.

'Can you believe this?' said my dad, mouth full and gesturing towards his slurry of food with a fork. 'And we get to go back! Be sure and go back, mind. We get to go back.'

My mother, who was breaking out in a sweat as she troughed down on her excess of salmon, came up for air. 'I don't know if I can, Tony!' she panted. 'I'm stuffed.'

'But you've got to go back, Brenda. We've paid for the plate. That's the whole point of a smorgasbord. You've got to go back.'

My mother, with the determination of a wounded soldier, dragged herself back to the table, half-heartedly tossed some beef on to her plate and slapped on an accompaniment of coleslaw and then staggered her way back. Throwing the plate down on the table, she then sat, cheeks bloated and burping, and made a short stab at squeezing some beef into her mouth before throwing down her cutlery, collapsing headfirst on to the table and conceding that she was now so full that she was giving serious consideration to the afterlife.

I too was struggling, stuffed full of cheese and pineapple chunks, and had leant back in my chair with my arms hanging hopelessly down in a vain attempt to aid digestion. As I looked round the restaurant, I realised that everyone was similarly swollen to bursting. People were slumped in chairs, broken by an excess of protein and salad dressings. One girl caught my eye. She was a little older than me and was wearing a pink tracksuit. Her hair was scraped back from her face, tied up into pigtails, and as she pushed her plate away from her, she assumed a facial greyness not unlike a piece of cod that's been left out for a week. This lunch would be the end of us all.

'I don't ever want to eat again as long as I live,' moaned my mother, half dribbling on to the tablecloth.

'Thank God the sea's not choppy,' commented my father as we waddled our way out to the shops. 'Can you imagine?'

But I couldn't imagine. I'd never been on a ferry before.

So far, so good. Our holiday was going so well that Tony, in a fit of excitement, had bought a giant Toblerone to celebrate. My mother was in her element, awash with a sense of achievement, and I was buzzing, bouncing with anticipation that within a matter of hours I was going to be in a different country. I didn't know anything about France and my only experience of it was from reading the Babar the Elephant books that my mother had told me were French. As the new coast came into view, part of me half hoped to see elephants on bicycles but, sadly, that childish fancy would never be satisfied. What I did know, however, were two sentences taught to me by my mother: the first was a catch-all to get me out of any manner of scrapes, '*Excusez moi, mais je ne parle pas le français*' and the second was, as far as my mother was concerned, more important than breathing, '*Où est la toilette, s'il vous plaît?*' That was it. That was all I was going to be able to say.

As we pulled into Cherbourg, a tannoy announcement boomed out telling us we were allowed to return to our vehicles, and with a genuine sense of expectation, we followed the long line of families worming their way down through the boat to the car deck. Because the stairways were narrow, there was a traffic jam of bodies waiting to squeeze themselves into the stairwell. My parents were immediately in front of me and as I looked behind me I realised I was in front of the girl in the bright pink tracksuit. The ship, which was still reversing into port, was heaving and starting with thick shudders, sending deep, resonating judders that rattled into my ribcage. Whether it was the frequency of the ship's final tremors or just the result of a very long sea voyage, we will never know, but at that moment, as the ship emitted a particularly deep, gut-churning grumble, the girl in pink vomited. All down my leg.

'Oh no,' said the girl's mother as I stood, horror-struck, staring at my splattered leg. The girl had a hand to her mouth and by the look of her, I wasn't entirely convinced that she was all done. Tony, turning round to see where the waft of puke was coming from, saw the state I was in and automatically assumed that I was the culprit.

'Oh dear,' he said, putting a hand on my shoulder and nudging my mother with the other. 'Probably all those cheese and pineapple chunks.'

Traumatised by the fact that I was actually covered with someone else's sick, I could only shake my head. Thankfully, the girl's mother piped up. 'No, it was Melissa. She's not a good traveller. I'm very sorry about your son's trousers. Will he be all right?'

My father was standing next to a particularly unflattering light, the sort that lays bare the soul of any who come near it, and as the woman nodded in my direction and assumed I was a boy, I could see the flicker of a decision settling itself into his eyes: sometimes, things just weren't worth explaining. As I stood and watched, my father returned the woman's gaze and said, 'Don't worry. He'll be fine,' and then pushed me towards my mother.

'I've got sick on my leg,' I whined as she held me out to look at me.

'I don't believe this,' said my mother. 'Will she be able to get changed, Tony? Where are the clothes packed?'

'Third layer up,' said Tony, sucking breath in through his teeth like a builder trying to break bad news. 'And we won't be able to get anything out. Not until we're off the boat. We'll have to wait till we get to a lay-by or a motorway service station. I haven't even got any tissue on me. Have you?'

My mother shook her head. 'And she'll have to sit in the front with us. She can't lie out in the back. She'll get sick on all the bedding. Oh! It smells AWFUL.'

By now I was leaning into my mother, face first and clinging to her cord jacket. If I didn't look down then perhaps it wasn't there, but the damp stickiness that was creeping down my leg and the acrid stench of vomit snapped me back to reality: I had the stomach contents of a constitutionally challenged girl in a pink tracksuit dripping down my leg and there was no hope of being cleaned up within the next half hour. This was my welcome to France.

I was crying by the time we reached Bessy. Not girly, frivolous tears: it was something more broken, more withered and torn, like Sisyphus, the man condemned to forever roll the stone up the hill only to have it roll back down again. I could see no end to my misery. I was on an infinite treadmill of misfortune and all I could foresee was an endless melancholic wretchedness.

'Come on,' said my mum, hugging me to her. 'As soon as we can stop we'll wash you down and get you changed. Don't worry. What an awful thing to happen. Just awful.'

I was in such despair that I didn't even pay any attention to the moment Bessy clanked off the ship's ramp and on to French soil. We had made it and I didn't care. Only two things could reverse my agony: a power hose and disinfectant.

'I must remember to drive on the right,' said my dad, winding down his window to get some air into the car. 'Don't forget to tell me to drive on the right. Drive on the right. Drive on the right.'

'I think our first priority is getting Emma clean, Tony,'

said Brenda, a little strained. 'So you can drive on the right as much as you like as long as you drive us straight to a toilet.'

'*Où est la toilette, s'il vous plaît?*' I sobbed, gripping my mother's arm.

'Yes,' nodded my mother, squeezing my shoulder. '*Où est la toilette, s'il vous plaît?* That's right.'

My mother, trying to keep my mind occupied, made small but valiant attempts to get me to look out the window. 'Look at that, Emma,' she said, giving my hand a tap, 'there's a French shop. And that's a French car. And that's a French man.' But I wasn't interested. My head was glued into my mother's armpit, the only haven from my immediate horrors. To make matters worse, everywhere seemed to be shut. We'd arrived in France during the long, languid lunch break that everyone seemed to indulge in, and as we drove through Cherbourg, it became increasingly clear that my rescue would be some time coming. In fact, we had to drive for a good twenty minutes before my father, spotting a lay-by with some rest facilities, screeched into it and slammed on the brakes. Brenda took me by the hand and walked me towards an oblong, concrete toilet block that I could smell from the moment we stepped out of the car. Years of neglect had taken their toll: there were no discernible signs of upkeep, bins exploding with rubbish and a wet, overpowering smell of sewage. The door into the ladies' block was heavy and metallic, the handle crusted with an unidentifiable solid green matter that crumbled into the hand, and as my mother opened it, an overpowering yet anonymous stench punched us in the face. It was the sort of smell you could taste and both of us instinctively covered our mouths with a hand. Our other problem was that, as soon as the heavy door clanged shut behind us, we couldn't see a thing. It was pitch black, a thick, stinking darkness like finding yourself at the bottom of a cesspit. 'Goodness!' exclaimed Brenda, startled by the depth of black. 'There must be a light in here somewhere. I'll just...' and her hand fell away from mine.

Disorientated by my, albeit temporary but total, blindness, I put my arms out and shuffled forwards. I could hear my mother to my left, running her hand over surfaces and muttering about how she couldn't now find the door and that if we both just stood very still then maybe our eyes would adjust to the lack of light. I was still shifting forwards, fingers aloft, when my tips came up against something cold and metallic. Applying pressure, the surface, which I could only assume was a door into a toilet, pushed away from me. Another powerful, reeking wave slapped up at me and, pulling the neck of my jumper up over my nose, I made small steps forwards. Letting out a small, muffled shout, I said, 'I think I've found a toilet.'

'Is there a sink?' called out my mother. 'Have a feel around.'

Again, moving slowly, I reached forward. My arms waved into an empty space. Bending my knees, I waved my arms lower, hoping, at least, to locate the toilet. If I could place that then the sink, if there was one, would be off to one side. But there was still nothing there. Concluding that I must be in a large, long cubicle I stood up and took a large stride forward. The edge of my flip-flop hit a ridge. Having not expected to come up against a small but significant raised surface, I stumbled, my bodyweight surging forward. My right leg, which had been trailing, automatically flung itself forward to stop me falling over, but as my foot came down, it sank away from me, plunged down into a stinking hole that sent me tipping over to the right. An overwhelming smell of faeces flooded over me and my right leg felt as if it was submerged in a thick, sticky mud. Except it wasn't mud.

I had found the toilet.

Having fallen leg first into the Turk-style hole in the ground toilet so favoured by the French, there was little I could do other than scream and suck myself back out of it. My right flip-flop was gone, my leg covered in shit. So just to recap: I had someone else's vomit on my left leg, and a whole host of strangers' shit on my right. Horrified and in shock, all I could do was scrabble backwards, struck down with panic, my heart pounding, the breath catching in my throat and my head pumping with a white, searing fear that felt as if my brain was boiling. As a child I was not naturally given to hysterics but in that moment, as I felt my mother's hand on my arm, her voice shouting through the deep fog of disaster and felt the outside light stabbing in as my father opened the door to see what was going on, I felt the eyes roll up into my forehead and I passed out.

I came round lying on the floor by the bins. My shorts were being pulled off me by my mum, and my dad, acknowledging that this was a bona fide emergency, had unpacked two layers of camping gear to get to the towels. I was catatonic, my breathing shallow. My parents were talking urgently and loudly but I couldn't take in anything they were saying, their words blurred away by the erasing childhood trauma that was sending my mind spinning. I had fallen into a toilet: a filthy, stinking, hell hole of a toilet. My nostrils were screaming and I could feel shit between my toes. Tears were pouring down my face and I was making no noise apart from the occasional broken-down, 'Hurgh...huh...huh' that pushed itself up from my guts and moaned out in ungodly grief. With nothing liquid to wash me with, my dad scraped at my legs with the towel until they felt as if they were burning. My mother, having thrown my shorts into the bin behind me, was kneeling by my head, stroking my hair and holding my hand. I was vaguely aware of my father's expression, a look of such intense revulsion that his face was con torted into a look of extreme pain. He was doing his best, but we needed to get to soap and water.

'If we put her in a bin bag,' suggested my mother, pointing to the back of the Land Rover, 'then we can drive on to a proper service station, a garage, anywhere. We've got to get her washed. Jesus Christ! Why does this only happen to us? Why?'

My dad, stopping what he was doing and holding out the shit-stained towel, stood up and looked down at me. 'Wrap her legs in a bin bag. Yes. Come on, Em. We can get through this. We can.'

Tossing the foul-smelling towel over in the direction of the bin, Tony paced to the back of the Land Rover. After wiping his hands on a small patch of dried-up grass on the roadside, he dug into the rear of the car and pulled out a large, black plastic bag. Flicking it open, he hooked one end under my feet, slid the bag up to my waist and gathered the ends together, where he tied them into a chunky knot. My lower limbs were sealed in. Crying and incapable, they stood me up and carried me to the car, disgusting wafts of hot, stinking air pumping up from the bag's edges. With both my parents' heads hanging out the windows and retching, we screamed off. Soap and water: it was all we wanted.

My deliverance came in the shape of an unshaven man in oil-stained overalls. Having pulled into a garage and bundled me out of the car, my father, carrying me over his shoulder, had run to the rear of the building where he found the proprietor sitting under a shaded veranda with a glass of lunchtime wine in his hand. A fat, dusty *saucisson* sat on a plate in front of him, the peeled skins heaped into a tidy mound. '*Au secours!*' yelled my father, pointing towards me. '*Ma fille fell down la toilette! Nous need eau! Eau pour le washing!*'

'And soap!' added my mother, who was fast on our heels.

'*Oui!*' yelled my dad, nodding his head with urgency. '*Et aussi le soap.*'

The man sat and stared at us. A mad English family had descended on his lunch hour and he wasn't remotely interested. '*Fermé!*' he mumbled, with a small wag of his finger. '*Je mange. Fermé, monsieur. Fermé.*'

'*Mais la fille,*' implored my father, putting me down and pointing at my weeping face, '*has had un accident. Dans la toilette. Elle est covered in merde. Et we need a pwoooosh, pwoooosh hose or something pour la laver. De les jambes. Le pwoooosh, pwoooosh.*'

'*S'il vous plaît,*' added my mother, because manners are manners.

Sensing that something was very wrong, although he would never know what, the man stuck his bottom lip out and blew a small, exasperated puff. Tapping a thick, unfiltered cigarette out of a crumpled packet in his overalls, he tossed it into his mouth and stood up. Lighting the cigarette, he then stuck his hands in his pockets and gestured with his head towards a standing pipe to which a thin, red hose was attached. '*Voilà,*' he said, in a deep rumble, cigarette stuck to his lip. '*Pour le pwoosh pwoooosh, uh?*'

'Oh thank God!' exclaimed my mother, pacing towards it. '*Merci, monsieur! Merci beaucoup!* Quick, Tony! Get the bag off her.'

Up till this point I hadn't registered the weather: a dry, sucking heat that had turned my legs into boil-in-the-bag monstrosities. Although my father had done his very best with the towel, the stench of something biblical burst out as he ripped the black bag open, a plume of stinking vapour hissing into the air. My legs, covered in angry brown streaks, had turned an unpleasant, sickly white and were peppered with greasy beads of sweat. If I could, I would have peeled my skin off with a rabbit knife there and then. At that moment it was inconceivable that I would ever be clean again.

The water from the hose was freezing but it brought a welcome numbness that enabled me to distance myself from my immediate physical predicament. If I concentrated on the stinging cold then I could forget why I was standing there in the first place. I had fallen into a toilet: I had actually fallen into a toilet. As my parents hosed and scrubbed me, I could hear cicadas singing in the grass, see the unshaven man smoking his cigarette and off in the distance two boys cycling circles in the dust: the world was carrying on as if nothing had happened. I had fallen into a toilet and everything had not come to a grinding halt, the earth had not fallen off its axis and the universe clicked on: my mishap was as nothing in the scheme of things. It was my first lesson in insignificance. I was placed in a clean pair of shorts and given a bottle of fizzy orange by the unshaven man. We drove on in silence. I never wanted to go into a public toilet again.

Our destination was Carnac, a small coastal town in Brittany famous for its beaches and its standing stones. Given that the remainder of our journey had been conducted in virtual silence, it was something of a jolt to arrive at the campsite, which was buzzing with noise and activity. To date, our experiences of campsites had been distinctly unimpressive but the site at Carnac was like an outdoor five-star hotel. Spread over six acres, the site was entered through a heavy wooden gate. Fields sloped down to our left, and up to our right and in front of us, about 300 yards from the entrance, there was a small, picturesque lake surrounded by woodland. 'Look at that,' said my dad, in an almost reverential hush. 'They've got rows of stones marking out the pitches. That's amazing.'

'And some are marked out with hedges!' pointed my mother. 'Imagine that! Hedges!'

I just stared blankly, disengaged and damaged. Something inside me had died, like the last spit of a candle, and instead, a dull, winter-heavy ache had moved into my ribcage, rendering me incapable of ever experiencing pleasure again. My mother, realising that I was in the grips of a terrible melancholy, sat me on her knee as Dad put the tent up. With my arms round her neck and my face pressed into her shoulder, I finally gave vent to my horrific experience, crying my brain out my nose until every last scrap of misery had been rounded up and sent packing.

'Now then,' said my mother when I was done. 'Do you want to help me set up the table and chairs?'

Arranging outdoor furniture was something we'd never been able to do before and my mother was in her element. Despite the fact she had very little to work with, Brenda was convinced that this holiday (minus the earlier unfortunate incident which could be dismissed as just bad luck) was going to be the pinnacle of her life to date. She had made it. We were on continental soil. The early-evening sun was casting a warm, pink glow and it wasn't raining. All about us French families were smiling and enjoying evening meals, their tables heaving with wine, barbecued fish, quiches and salads. This was where Brenda wanted to be. This was the line where the misery of previous holidays came to a dead stop. 'I think', she began, one hand on hip, 'that we'll have the table over here, in the shade. Just under the tree. And then the cooking stuff can be over there. But with the windbreak round it because no one wants to look at cooking stuff. And if we put the chairs here then we can all enjoy the view. Of the other tents. So that's what we'll do. Tony!'

My father, having been given strict instructions of what

was to go where and next to what, jumped to it. In no time at all, the three of us were sitting, staring at our temporary home. 'Look at that family over there,' said my mother with a nudge. 'They're eating mussels. On a campsite. And they've got an apple tart. Incredible.'

The smells that were wafting from every direction were heavenly: thick, meaty odours of herby roasted chickens and charcoal-grilled steaks saturated the air. 'All these smells are making me hungry,' said my mother, nose aloft. 'What are we having for dinner, Tony?'

'Tin of Spam,' said Dad, trying to make that sound as exciting as possible. 'And piccalilli!'

'Is that it?' asked my mother, turning to look at him. 'Do you not think we deserve a treat? You know, after the day we've had.' My mother threw a surreptitious nod in my direction.

'Spam *is* a treat,' said my dad, folding his arms. ''Em loves Spam. Don't you?'

'Not really,' I said, scuffing at the brown grass beneath my feet.

'Well, all right then, we'll have corned beef instead,' suggested Tony. 'Everyone likes corned beef.'

'I don't,' said Brenda, taking off her sunglasses to give my father a proper once over. 'Haven't we got anything a bit, you know, less 1950s?'

My father, who hadn't told my mother about his secret stash of tins, fidgeted in his chair. 'You never told me you didn't like corned beef,' he said, before adding, 'because if you didn't then you should have said. Because that sort of thing is important. You eat it in sandwiches at home.'

'When I'm desperate, yes,' nodded Brenda. 'But if you said to me, "Ooooh, let's go out for a meal. Let's have something nice. It's a special occasion," am I going to go, "Yes! I'll have a corned beef sandwich? Or a corned beef salad? Or corned beef with anything?" No. I'm not. And I detest Spam. It's revolting.'

My father, who had assumed a slightly pallid hue, sighed a little and ran a hand across his forehead. 'The thing is,' he mumbled, 'Dave Cox told me that in France food is really expensive, especially the meat, and you never know what you're getting because some of them eat horses. And he told me to stock up on tins and bring them with us. So that's what I've done.'

'Dave Cox told you to do this?' interjected my mother, not yet grasping the enormity of the situation.

'Yes. And so I did that. And we're on a pretty tight budget. What with getting Bessy. And the cord jacket.'

'Leave the cord jacket out of it.'

'And so we've got all the food we need for the holiday. And it's in that box. And it's mostly corned beef. And Spam. So that's what we've got. There. I've said it. And that's that.'

My mother, who had gone dangerously quiet, pursed her lips and got up to investigate. The large cardboard box to which my father had pointed was sitting, unopened, in front of the tent, a large piece of tape sealing its top rim. Taking one edge of the tape between her fingers, my mother picked at it until she had an edge and then ripped it off in one rasping yank. Reaching in and taking a tin in her hand, she looked at the label. 'Corned beef,' she said, shooting my father a glance. Then, putting that tin on the floor, she picked out the others. 'Corned beef. Corned beef. Corned beef. Corned beef. Spam. Onions. Corned beef. Spam. Spam. Piccalilli. Onions. Spam. Corned beef. Spam. A tin of tomatoes. Spam. Corned Beef. Onions. And, wait for it, corned beef. Well. What an extensive range, Tony. We're in France, the gastronomic centre of the world, where everyone is eating shellfish and things in sauces. And what have we got to look forward to? Corned beef and pickled onions.'

'And a tin of tomatoes!' protested Tony. 'There's a tin of tomatoes in there.'

'So sorry,' said my mother. 'And a tin of tomatoes. I can barely wait for that. I must send Dave Cox a thank-you note when we get home. Don't let me forget.'

And so we sat, with our three metal camping dinner plates languishing before us on the table. The plates had been picked up by Dad from an army surplus store and were made of aluminium and divided into three triangular compartments. In one compartment we each had two pickled onions. In another we had a dollop of piccalilli. And sitting in front of us, in the centre of the table in pride of place, was a plastic side plate in the middle of which sat a jelly-covered, fat-mottled rectangle of good corned beef. We all sat and stared at it. A French man, carrying some bread and a bottle of wine, strode past. He looked at us, waved and shouted, 'Bon appétit!'

A gesture that was greeted with the weakest of smiles.

I had had a fitful night, dreams filled with nightmarish visions of cavernous holes and filth. My natural *joie de vivre* was still to be recovered, leaving me subdued and nervy. Waking up to my first holiday morning where we didn't have to instantly pack up and go home was a revelation: I had wandered round, tousle-haired and sleepy-eyed, and watched as Dad lit the camping stove and boiled some water for coffee. Not only that, but he'd gone to the campsite shop and brought back three crescent-shaped pastries, telling me they were 'croissants', an unheard-of delicious, crumbly flaked delicacy that you could only eat in France. We ate them in wonder: it was unbelievable that you could eat cakes for breakfast. People were wandering past carrying wash bags and towels: it was a muffled, creeping start to the day and it suited my mood perfectly. I had refused point-blank to go into the toilet block and so was reunited with the bucket for my morning ablutions, an arrangement that, thankfully, managed to pass without incident. The weather was perfect: high blue skies, the hint of a sea breeze; it felt as if there had been a shift in the sands. Perhaps, after the shakiest of starts, we might be able to enjoy our holiday.

There was much to see in the area and, before we headed to the nearby beach, Brenda had insisted that we pay a visit to the famous Carnac stones. I had previously been to Stonehenge in England on a short weekend away and so was familiar with odd, ancient standing stone sites, but this was on a much bigger scale. Carnac was not just a circle of stones in the middle of nowhere; here the stones seemed to go on for ever. Light grey and covered in a dark patchwork of lichen, the stones sat perched on a bed of sun-scorched grass, a hefty queue frozen in a march to who knows where. Mum, determined to 'feel the energy', was dancing about with her arms in the air. Dad, doing his level best to walk as far away from her as possible, was distracting himself with a battered guidebook he'd borrowed from his school's library. 'According to this,' he said, tapping a page with his finger, 'there's somewhere called the House of the Dead. And there's a big massive stone somewhere. And one shaped like a hand. And there's more than three thousand stones. And there's a tumulus, which is like a massive grave. I'd quite like to see the House of the Dead. Wouldn't you?'

The megalithic stones of Carnac were the stuff of legend. Giant menhirs laid out in lines that defied explanation or reason. The alignments were a mystery in themselves: locals would happily tell you that the stones were once an entire Roman legion that had all been turned to stone by the great wizard Merlin. That was why they stood in such rigid rows, all to attention, waiting for the day when another wizard would return and transform them back into their human bodies. The thought that the stones were men trapped in solid form gave the alignments a haunted, saddened air and I was spooked from the off.

'It's so mystical, isn't it?' declared my mother, as we stood regarding the aspect. 'I think I'm going to pretend to be a priest and summon up the spirits of the moon and the sun. It almost feels rude not to.'

'Please don't,' said my dad, who was mindful that there were other people in the vicinity.

I was starting to feel a little unnerved. My mother was skipping like a lunatic, face upturned to the sky, and my father was trying to track down something straight out of a Hammer House of Horror movie. 'I am a wizard!' sang my mother, leaping out from behind a stone. 'And I command you all to turn back into men! Arise! Arise, ye mortals!'

'Jesus,' said my dad with a start. 'You almost gave me a heart attack. Don't jump out on people. And don't do the wizard shit. It's a bit...I don't know...a bit weird.'

'Join my coven!' yelled Brenda, dancing on the spot. 'And bring the stones back to life. Come on, Emma! Let's pretend we're wizards!'

'No thank you,' I said, hunching my shoulders a little. 'I don't want the stones to turn back.'

'But don't you want to be a wizard?' asked my mother, still dancing. 'It's very powerful! Think of all the magic!'

I shook my head and kicked at a patch of blood-red heather. 'Never mind that,' said my dad, flapping his guide-book in Brenda's direction. 'What about the House of the

Dead. Ooooooooooooh. House of the Deaaaaad! Hoooouse
of the Deaaaad!'

'It's not really a house with dead people in it, of course,'
explained my mother, panting a little and staring down at me.
'It'll just be a configuration of stones they've decided to give
a slightly frightening name to. That's what tourist boards do.
It's their job.'

'Hoooouuse. Of the Deeeeeaaaaaad!' wailed my dad,
trilling his fingers in the air.

'The stones won't really come back to life, will they?' I
asked, looking about me nervously. 'A wizard won't come,
will he?'

'Probably not. But we can still have a dance round the
stones,' said Brenda, kicking up her heels. 'There's a great big
flat stone over there. Let's go and dance round it and pretend
we're pagans.'

'What's a pagan?' I asked, scampering after my mother.

'Someone who believes in lots of Gods!' shouted my
mother. 'Like the Romans. Nowadays everyone just believes
in one God, which is extremely boring. But when these
stones were put here, everyone believed in lots of Gods.
Maybe each of these stones *is* a God? What do you think
about that?'

'What is this stone a God of?' I asked, pointing at a
particularly squat, fat-looking menhir.

'Cakes,' said my dad, who was tramping close behind.

'And what about that one?' I asked, gesturing towards a
small, thin stone that seemed to curl out of the ground.

'That is either the Aniseed Twist God,' opined my father,
'or the God of Wall Screws. Could be either. No way of
knowing.'

Having visited the stones, our next port of call was to
head straight to the beach. There were five beaches at

Carnac Plage, and we had chosen to head off to the Plage Men Du, a smaller beach to the east of the main Grande Plage that was a little more secluded and a little less hectic. My only experience of sea and sand had been of grey skies and churned-up, sickly-looking surf, but here the water was a crystal blue and the golden sands were as soft as Egyptian cotton. As I kicked off my plimsolls and my feet sunk into the hot, thick sand, I was overwhelmed with an urge to run through it as fast as I could, arms outstretched, careering from left to right, jumping over sandcastles and leaping from wet to dry. Everything about the beach felt like a celebration. I loved it.

Brenda was also brimming with delight. Here she was, at last, lying on a towel, sunglasses on, heat beating down. 'Look at that,' she said, pointing towards a shimmering in the distance, near to the ground. 'Can you see how everything looks a little distorted and it's all wavy and wobbling? That's heat. That's what it does when it's hot. You don't get that in Wales.'

'That's not true. I saw that in Swansea once,' piped up Tony, who was unpacking our lunch. Today, it was Spam with a side order of onions, topped off with a bit of French baguette. Dad quickly made sandwiches and I stood, fidgeting on the spot, trying to eat it as quickly as possible. As I munched away, I looked around at the other families on the beach. Yet again, we were the poor relations: some of them had tables, all of them had chairs, there were parasols, windbreaks, and one family, immediately to our left, had set up a large awning under which they had managed to erect a trestle table where they were all sitting enjoying a whole barbecued salmon. Brenda could only look on with the sort of longing reserved for orphans hung in cages over a perfect family Christmas. They had outdoor-cooked fish and chilled wine; we had pulped pig's testicles and a bit of orange squash. Still, at least the sun was shining. Finally, it felt like a proper holiday.

Our week in Carnac fell into a steady routine: a trip in the morning followed by beach in the afternoon. Every morning we would drive to a different town, where Dad would take endless photos of door knockers and buildings and engage wizened old ladies in a peculiar form of Franglais: '*Bonjour. Deux bottles lemonade, s'il vous plaît.*' Mum would wander, holding my hand, sighing at the occasional clothes shop and then opining loudly on what it must have been like when the Nazis were in Brittany and whether she would have been in the Resistance. Conclusion: only if they'd given her a rakish beret. Because the beach was so near and so wonderful, we spent little if no time at the campsite, a fortunate state of affairs given that the camp swimming pool looked as if it was permanently full of urine. I spent the long, hot afternoons running around finding random playmates, leaping in and out of the gentle breakers and clambering across rock pools, constantly amazed by crabs and anemones and all manner of salty secrets. Dad, who wasn't one for sitting and doing nothing, would busy himself by building amazing sand sculptures of racing cars and planes for me to sit in. Brenda would lie on her towel, soaking in the vista, and occasionally wander down with me to the water's edge, where she would hold on to the back of my shorts to stop me from 'being carried away by the current' – even though there was no current, it was a slow shelving beach and I was only standing up to my knees in water. We saw a firework display, sat one evening in the harbour listening to the wind rattling through the ship masts, played badminton and *boule*, sat, face dripping with juice, as we enjoyed the fattest peaches I'd ever seen and danced and clapped along to a passing street band: all of it was magical.

When we came to leave, I felt genuinely sad. Even though

the holiday had got off to the worst possible start, I felt refreshed, scrubbed clean by the sea air. Had the Holiday Gods, after my leg-down-the-toilet sacrifice, been appeased? Were my trials now at an end?

'Goodbye, campsite!' we had all shouted as we drove out of the large wooden gates for the last time. 'Goodbye, stones! Goodbye, Carnac!' I had elected to sit in the seats immediately behind my parents for our grand exit. I had wanted to wave everything off properly and I sat, half kneeling, so I could lean out the window and say goodbye with ease. 'Shall we sing a song, Mummy?' I had asked, sitting back down but leaving my arm trailing out the window so that I could feel the warm air billowing in the palm of my hand.

'Yes!' she declared, as if the thought had passed her by. 'We haven't sung any songs on holiday this year. What shall it be? Let's choose and then we can sing it all the way home.'

'What about "Tie a Yellow Ribbon"?' suggested Tony. 'We all know that one. And it's about going home.'

'Perfect,' said Mum and off we went, singing it as loud as we could. We'd got about halfway through the second verse when Tony, looking at the petrol gauge, stopped singing. 'Hmm,' he said, 'I think I ought to fill up sooner rather than later. There's a garage over there on the left. I'll do it now.'

Almost all our holiday funds had gone on petrol and as Dad filled Bessy to the brim, Mum popped her head out the window. 'Do you have to fill her right up?' she asked. 'How much money have we got left? Will we have enough to do some shopping on the boat?'

'I'll have about ten francs left after this,' said Tony, eyes watching the petrol pump. 'And yes, we do need to fill her up. We'll only have to do it again if we don't.'

My mother, giving out a little sigh, thought about that for a minute and then, popping her head out again, said, 'Did you know how much petrol was going to cost when you bought the car?'

'Brenda,' said my dad, sensing a pointless row brewing. 'We've got to buy petrol and that's the end of it. How else are we going to get home? We can't put lemonade in the tank, can we?'

I knew to keep well out of this one. It was a small storm that had been threatening to burst forth all week, mostly every time my mother was presented with another tin of corned beef. 'I mean, it just seems to me that we've spent way too much on petrol,' continued Brenda, as Dad got back into Bessy. 'Isn't petrol cheaper in England? Couldn't we have brought petrol with us or something? We could have brought petrol instead of bloody tins of Spam. That's what we should have done.'

'Brenda!' retorted my father, sparking up the engine. 'You can't carry a week's worth of petrol in the back of the Land Rover. Do you have any idea how much petrol that would be? And what are you going to carry it in? Think of the fumes. Don't be ridiculous.'

'I'm not being ridiculous,' snapped my mother, as Tony edged out of the garage. 'But we've had to live on bloody rations all week. On our holiday. Because of bloody petrol.'

As my parents rattled on, distracted by their minor argument about petrol, none of us had noticed.

We were driving on the wrong side of the road. My father, engrossed in a needless tiff, had pulled out of the garage and forgotten to drive on the right. Not only that, but we were heading towards a humpbacked bridge at speed. With the road ahead of us obscured and my parents still snapping at each other, we rattled onwards. But coming towards us, also at speed, was a German car towing a caravan. The first we knew about it was the blaring horn followed by the sharp swerve to the right, followed by the snap of a grazing impact, followed by the jolt forwards that threw me off my seat, followed by a cacophony of expletives, after which we came to an unceremonious stop. I was lying on the floor and was vaguely aware that my head hurt. My mother was saying 'Jesus Christ' a lot, my father was panting, and somewhere behind us I could hear a German voice shouting, '*Scheister Englander!*' Thankfully, Dad had managed to swerve away just enough for the crash not to have been considerable, and on inspection, Bessy had only lost the top of one rivet. The German car, on the other hand, had come out of the sorry mess slightly worse and a whole right-hand wing had caved in. I had also not come out of it unscathed, and as I struggled off the floor and sat back in my chair, I was instantly aware that I had blood pouring out from a cut at the top of my forehead. I had struck my head on the metal handlebars in front of my seat and, while my life was not threatened, I was in a bloody, sticky mess.

We had come full circle. I was bleeding again. I sat on the ferry wearing one of my mother's sanitary towels strapped to my forehead with a bandage.

I might be wrong, but I don't think it was quite the chic look my mother had been hoping for.

Chapter Five

Not so Quiet on the Home Front

Stevenage had served its purpose. As a bridging home, Jessop Road had done us proud, but it was time to upgrade. Thanks to the new Stevenage Development Corporation and their policy of selling council houses to sitting tenants at a discount, my parents were able to buy our home for the paltry sum of three thousand pounds, sell it swiftly for nine thousand and so shift ourselves sideways to neighbouring Hitchin.

Hitchin was an altogether better prospect: a historic market town, it was the polar opposite of the concrete right angles of Stevenage. Centred on a magnificent church that dated from the thirteenth century, Hitchin was a chocolate box of tucked-away inns and timber beams, exuding a quiet yet confident prosperity. If Stevenage was the brash young buck, then Hitchin was the well-dressed uncle laden with cake. It even had a shop where they made their own pork pies, an eye-boggling fact that left my father reeling. 'They're HOMEMADE?' he had squealed, shaking his head. 'They're HOMEMADE, Brenda. HOMEMADE!' My mother had heard enough. Any town with a shop that made its own pork pies screamed the word 'classy'. They even had their own chutneys. It was perfect.

Our new house was a two-bedroom curiosity gripped to a steep slope that started with a cherry tree at the front and slipped away to a vegetable patch at the back. We had moved in just as the cherry tree was in blossom, thick, wonderfully pink flowers carpeting the front lawn, tumbling into heaps that I happily scuffed through in my bare feet. We even had our own driveway where we could park Bessy, a luxury that felt beyond posh. And at the top of the property, perched on the driveway, there was a voluminous lavender bush wafting wondrous perfumed clouds that would catch you unawares on warm summer evenings. My mother, forever with an eye on the current trends, wasted no time in filling the house with up-to-the minute 1970s furniture, all bought from Habitat and most of it orange. Not only that, but she forged ahead with a flurry of home improvements that included replacing the beautiful iron fireplace with a disgusting stone one that looked as if someone had broken up bits of Stonehenge and plonked them in our living room. On the flimsiest pretext that she had 'read about them in *Nova*', she also insisted on having a serving hatch, complete with sliding door, fitted between the kitchen and the living room – a feature she thought so very modern that it was practically her pride and joy. Anything that could be passed through the serving hatch would be passed through the serving hatch, even if no one wanted anything, accompanied with the requisite sigh of intense satisfaction: Brenda couldn't have been happier.

I, on the other hand, was not. Uprooted from my school and my immediate playmates, I was desolate and had slipped into a depressive state so deep that not even the unexpected present of a Six Million Dollar Man doll could lift my spirits. 'Look at that, Em!' my dad had encouraged. 'If you roll back the skin on his forearm, you can see his hidden circuits.'

'Roll back the skin on his *what?*' shouted my mother, through the serving hatch.

'Forearm,' repeated my dad, 'fore*arm*. And he's got X-ray vision. Through this one slightly spooky eye. You can look through the back of his head. Look at that. Buhduhduhduhduhduhduhduh! Good outfit too. Look, he's wearing trainers. Brilliant.'

But I was unable to share my father's enthusiasm for this hot-off-the-press toy. I was in mourning for Helen and Fat Julie, my best friends at school, both of whom, sadly, I would never clap eyes on again. So, instead of enjoying the rollable delights of prosthetic skin on a man who had been brought back from the brink of death simply because they 'had the technology', I sat for hours on the bottom step of the stairs, head in the crook of my elbow, weeping. As I stared out at the large privet hedge that ran the length of our front garden and kept us sealed away from the rest of the street, I found myself longing for the openness of the Jessop Road estate. Moving up the social ladder was a gradual retreat from the rest of the world: the better off you were, the less people you had to look at. Every glimpse out the window at my Stevenage home would be filled with incident, something to tell my mother, but here, it was just a hedge that, towards the end of every day, cast the longest of shadows and left you cold, even though the sun was still shining. For me, the move to Hitchin brought with it the painful realisation that I was an only child. Suddenly I had no one to play with.

My solitude, however, was short-lived. I was packed off to Whitehill, the junior school at the bottom of our road, where I was welcomed by a beaming Welshman with red cheeks. He was the headmaster and the fact he was Welsh, like my dad, was something of a comfort. I had joined late in the school year and so was coming into a classroom where friendships and cliques were already formed. Bizarrely, I was the only blonde-haired girl in the class and, as I was swept in, I was aware that not everyone was necessarily going to be pleased about that. One girl, sitting near the front, was staring at me. I stared back. She had a squashed-up face like a potato and was wearing the sourest of expressions. Seeing that I was returning her solid gaze, she took matters to the next level and stuck out her tongue. I had been thrown into the lions' den. I was on my own.

'Why don't you sit over there next to Simon?' suggested Mrs Jones, my new form teacher, pointing a finger in the direction of a skinny-looking lad with a mop of dishevelled hair. I turned and looked at him. He already had his head in his hands and was pulling a face that suggested either he had incredible stomach pain or he didn't want me anywhere near him. 'Simon will show you where the pencils and the paper are,' said Mrs Jones with a smile. 'Won't you, Simon?'

Simon couldn't have looked less inclined to show me where the pencils or the papers were if he tried. Without speaking, he scraped his chair back and marched me over to a corner of the classroom, where he pointed randomly and carelessly towards a drawer and a couple of pots. He muttered something about 'crayons' but his heart wasn't in it. He absolutely hated me. It was official: I had met my first boyfriend.

I had only been at my new school a week when I was given the letter to take home to my mother.

'Dear Mrs Williams,' it read. 'We are currently planning our annual school trip for the first years. This year we will be taking children to Cuffley Camp near Potters Bar, where the children will enjoy a five-day camping holiday with lots of extra activities. Activities will include:

Enjoying nature trails

Learning cooking and cleaning skills

Fireside singalongs

Morning outdoor courses, including Flowers and Plants, Map Reading and Orienteering, Building Skills, Woodland Study and Pond and Small Mammal Investigation

We do hope that...' (my name then appeared in hand-written form) 'will be able to join us for what we hope will be a very enjoyable and rewarding week. If you are happy for your child to come on this great activity holiday then please fill in the form below and return it with your cheque for the holiday in the envelope provided. Thank you.'

Brenda, having read the letter, tossed it on to the dining room table. 'Over my dead body. There is no way, NO way, Emma is going on a camping trip to the middle of nowhere to get crushed by a tree or drowned in a pond. She's only seven!'

'Potters Bar isn't in the middle of nowhere,' said Dad, picking up the letter and having a look. 'It's about five miles from the M25. And there'll be teachers there. And instructors. I don't know. I think it would be good. It's important for her to have experiences. And she's used to camping. She'll enjoy it.'

Two weeks later and I was struggling, suitcase dragging behind me as I tramped into one of the twelve 'villages' in Cuffley Camp. We were in Brackendene, a small, glade-like clearing hidden among a density of hornbeam trees. There were several light green canvas tents arranged at intervals around the site. In the middle of the clearing were the remnants of the previous night's fire with logs arranged around it for people to sit on. Behind the fire there was a large awning that served as a group shelter and beyond that a covered cooking area. Off to the left, sitting alone on a mound of earth, was a small wooden shack. 'What's that?' I asked a man in combat trousers who had led us into our camp.

'Night toilet,' he said, casting a glance in the shack's direction. 'You'll all take it in turns to clean it. That'll be one of the skills you learn.'

It was the night toilet. The NIGHT toilet. As I stared at it, a creeping fear attached itself to the base of my neck. My track record with outdoor toilets was woeful and that was during the daytime. Having to tackle one during the night didn't bear thinking about. Still staring at it, I resolved there and then that I wouldn't set one foot in it. I had made up my mind: I would not go to the toilet for the next five days.

I was going to be sharing a tent with four other girls, one of whom, much to the displeasure of a girl called Jane, was widely regarded around school as 'the stinky one'. Jane, whom I hadn't met before because she was in a different class, was sparing nothing in her anger at being shoved in the 'Pongo tent with Pongo', which, to be honest, created an atmosphere from the off. I was still the new girl so I made every effort to keep out of it, concentrating instead on trying to open my suitcase, which I couldn't do and had to be satisfied with it remaining half unzipped for the rest of my stay. In the meantime, 'Pongo' was already in tears and a girl called Barbara was threatening to wet her pants because the fourth girl in our tent, Paula, had kept herself amused by knotting all the string ties that did up our door, meaning none of us could get out. After fifteen minutes of calling for help, a boy called James had fetched a teacher and we were finally released, sadly not quick enough for Barbara, who was now also in tears. As starts of holidays go, it was special.

Our days at Cuffley Camp were strictly structured: in the mornings we would have an organised activity with an educational twist. We studied invertebrates and where you could find them, an exercise marred by the boys' insistence on stamping on worms at their top end so that their innards shot out their bottom end, hitting any girl in the vicinity. We also enjoyed pond dipping, where we sank jam jars into murky waters and then examined what came out: to conclude, mud and some bits of twig. Simon claimed to have found a frog, but, unable to back that up with hard evidence, was forced to retract, while James's wild assertions that he had almost 'caught a badger' were dismissed out of hand. We also turned our hands to den building, where we were split up into our tent teams and told to 'make yourselves a waterproof shelter using only what you find on the forest floor' – a challenge that was tested to the full when James asked whether he could use the 'soggy socks' he'd just found. Answer: not really. After gathering as many sticks and bits of bracken as we could, we made a half-hearted attempt to give our den a sense of structure. But given that Jane had insisted on using Pongo as the leaning point on which all our sticks rested, I didn't hold out much hope that our effort would pass muster. A condition of the challenge was that we all had to be able to get inside our dens and then stay dry while water was poured on the roof. This meant that our human tepee arrangement was swiftly abandoned, not least because Barbara had been on a quick reconnaissance wander and come back to report that the boys had managed to make box-like dens by plunging sticks into the forest floor and draping bracken over the top. What Barbara had failed to spot was that the boys' bracken was lying on top of a latticework of more sticks. Still, that wasn't going to bother us now. We were going to drape bracken like it was going out of fashion.

In retrospect, it probably wasn't the wisest of decisions to let James be the waterproof tester. Olive-skinned with big brown eyes, James was the sort of boy you knew would grow up to melt hearts left, right and centre, but at the age of seven, he was a helter-skelter of shaken pop, forever fizzing over. The instructor, having asked for a volunteer and been rewarded with a bouncing James, had handed him a large saucepan of water and told him to pour some of it on to the roof of each den. What James had failed to understand was that he was only required to pour a small amount of water, so when he came to our den, inside of which the four of us were squashed in considerable discomfort, he lifted the saucepan and emptied its entire contents over the top. We were soaked to the skin.

Dripping wet and freezing, Jane was adamant that James would be made to pay and it was down to the rest of us to come up with an appropriate retribution. 'We've got to get him back,' she said with a determined stamp of her foot. 'Something really horrible. REALLY horrible.'

'We could tell him it's his turn to clean out the night toilet, when it isn't, suggested Barbara.

I didn't have a suggestion to make. Instead, I was engaged in an arm-cramping wrestle with my suitcase as I tried to pull some dry clothes out of the small gap I'd managed to open. It had taken me ten minutes to get one T-shirt out and I had been so exhausted by the effort that I made my second decision of the holiday there and then. I wouldn't get changed for the rest of the week; I would battle on in the clothes I was standing up in. The T-shirt I'd managed to extricate from my suitcase turned out to be my favourite. It was bright yellow with the characters from the cartoon *Top Cat* emblazoned across its chest. As I pulled it on, I knew I looked good and so allowed myself a small, lying-on-my-back sprawl so as to show it off to its best advantage.

'Wow,' said Jane, casting me a glance. 'I love *Top Cat*. Who's your favourite?'

'Benny,' I said with the coolest of nods. 'He's the best.' Jane liked what she was hearing and came to sit, cross-legged, next to me.

'Do you know swear words?' she asked in a conspiratorial tone. 'I do. I know bugger and fuck.'

'I know bugger and fuck, too,' chipped in Barbara. 'And bloody.'

'Everyone knows bloody, Barbara,' retorted Jane. 'It's not even a swear word.'

'It is,' complained Barbara. 'Bloody is a swear word.'

'And bastard,' said Paula, shuffling over to join us. 'My mum says that all the time.'

'What do bugger and fuck mean?' asked Pongo, who was still trying to get bits of bracken out her hair.

'Well fuck means going for a poo,' said Jane with a knowledgeable air. 'I know that because my big brother told me.'

'*Fuck means poo?*' questioned Pongo, stopping what she was doing.

'Yeah,' said Jane, nodding authoritatively. 'And bugger means something to do with a boy's willy.'

'Errrrrrrrrrrrrrrrrrrr!' we all yelled, disgusted.

'I saw Nicholas's bugger once,' whispered Barbara, leaning forward. 'He showed it to me at the pegs after country dancing.'

'Errrrrrrrrrrrrrrrrrr!' we all screamed again.

'Nicholas showed ME his bugger too!' boasted Jane. 'AGES ago. I've seen loads of buggers.'

'What does a bugger look like?' I asked, because as far as I was aware, I had yet to see one.

'Like a sausage with a hole in it,' explained Jane. 'Mostly just disgusting.'

'Errrrrrrrrrrrrrrrrrrrrrrr,' we all went, because it was true.

'Anyway, listen. What are we going to do to James?' asked Jane, bringing the conversation back to its original purpose.

'We could put pepper in his pants,' suggested Paula, 'and make his bugger hurt.'

'I still think the night toilet thing is the best,' pondered Jane. 'But it needs to be a bit worse. Let's shut him in it and not let him out?'

'Yeah!' cheered Barbara and Paula.

'OK. So we're going to shut him in the toilet. So here's the plan. One of us has to get him to the toilet. Emma, that can be your job. And then me, Barbara and Paula will hide round the side. And then when he's inside, you shut the door and hold it while we put a stick in the handle.'

'What about me?' whined Pongo. 'What will I do?'

Jane turned and gave her a withering look. 'Oh I don't know. Look-out or something.'

'You can come and get James with me if you like,' I said, sensing another bout of tears that we could all do without. Pongo seemed appeased. We all knew our part. The trap was set.

We decided that the best time to strike was just after the evening campfire when everyone had had their cocoa. Parents had been instructed to provide their children with an appropriate mug for night-time beverages but, because I couldn't get into my suitcase, I didn't know whether I had an appropriate mug or not. Being seven, it didn't cross my mind that I could discuss this small and easily solved problem with a grown-up and so I declined the cocoa, even though I was desperate to have one, a trend that continued throughout the week. 'I've never met anyone who didn't like cocoa,' said my teacher, a statement that elicited no response from me because neither had I. We had spent a good hour sitting round the campfire, singing songs like 'She'll be Coming Round the Mountain' and 'Red, Red Robin' and staring, half-hypnotised, at the flames as they licked up against the night sky. The smell was delicious, pine crackling through the air, and the heat was tremendous, a fact I was grateful for, given that I was only in my T-shirt. As the fire died down and children started shifting towards their tents, we knew our moment had come. 'Quick,' hissed Jane, giving me a nudge. 'Get James before he gets to his tent. We'll go hide behind the shack.'

As Jane, Barbara and Paula scampered off to take up their post, Pongo and I made a beeline for James. We had already decided that I would do most of the talking, as a rumour was going round that James slightly fancied me even though it was quite clear that I was Simon's girlfriend. Simon didn't know I was his girlfriend but that was a minor technicality I was prepared to ignore. 'James,' I began, tapping him on the arm. 'You have to come up to the night toilet. Miss said. We've got to clean it.' Pongo, who was standing a little behind me, stared on.

'Oh no!' said James, jumping about a bit. 'I had to do it yesterday as well! Come on then,' he added with a sigh. 'I'll show you what to do.' We were home free. Now all we had to do was get up to the shack and stick him in it.

'Where are you three going?' asked an adult voice suddenly. We froze. It was our form teacher, Mrs Jones.

'Up to the night toilet,' said James, hopping on one foot.

'Why are you all going together?' she asked, eyes narrowing. 'What are you up to?'

And it was at this point that Pongo, thinking that this was her moment to shine, piped up with, 'We're going to the shack for a fuck, Miss!', which, by the look on her face, was a sentence Mrs Jones was never expecting to hear. We were sent to bed. And none of us got any marshmallows.

We were facing a swift turnaround between my school trip and our own family holiday. France was out of the question this year, partly because we had moved and the family budget was lying bludgeoned to death on the living room carpet, but primarily because of the increase in terrorists hijacking planes and bombing 'anything a bit English', according to my mother. The IRA was getting busy and in June had even managed to explode a bomb in the Houses of Parliament, an incident that convinced my mother that nowhere was now safe. Wales was out of the question, Scotland wasn't an option and so Brenda settled on Cornwall, reasoning that there would be no way the IRA would ever bomb Cornwall because 'everyone loves clotted cream'.

The journey down to Cornwall had been an uncharacteristically quiet one. My parents, who had been to a wedding reception the night before, were in the grips of appalling hangovers and so that year's holiday song, 'Waterloo' by Abba, was enjoying a blanket ban. My dad had the grey pallor of a man who'd opened one too many Party Sevens packs of beer, while my mother, who seemed incapable of removing her hand from her forehead, remained hidden behind a large pair of sunglasses. We had moved out at an ungodly hour which, given the state my parents were in, was bordering on madness, but my father was so determined to beat the rush of traffic flooding into Cornwall that he was clearly willing to risk life and limb to get there. I don't think anyone spoke until Bodmin Moor: all our toilet and petrol stops had been negotiated using nothing more than primeval grunts. But as Bessy rattled over the cattle grid that marked the edge of Cornwall's most dramatic moor, it was if the landscape jolted my parents back into the land of the living.

There was no doubting it, the moor was spectacular. The skyline was dominated by striking granite tors and slopes strewn with stone litter. Desolate expanses of marshy moorland stretched ahead of us, its unrelenting breadth broken with the occasional Cornish wall, bridge or cottage, all built from tumbled-down granite, as if anything that had tried to leave the moor had been dragged back. It was a place trapped in time, elemental and stubborn.

'Isn't this lovely?' said my mother, commenting as we drove past a particularly impressive outcrop.

'Look, ponies over there,' added my dad, pointing off to the left with a small, gruff clearing of his throat. 'Can you see them, Emma? They're wild ponies.'

I craned over to see three short, stocky ponies, manes flapping in the wind. They were some distance away, standing still, like moorland furniture.

'Do they just live here on their own?' I asked. 'Don't they live in stables?'

'No,' said Dad with a shrug. 'I expect they sleep under trees or lean up against a rock. Horses can sleep standing up, like cows.'

'Bit spooky, isn't it?' managed my mother after a deep swallow.

We hadn't pre-booked a campsite this year, deciding instead to let the fickle finger of fate weave its magic. Given that fate had been dealing us continual body blows for the past four years, this might have seemed like madness but, sadly, we were unaware that we were at the mercy of capricious powers. So, as we pulled into the campsite at Praa Sands, we were all agreed: it looked lovely. The campsite was positioned just behind the beach, a sprawling, golden expanse much favoured by surfers and holidaymakers, and when we arrived it was virtually empty. With no more than forty tents spread over the spacious site, we were confident that this would be a delightful and peaceful spot. 'This is great, isn't it?' said Dad, as he got up the tent. 'We've got masses of space, no one near us. This is going to be lovely.'

My mother, never the easiest to please, was forced to

agree. 'It's so nice that we can see the sea from the tent, isn't it? What a treat.' And it was. We would be sleeping, our nostrils filled with sea spray and our ears soothed by lapping waters. This holiday was already promising to be bliss on stilts.

Because my parents weren't quite over their hangovers, they decided that the best way to blow away the cobwebs was with a bracing walk. The village of Porthcurno, a few miles from Newlyn, was our starting point. Dad, armed with an ordinance survey map, had decided that we were going to begin with a quick tour of the Minack Theatre, then head east along the headland to Logan's Rock and then turn back to go down on to Porthcurno beach. He had suggested but been denied a trip to the Porthcurno Telegraph Museum because my mother had absolutely no interest whatsoever in 'knobs and wires' and quite rightly pointed out that, in a democratic family unit, 'just because one of us wants to stare at Morse code machines for two hours doesn't make it a fun day out'. Dad, a little crushed, had tried to protest but his pleas about there being 'tunnels and everything' fell on deaf ears.

The Minack Theatre, on the other hand, was an altogether different proposition. Carved out from the cliff side, the open-air amphitheatre was spectacular. Standing at the top by the entrance, we saw the theatre plunging away from us. Grass rows melted downwards at a sheer angle towards the stage, a flattened semicircle that curved itself to the cliff edge and hung on who knows how. It was an incomprehensible accomplishment made all the more amazing by the fact that the whole thing had been built by one tiny woman called Rowena Cade.

'How did she do all this?' wailed my mother in abject astonishment. 'I can't even manage a rockery. And look at her...' she added, pointing to a picture of a stick-thin woman, white hair billowing, sitting in an upturned wheelbarrow.

'She doesn't look as if she could lift a stick, let alone drag twelve-foot timbers up from the beach. That's what it says she did. She dragged twelve-foot timbers up from the beach. On her own. That's ridiculous. Oh God! It is VERY steep. Be careful, Emma. Oh God! It's giving me vertigo! Oh! Tony! Ohhhhh!'

My mother, disconcerted by the plummeting drop towards the stage, had got down on her knees and was trying to crawl backwards on her belly while grabbing hold of any available grassy tuft. 'Look at those,' said my dad, pointing over to a second tier of seating to our left. 'That's amazing. Can you see them, Emma? She's carved individual seats out of stone. It's unbelievable. And look down there! To the left of the stage! It's like a proper box! Like you see in the theatre! Incredible!'

'Tony!' wailed my mother, who was now lying prostrate across two seated tiers. 'Never mind that! Help me! I'm paralysed with fear! Paralysed!'

'But it's not that bad,' said Dad, looking back up at her. 'If you come down a bit further, it might be a bit better.'

'Tony!' screamed Brenda, clasping her eyes shut. 'I can't move! Do you understand? You'll have to help me back up to the top. I can't do it. Ohhhhh! Just help me. Please!'

My father gave out a sigh and trudged back up the slope. Taking my mother by the hands, he half-led, half-carried her back to the top of the theatre. As I sat, perched on a stone seat and letting my legs dangle, I watched as my parents scrambled back up the cliff side, my mother screaming with every step, as if the world was ending. Other people were stopping what they were doing to look at her. One man even decided to take a photo. Something I hadn't felt before stirred in my innards. I couldn't quite put my finger on it but whatever it was, I didn't like it. But the Holiday Gods knew what it was. It was the short, sharp punch of mortification. I had taken my next, vital step towards my teenage years: my parents were becoming embarrassing.

The rest of the walk had been a disaster: Brenda had spent most of it in tears, convinced that she was about to tumble headlong over the cliff at any moment, but with nowhere to go other than up or down, her hands were tied. I had tried to pretend I had nothing to do with my parents by scampering ahead, the thin, rocky line of mud weaving through tall bracken and giant rhubarb, some of whose leaves were larger than me. We had made it to Logan Rock, a massive slab of granite that could be rocked from side to side, and while Dad had a small go at nudging it, my mother embedded herself into a patch of heather and begged him to stop. 'Please, Tony,' she whined, bent over and broken. 'Don't touch it. What if it rocks back and crushes you? Or Emma! It could rock back and crush Emma. Leave it alone. It could fall off the cliff and take you with it. Or take Emma with it. Come away, Emma. Don't even look at it. Oh God. Is there another way out of here? Have we got to go back up that track? Oh God.'

I was paying little if no attention to my mother's seamless moaning. I was enraptured by the views, the smells, the gulls floating on the wind and the warm breeze rippling over my arms. Masses of tiny purple flowers clustered out from the rocks and there were endless butterflies skipping over the tops of the bracken. The sea below us was a turquoise blue and tall peaks of spray tossed off the surf, dancing like the souls of long-lost fishermen, there for a moment and then evaporated, sucked back into the sea. I loved the way the water crashed against the rocks, how the sun sparkled on the sea, and I delighted in the boats that bobbed and rolled in the distance, balloon-like swarms of gulls at their heels.

Standing there, staring out and twisting a long piece of grass between my fingers, I felt liberated and at peace.

The walk down to Porthcurno beach had turned into something of a dash, so desperate was my mother to be back at ground level, and as we touched down on to the white, dust-like sand, there was relief all round. Small groups of people were clustered on the beach, not families, but young men and women in their twenties, a lot of whom seemed to be wearing green parkas and khaki-coloured hats. Around them a few poles were sticking in the sand, at the top of which flapped a black flag with a white cross. Dad had bought us all a round of ice creams with flakes, and as we sat, licking away, I found myself staring at the disparate group in front of us. I tugged Dad by the sleeve. 'Does that flag mean they're pirates?' I asked.

'No. That's the flag of Cornwall. You know how the flag of Wales is red with a dragon? Well the flag of Cornwall is black with a white cross.'

'But Cornwall isn't a country, though,' I said, a little puzzled. 'How come it's got a flag?'

'Well some people say Cornwall *is* a country. And they want to be independent from England. In fact, some people don't even call Cornwall, Cornwall. They call it Kernow. Which is the Cornish word for Cornwall. Like Cymru is the Welsh word for Wales.'

'People speak in Cornish?' I asked, baffled.

'Tony,' said my mother, whispering. 'You don't think this is some sort of rally for that group? You know, the Free Cornish Army lot? Do you think it's safe to be here? Honestly. Everyone's gone independence-mad these days.'

'The Free Cornish Army isn't real,' said Dad. 'It was a hoax. It was a bunch of students on rag week. They set up fake passport controls to get into Cornwall. It was just a bit of fun.'

'Are you sure?' asked Brenda, eyeing up a bearded man with suspicion.

'Yes. There is no such thing as the Free Cornish Army. I remember reading about it. They were students from Plymouth mucking about. Do you want your flake, or can I have it?'

My mother, however, was unconvinced. Once she got hold of an idea she held on to it like a terrier holds on to a rat. 'I've seen *The Wicker Man*,' she whispered, as if that made her an expert. 'And trust me when I say that things are taking a sinister turn. I think we should talk in slightly Cornish accents from hereon. Just to be on the safe side. Emma, say, *Can Oi gooo to the toylit, pleeeease?* Say it like that.'

Brimful with sea air and legs glowing from our clamber, we were in a fine mood as we drove back to the campsite. Brenda, despite her brush with terror, was keen to give an outing to our holiday song, even if we did only know the words to the first line and the chorus. By the time we pulled back into the campsite, we were roused and laughing. But our mood was about to be shattered. We had left an empty and spacious campsite, but we had returned to a shanty town. 'What the bloody hell…' said Tony, looking out at the crush of tents that had been crowbarred on to every available square foot of grass.

'Where has everyone come from?' squealed my mother. 'There must be three hundred tents here. Oh God,' she added, noticing that the vast majority of the new campers were hippies and teenagers. 'There's not a music festival on we don't know about, is there? Tony? Where's our tent? It's vanished.'

Thankfully, our tent had not disappeared but was now crushed in the middle of four surrounding tents, all of which were occupied by spotty youths with radios glued to their ears. Music was blaring every which way and two of the tents were so close, there couldn't have been more than a foot between us and them. There was nowhere for us to put up our table and chairs and the view to the beach was now totally obscured. We were surrounded by sixteen-year-olds on their first holiday without their parents: this was going to get ugly.

By my reckoning there were six lads in the four tents immediately around us. One boy, thin with trousers that didn't quite fit him and a mass of lanky hair, was already face-down on the grass. He might have been sleeping, but the presence of a plastic jug of scrumpy in his hand suggested otherwise. No one was paying the slightest bit of attention to him but instead were arguing about how to make roll-up cigarettes without roll-up paper which all of them, so it would appear, had forgotten to nick from the campsite shop. The largest lad, a beefy-faced boy, wearing a Jimi Hendrix T-shirt that looked as if it might explode off him at any moment, was trying to persuade a cooler-looking boy with curly blonde hair that they could use toilet paper to make cigarettes but, going by the blonde-haired boy's response, that 'that was the same as kissing shit', I guessed that idea was a non-starter. Another boy, wearing nothing but a grey pair of pants, was sitting on the floor just to the left of our tent. Rather alarmingly, he was trying to stab open a tin of baked beans, wedged into his crotch, with what looked like a bread knife. Tony, who was wincing every time the lad slammed the knife downwards, decided to take matters into his own hands. 'Do you want me to open that for you?' he asked, shouting over to the boy. 'I've got a tin opener.'

Glancing up through a dense and greasy fringe, the teenager stopped what he was doing, muttered something incomprehensible and held out the tin in the direction of my dad. I had chosen to stand as close to our tent as possible and hold on to one of the guy ropes. I was not used to teenage boys and until told otherwise I was prepared to treat them with the utmost suspicion. The boy, who had wandered over in our direction, was now slouching within five feet of me. His skin was pale, his body bony and, as I stood staring at him, I couldn't help thinking that he looked like a giant, uncooked chicken wing. As my dad took the tin of baked beans from him, he stood, shoulders hunched and sniffing. I couldn't take my eyes off him. He was like something from outer space.

Brenda, meanwhile, had retired to the sanctuary of the inner tent where she was standing, hands on hips, wondering what to do. Having been transfixed by the baked bean incident, I had joined her in order to discuss what I had seen. 'He was just wearing pants, Mum,' I said in a shocked whisper. 'They weren't even swimming trunks. And he smelled of socks. Which was strange because he wasn't wearing any.'

My mother was clearly agitated. 'Tony,' she hissed with an urgent wave of her hand. 'Come here a minute. What are we going to do? I don't want to spend a week surrounded by teenage boys in pants. They'll be drunk, they'll be smoking who knows what, and what if they find some girls? Then what?'

Dad, who was best placed to understand the workings of the young male mind, patted at the air in an attempt to be reassuring. 'Calm down,' he soothed. 'Once they've settled themselves in they'll be fine, and we'll barely know they're there. We'll be out all day. They'll be out all day. They'll probably be out for most of the night. If they get a bit rowdy then I'll have a word. Let's not worry too much about it.'

'Tony,' said my mother, fixing him with a special stare, 'there's a teenage boy unconscious right outside our tent and they're trying to smoke drugs. We've got nowhere to sit and have our meals and instead of a lovely view down to the beach I am now staring at a sea of spotty backs. I think we should go to another campsite. I do.'

'But Brenda,' said my dad, leaning in a little to talk quietly, 'this is Cornwall. Everywhere is going to be packed. It'll be fine. Let's give it a couple of days at least. See how we go.'

'That boy had loads of spots, Mummy,' I said, because I was on her side. 'Just loads.'

'I know,' she said, putting an arm round my shoulders and sighing. 'I know.'

The atmosphere was tense. Dad had managed to squeeze our small, two-ring gas stove into a tiny gap at the back of our tent and, having cooked our supper, we had sat inside the tent on three chairs, eating tomato soup with only the bucket to look at. 'This is nice,' had said my mother in a tone that some might call sarcastic. Outside, the boys were discussing how they could get hold of a 'porno mag'.

'What's a porno mag?' I asked.

'Never mind,' said my mother.

'I know,' said Tony, anxious to change the mood. 'Let's go for a little walk. We could have a stroll on the beach. Watch the sunset.'

'Good idea,' nodded my mother. 'Anything to get away from these wretched boys.'

'Wretched,' I said, agreeing with a solemn shake of my head.

I decided to walk barefoot to the beach, a luxury my mother indulged because of our proximity to it, and as I jumped and hopped through the coarse, grassy dunes I marvelled again at the liberated abandon that Cornwall seemed to have instilled in me. As we tripped on to the still-warm sand, a clutch of surfers were jogging down to the shoreline, boards tucked under one arm. I had never seen anyone surfing before and thought it incredible and exotic. Scampering after them, I ran down to the sea to watch as they dived into the tumbling breakers, lying face-down on their boards and paddling like fury to get beyond the waves. Other surfers sat, bobbing in the distance, sitting upright in their all-black wetsuits, checking over their shoulders and waiting for a swell. The sun was softening on the horizon, sending pink darts across the skyline. As the surfers grabbed the best of what the early-evening waters had to offer, I darted across the edge of the sea as it stretched up the beach.

I had been running for about five minutes when I felt a sharp, sudden stab in the ball of my foot. My parents were higher up the beach, wandering at the top of the dunes and as I pulled up, shocked by the unexpected jab, they were unaware that I was in any sort of difficulty. Looking at my foot, I could see it was bloody and that something sharp and jagged was sticking out of the wound. I had run, at full pelt, on to a broken piece of shell that was now embedded in the soft pad just beneath my big toe. Blood was trickling down the length of my foot and as I ran my finger over the wound, thick, glutinous blobs oozed out, dripping into a sticky heap on the sand. I knew I had to pull the shell out and, knowing it was going to hurt, I pinched the shell quickly and gave it a sharp tug. The pain was momentarily excruciating and I let out a small yelp, not least because I was surprised at the significant gush of blood that followed. My instinct was to put my foot into the sea; my dad had told me that sea water was good for horses' legs. So I hopped to the surf and wriggled my foot in it, watching as wafts of red clouds were sucked away. One thing I was certain about: there was no way I was going to tell my parents. I had had a job persuading my mother that I was allowed to come out with no shoes on and if she knew I'd hurt myself I'd be in trouble. No one was going to know about it.

That, of course, was easier said than done. I had an open wound on the flat of my foot and I was leaving pools of blood with every step. Hobbling towards my parents, I was convinced that I could keep this sorry mess quiet and so, with the gash in my foot packed with sand, mud and a few stray blades of grass, we made our way back to our tent. We went via the campsite shop, a low-to-the-ground shack that seemed to be full to the brim with cornflakes and not much else. As I stood waiting for my parents as they negotiated essential requirements like milk and a loaf of bread, I was alarmed by the intense throbbing in my foot. It really hurt. Worried that my parents were going to notice me limping, I decided to make a declaration. 'I'm going to hop on one leg until bedtime,' I said, just to make sure we were all on the same page.

'That's nice,' said my mother, staring at a packet of butter.

'Look at this,' said my dad, choosing to ignore me. He was pointing at a hand-drawn poster that read, 'Breage Village Fete. Hog roast. Pony rides. Bale toss. Lots of fun for the family. This Sunday.'

'Shall we go?' he asked, tapping it with a finger. 'It looks good. Especially the hog roast. That sounds nice.'

'Yes,' said Brenda, casting an eye over it, 'why not? You still hopping, Emma?'

'Yes, thank you,' I answered.

The boys had disappeared when we got back to the tent, a significant relief that meant my mother could relax and enjoy herself for a few hours before the inevitable late-night teenage cacophony started up again. Given that I was experiencing new levels of agony, I had pleaded semi-exhaustion, got into my pyjamas and retired to the inner tent, where I had rubbed some of the dirt out of my foot with the sleeve of a jumper. It didn't look pleasant: an angry black bruise was spreading from the base of my toe downwards and the wound, crying out to be cleaned, was tender and howling. If

I put a sock over it, I reasoned, then I wouldn't have to think about it till morning. So that's what I did.

The music kicked in around midnight. I had woken, vaguely aware that a radio was playing somewhere behind us to the left and that two of the boys were singing along with a sense of appropriate teenage angst. Not only that but someone, probably the boy who had been face-down on the grass earlier, was vomiting loudly by our tent very near my head. Layered over the top was a small but nevertheless persistent argument about some stolen fags. We were being battered in a cage of noise. 'Oh, Tony,' moaned Brenda with a deep and desperate sigh. 'I can't bear it. I actually can't bear it. This is going to go on for hours. Can't you go out there and ask them to be quiet?'

My father, who had wrapped a jumper round his head to block out the dread wailings of the singalong to the Bay City Rollers' song 'Shang-a-lang', didn't need asking twice. Leaping over my mother and unzipping the inner tent with a fury, he stormed to the outer door. 'Lads!' he shouted, sticking out his head. 'There are people trying to sleep. So pack it in!'

The boys, deafened to reason by a surfeit of cheap cider, took it in turns to shout back. 'We're on holiday!' yelled one, who sounded in a state. 'We can make as much noise as we like!'

'Yeah!' shouted another. 'Go and pony on your own patch!'

'What does that mean?' I asked Mum, who just shook her head at me and raised her eyebrows.

'It's one o'clock in the morning. Turn it off, lads!' battled on Dad, in as stern a voice as I had ever heard.

At this point we were only able to hear a somewhat muffled noise, but it was fair to say that something approaching an undignified scuffle was in full flow. My mother, sensing that Tony had got himself involved in a physical entanglement, jumped off her air bed, grabbed the trowel that Dad used to loosen the ground for the tent pegs and joined my father in front of the tent. Alarmed and fascinated, I sat up and quite clearly heard my mother threaten to use the trowel if they didn't all shut up. Quite what damage she thought she was going to do with a trowel was, thankfully, a question that remained unanswered and, after a sustained period of name calling, everything died down and my parents returned to the safety of our sleeping quarters.

'Well, that told them,' said my mother, still brandishing the trowel.

'Little shits,' added Dad, who was still fired up. 'I can't believe he tried a kung fu kick on me. Can you believe that? A kung fu kick!'

'Yes,' added my mother, plumping up her pillow. 'But he did miss you by a mile. And actually,' she added as an after-thought, 'I think he quite hurt himself.'

We'd had our first tent rage incident. Rock and roll.

My foot was in a terrible state. Overnight it had swollen and was now throbbing with the deep and painful intensity of an infection taking hold. Even though I was obviously in physical torture, I was still reasoning with myself that my parents could not and would not know about it and so, instead of asking for immediate medical assistance, I pulled another sock over it and hoped for the best. The Breage village fete was, at first sight, a clutter of stalls and bunting crammed on to the central village green, splattered with ladies carrying cakes and children smeared with jam. A girl in a thick checked shirt was wandering around with a pony and off to the left a smoky, intense aroma was floating off a hog roast slowly rotating over a low charcoal fire. My dad, who had a natural predilection for anything meaty, had wandered over to stare at it, salivating like a Pavlovian dog. The furthest I'd had to walk that morning was from the tent to the Land Rover and the prospect of an entire day scampering around on a rapidly degenerating foot was filling me with considerable dread.

Thankfully, an opportunity to sit down presented itself almost immediately. Tony, who'd got chatting to the burly man in charge of the hog roast, had discovered that there was going to be a bale toss and that the winner got to take a whole leg of hog home. 'A whole leg, Brenda,' he had told us, wide-eyed and rubbing his hands. 'They're starting in five minutes. I've put my name down. A whole leg!'

My mother said nothing but instead shot me a glance that seemed to span the centuries: men, it would seem, were prepared to do anything, however foolish and impossible, for pork.

To get himself in the mood, Dad decided to warm up with a bit of hammering. Next to the usual village fete tombola and the compulsory throw-the-wet-sponge-at-the-local-joker, there was one stall that was verging on the peculiar. 'Bang the Nail in the Log!' yelled the banner and that was precisely what you had to do. Each competitor was handed a six-inch nail and invited to bang it into a large, upturned log. The person who banged the nail into the log with the least amount of strikes won a fiver and a pair of Wellingtons, so there was everything to play for. Tony, riding on a surge of masculinity, handed over fifty pence and then stood in line, waiting to have his crack at the log. Having had a quick look at the wooden stump in question, Tony had noticed that there was a thin fissure running down one side. If he could put the tip of the nail in that, he reasoned, he would be giving himself a head-start. As Dad stood, throwing me the occasional thumbs up, I was on the verge of passing out. The pain in my foot was now so intense that I was breaking into a sweat and fighting not to go cross-eyed. My mother noticed that I was in some distress and clamped a hand to my forehead. 'You're very hot, Emma,' she said. 'Are you all right? Do you want to take your jumper off?'

I gave her a feeble nod. 'Just feel a bit warm,' I mumbled and stood, arms in the air, as Brenda pulled the jumper over my head. She looked at me again.

'Are you sure you feel all right?' she asked again, giving me a thorough scan. 'You don't feel ill or anything?'

I shook my head and sat down in front of the log. 'I just want to watch Daddy,' I said, relieved to be off my feet. 'I'll just sit here for a bit.'

My mother stared at me with nothing but suspicion. 'Well, all right,' she said, giving me a small stroke on the head. 'But tell me if you're not feeling well. You just look a bit...funny.'

Funny wasn't the half of it. A fever was taking hold and every time I put any pressure on my foot it was like being stabbed with a knife. A sticky wetness was starting to seep its way up my sock. I didn't want to look at it. I didn't want to know what it was.

The men in front of my dad had all brought their own hammering techniques to the table. One had taken his time, with slow, methodical taps. Another had gone for bashing the nail but from a greater height. 'Five strikes!' shouted the round-faced woman in charge. She was very jolly and was wearing an all-in-one brown nylon catsuit, which, given her shape and size, was probably not the best of choices.

'What's the best so far?' asked Dad, as she handed him his nail and the hammer.

'Three strikes,' she said. 'That's what you've got to beat.'

'No chance,' said the man behind Tony. My dad turned

to look at him, a little startled by the outburst. The man stared right back and folded his arms to show he meant business. He had a swarthy look to him, unshaven and with a mass of uncombed hair. He was wearing a dirty white shirt, sleeves rolled up to the elbows and scuffed, denim flares. He was also wearing a belt buckle. It was of a skull.

Perhaps it was the presence of the large, tarnished silver skull that did it, or the tattoos that ran up both forearms, but whatever it was, my dad was paying attention. Tony turned the other cheek and placed his nail on the log. 'You're allowed one tap to get it standing,' explained the lady. 'But just a tap, mind.'

Tony tapped his nail into the crack in the wood as planned. He wasn't looking for precision, nor was he looking for beauty. All he was looking for was cold, brute strength and, with his nail in position, he raised the hammer way above his shoulder and with one mighty and primeval roar, he brought the hammer crashing down.

He missed.

Realising his basic error, something snapped inside him and I watched, momentarily distracted from the torment raging in my sock, as my father went bananas. Down the hammer slammed! Again he missed the nail. Up the hammer went, down it came, blows smashing into the log, my father screaming like a man possessed. As the nail's head finally settled into the surface of the log, he stopped, turned to the lady and panting said, 'How many?'

'Twenty-four,' said the lady, not quite able to look my father in the eye. Something told me we wouldn't be getting the Wellingtons.

'Are you sure you want to do the bale toss?' asked my mother as we wandered over to the two rugby-style posts that had been erected in the centre of the green. 'It seems to me that it might be something best left to the locals. There're a lot of Cornish flags up. And you know they don't like outsiders.'

My father, wearing the deep scowl of a man who wished he had bigger forearms, was paying little attention. The man with the silver buckle was still laughing behind us and, even worse, he was also heading over to the bale toss. Things were about to get personal. My foot, meanwhile, was burning, the throbbing so intense that I was finding it difficult to think. I had tried walking on my heel to alleviate the pain but, by hobbling, I was attracting the attention of my mother, who had started to take a sharp interest in me.

'Are you sure you're all right?' she asked again. 'And why are you walking funny?'

I was about to rustle up an excuse about a stone being in my plimsoll but, unable to muster the strength, I settled for a small shattered expression and buckled slowly to the floor instead. Before my mother could respond, events at the bale toss took over. My dad, who had rolled up his sleeves, was about to take his first turn. The aim of the challenge was to toss a bale of hay on a pitchfork between two horizontal bars, the lower of which was set ten feet from the ground, while the higher bar was at twenty feet. As players who failed to toss their bale between the bars were eliminated, the lower bar was moved up so that the gap between the two gradually became smaller. There seemed to be a particular knack to tossing the bale successfully and it was quickly apparent that anyone without immediate experience of working on a farm was at a distinct disadvantage. As my dad stepped forward and took hold of the pitchfork, the man with the skull buckle shouted out. 'This'll be a laugh!' he yelled, gesturing towards Tony with a dirty thumb. 'Took twenty-four goes over at the nail log!'

Whether my dad meant to do it we will probably never know but, plunging the pitchfork into the bale, he swung the whole thing from left to right. The bale, which should have gone upwards, arced sideways, slid off the end of the pitchfork, and in a sudden and unexpected twist, flew straight into the face of the man with the belt. Knocked on to his back and with a considerably bloodied nose, the man was fast on his feet and striding towards my father with a clenched fist. 'I'll bloody have you!' he was yelling. Dad, realising that he was going to get thumped, dropped the pitchfork and prepared for the worst.

'It were an accident!' shouted a voice from the crowd, but it was too late. Before Tony could do anything about it, he'd been lamped full on the chin. Dad, who had proper Welsh rugby blood flowing through his veins, sucked in the punch and turned to thump one back, but as he ran at the buckle man in a half-bent scrum manoeuvre, a small phalanx of Morris Men moved in and hauled them both apart. For some inexplicable reason, the Morris Man with the pig's bladder then decided that the best way to dissipate the tension would be to do a few quick Morris Man dance steps and hit both the buckle man and my dad over the head with his animal innards balloon, an act that was greeted with a ripple of polite applause from the crowd.

Brenda, appalled and exasperated, reached down to take my hand. 'Come on,' she said, 'I've seen enough. Let's go!'

My father, extricating himself from the clutch of white-clad men covered in bells, poked a finger at the buckle man and shouted, 'You're mad, pal! Mad!'

'Tony!' shouted my mother again. 'We're leaving! Emma, get up please. We're going.'

But I couldn't get up. Something in my foot had burst, like a carcass that's been left in the sun. 'My foot...' I said weakly and pointed towards the sticky liquid that was spreading up my sock.

'Oh my God,' said my mother, bending down and looking at it. 'What's happened? What is this? Give me your foot. Let's get your plimsoll off. Oh God! Tony! Look at her foot!'

My foot had turned septic. Green pus was oozing out of the wound and my foot was covered in what looked like thin, stinking yellow gravy. My father carried me over to the obligatory St John Ambulance volunteer, a bald man with tiny teeth. I was sweating and close to fainting.

'This wound's infected,' said the volunteer, having given me an examination. 'All I can do is clean it up and dress it. But she'll need antibiotics and bed rest till it's healed.'

As we returned to the campsite, we discovered that the boys, who had been asked to leave by the campsite owner, had not gone without a parting shot. They'd let our tent down and tipped the contents of the bucket all over it. It was the end of another shitty holiday. Literally.

Chapter Six

*Fruits*ᵈᵉ***Merde***

'Let's go on a road trip!' suggested Brenda. 'You know, a proper one. Where we take ages getting somewhere and then take ages coming back. But coming back a different way. So we see more things. Let's do that.'

'When you say "ages",' said my dad, who was peeling a potato, 'how long do you mean?'

'I don't know,' answered my mother with a shrug. 'Three weeks?'

'So, like a week to get to a place, a week at the place and then a week coming back from the place?' asked my dad, thinking out loud.

'Yes!' nodded my mother. 'Exactly like that. And the other thing about making it three weeks,' she added in a whisper, 'is that if anything goes wrong, then you know, we've got more time to try and forget about it.'

We were now so used to disasters happening to us on holiday we were actually factoring them into our plans. A three-week holiday sounded enormous and exorbitant but due to a government review the previous year that had given teachers an incredible 30 per cent pay increase which had been followed with a 29 per cent pay rise in 1975, somehow my parents were rolling in it. 'We've saved a hundred quid this month!' Dad would squeal, shaking his head in disbelief. For the first time in their lives, my parents had money to burn. And burn it they would.

Brenda, who had long fantasised about sun-kissed balconies with stunning views, had seen an advert in one of the Sunday papers. It was for the holiday village of La Presqu'île in Port Barcarès, a small town in the South of France just shy of the border with Spain. She had sent off for the brochure, elated by the prospect of a proper bed and no communal showers and, after a quick five-minute flick- through its silky pages, had ordered my father to book a studio flat sharpish. 'It hasn't just got one restaurant, Tony,' she had gushed, throwing open the relevant page and tapping it with some urgency. 'It's got two!'

Dad, on the other hand, was in charge of the tour there and back again. He was in his element: any excuse to stare at maps all day and he was in ecstasies. He spent hours writing down place names, making lists, rearranging them, crossing some off, adding new ones. He even worked out mileage between stops, calculated petrol cost and gave each town a star coding according to 'things of natural and unnatural interest'.

'When you say "unnatural interest",' asked my mother during the family presentation, 'what do you mean by that?'

'Anything man-made,' explained my father, who had pinned his map of France up on a cork board and was point- ing at it with a wooden spoon. 'So that would include the cathedral in Orléans, the amphitheatre in Arles and the palace in Fontainebleu. As opposed to the things of natural interest, by which I mean the Loire river and the Camargue. And also the Pyrenees.'

'I see,' nodded my mother. 'Please continue.'

Tony was giving a presentation. He'd even put on a tie, a small gesture that my mother found hilarious, but not as hilarious as when Dad said, 'Welcome. And thank you for coming', which my mother laughed about for a good fifteen minutes. Dad had set up his map at one end of the dining room and arranged chairs at the other end, which we were invited to sit on. I was a bit put out at having to attend because 'The Waltons' would be starting in five minutes and the ongoing struggles of John Boy and Jim Bob were of far more importance to me than where we would be spending three weeks of our summer. The map, pinned up in front of us, had our route marked out in felt-tip pen with the stopover towns ringed in red. It all looked very professional.

'Our longest day of travel,' explained Tony, following the line on the map with the spoon, 'will be our first. As you can see, we will arrive in Calais at around 11.30, push on past Paris taking the Périphérique, and then onwards...'

'*The Périphérique?*' asked Brenda, holding out a flat palm. 'Isn't that the AWFUL road where everyone dies?'

'Well not everyone dies, Brenda,' answered my dad, tapping the map in the relevant place. 'Because no one would go on it. I mean some people die but then some people die on every road. So, taking the Périphérique...'

'Do we have to go on it?' asked my mother again.

'Well, yes,' said my dad, looking baffled. 'I've coloured it in.'

'Yes, but that doesn't mean...'

'I've coloured it in,' said my dad again, a little firmer. 'Good. So we will push onwards to our first stop at Andonville from where we will be able to visit Orléans, which is jam-packed with things of unnatural interest.'

'Can I go and watch "The Waltons", please?' I asked, fidgeting.

'Don't you want to know where we're going?' asked Dad, stunned that I wasn't fascinated.

'No,' I said, getting up and moving to the door. 'I want to know if Jim Bob's all right after the guinea pig died.'

Sometimes, you just have to prioritise.

*

Knowing that we had a long and potentially boring journey ahead of us, I had packed my section in the rear of Bessy with as many distractions as space would allow. As I lay on top of all the camping gear, it was possible to position myself so that I was totally obscured from view and, given that my interest in everything my parents were up to was beginning to wane, I was glad of the limited privacy. I had started to read Roald Dahl books and had brought three titles with me: *James and the Giant Peach*, *Charlie and the Chocolate Factory* and *Charlie and the Great Glass Elevator*. I had also brought my favourite annual, *The Goodies File*, which I regarded as subversive and extremely grown-up, and to wash it all down, a small Mickey Mouse Pez dispenser which doubled up as a secret communication device with spies and spacemen. Because I was so engrossed in my *Goodies* book, I spent little if no time paying any attention to the scenery. I had looked out the window for a brief time as we left Calais but other than the striking tower of the Flemish-style town hall, there was little of any interest. Much of Calais had been razed to the ground during the Second World War and as a result was a series of low-roofed corrugated warehouses and not much else.

In any event, there wasn't much to look at between Calais and Paris; it was motorway all the way. The only thing of note was that we had to pay to drive on the road, a concept I found bizarre, and I watched, intrigued, as we pulled into the regular toll stations dotted along the length of the motorway and Mum and Dad scrabbled about for loose French change. Brenda found motorway travel unpleasant and stressful and had spent the first few hours of our journey working herself up into a small stew about our impending drive on the Périphérique, the notorious ring road around Paris. Brenda hated busy roads at the best of times and had once wailed to a friend that a journey had been particularly horrific just because

Tony had had to 'overtake four lorries! FOUR!' She had been sitting, staring at the road map for at least half an hour. 'French drivers are mad, Tony,' she had argued as we approached the point of no return. 'They're nervous drivers. And that makes them agitated. So all they do is keep their foot on the accelerator. That's all they can do. They don't even know where the brake is. In fact, I'm not even sure they've GOT brakes in French cars. And if they're not accelerating then they're tailgating. And we can't go that fast. And what if we need to brake and they're tailgating? And accelerating at the same time? What then? They'll go into the back of us. That's what. And what if we need to move out? What if we need to overtake something and we can't? Because the French won't let us out. They'll be too busy accelerating. And being agitated. They're extremely agitated. It's because they drink so much coffee.'

'Have you finished?' asked my father in a weary tone.

'Not really,' answered my mother, chewing her lip. 'Can't we just not go on it? Please? Can't we go another way?'

'Brenda,' snapped my father, gripping the steering wheel, 'there is no other way. This is the way. If we need to overtake then we'll overtake. If we need to move lanes we shall move lanes. I am perfectly capable of driving on a busy motorway.'

'But this is a French motorway,' whined my mother. 'With French people on it who've drunk too much coffee. They're permanently livid. And you know how much they hate the English. They didn't even want us in the EU. This is their revenge. Accelerating and tailgating. This is how they get us back. There must be another way. If I just have another look at the road map then maybe I can…'

'Well you'll have to look quick because this is our exit,' said Dad, pointing to a large sign in the distance that signalled the beginning of the infamous ring road: a gesture that was met with a sudden and alarming scream from Brenda.

'Is this road really dangerous?' I asked, turning on to my belly and leaning on my elbows.

'Yes!' wailed my mother. 'Your father wants to kill us all!'

'No,' said Tony with a sigh, 'it isn't. It's just busy. There's a difference.'

'Oh Mary, mother of Jesus!' screamed my mother suddenly, as a car undercut us at the exit and screeched off, zigzagging its way through the traffic. 'See!' yelled my mother, shoving my father in the arm. 'See that? They're all mad! Mad! They're doing it deliberately! They don't want us here! They want all their cheese and wine to themselves! Oh! Look out!'

Another car had wailed up our inside, horn blaring, forcing us to move quickly into the adjacent lane. It was quite a swerve and my dad, who up till this point had let my mother's incessant laments wash over him, was visibly rattled. 'Jesus,' he muttered, straightening the Land Rover.

'I told you, Tony!' cried my mother, clasping a hand to her forehead. 'We're going to die!'

We were now trapped in the wrong lane. If we didn't get out of it we were going to be dragged down a slip road into the centre of Paris. The problem we now faced was that, because Bessy lacked the requisite oomph for a quick manoeuvre, we couldn't pull out. Cars were zipping past us at a relentless rate and, since we were relatively slow, we also had a tailback of French drivers stuck behind us who were more than happy to let us know about how angry that made them. 'Everyone's beeping us, Dad,' I pitched in helpfully, looking out the back window.

'We've got to get out of this lane!' my father yelled suddenly. 'Bloody wing mirror! It's set for England! I can't see the inside lane! Brenda, you're going to have to tell me when I can move out! Open up your window, stick your head out!'

'Oh, Jesus!' howled my mother. 'Jesus! Jesus! Hail Mary full of grace! The Lord is with thee...'

'No!' said my father, gesturing violently to get her window down. 'Not "say a bloody Hail Mary", we need to get out of this lane! Come on!'

Cars were now blaring their horns every which way. Some drivers were even slowing down to shout at us before speeding off. No one in France, it would seem, was prepared to even contemplate travelling at less than ninety miles an hour. The man in the car immediately behind us, now so close I could actually see his nose hair, was gesturing so angrily at us that if he could have forced us into the concrete barrier and watched as we all burnt to death it still wouldn't have been sufficient punishment. Every time Dad tried to move out a little, we were forced back in. Every time we tried to slow down we were beeped from behind. 'It's no good!' yowled my mother, head out the window. 'No one's going to let you out! What are we going to do? Oh!'

'Right!' roared Tony. 'I've got to change lanes. I've got to do it now. Hold on! I'm going to sound the horn and move out! If they hit us, they hit us. Bessy'll keep us safe! Emma, get down!'

With one hand he pumped down on Bessy's horn, a loud, thick klaxon that rattled off every car in hearing distance, and with the other he swerved the car over to the left. A host of brakes screeched behind us, followed by an orchestra of beeps and a sea of men's heads and arms raging out of drivers' windows. Somehow we had done it and avoided a multi-vehicle pile-up. 'Arse off!' shouted my dad in his thick Welsh accent, as every car that then passed us registered their displeasure. 'Up yours!'

My mother turned to shoot me a look over her shoulder.

'What did I say?' she asked, raising an exasperated hand. 'What did I say?'

I, however, chose to remain silent. We were beeped all the way to the exit.

By the time we reached the campsite in Andonville, everyone was tired. It was a small affair, only ten or so tents spread out over a space of parched grass that backed on to a field growing Christmas trees. We decided to pitch our tent to the right of the site, up against the edge of the field where the smell of the fledgling pine was at its most fragrant. The campsite was run by a fat Madame who lived in a little onsite condominium which doubled as an office and shop. As we drove in, I had seen her pop her head out the window. Nobody and nothing got past the Madame. Before Dad could get the tent up, he had to register – a complicated process that involved a multitude of identity cards, including not just passports but the specially-applied-for Carnet Camping International Card, which Tony brandished with pride because it proved he was a 'proper camper'. What it didn't do was speak French for him. Given that his grasp of the language was flimsy and the Madame had the patience of a mosquito, we were treated to a protracted negotiation during which Dad tried to explain what he did for a living through the power of mime while the Madame stared at him through voluminous fleshy eyelids, threw her hands in the air and said '*Bouf!*' a lot.

'She thinks I'm a professor,' said Tony, shooting me a wink. 'A professor! Look at that! That's what she's written on the card.'

'*Professeur* is French for teacher,' said Mum, sitting in Bessy with the door open.

'Oh,' said Dad, a little crestfallen. 'Still. Professor, eh? And she sold me some pâté. We can have it for supper.'

'What sort of pâté?' asked Brenda, head falling to one side.

'*Pâté de tête*,' said Dad, holding a small bag aloft. 'She said it was *très bon*!'

'*Pâté de tête?*' quizzed Mum, lip curling a little. 'That's head pâté. Oh, Tony. Brain pâté? Has it got bits of brains in it?'

'It just looks like pâté,' said Dad, giving it a sniff. 'It smells nice. It doesn't smell of brains.'

'What do brains smell of?' I asked, looking up from the French comic my mother had got me at a service station.

'Something disgusting, I expect,' piped up Mum. 'Let me look at it...Tony...there's bristly bits in it. Look at that. Not gristle. Bristle. It's pâté made from a head.'

'Head of what?' I asked, scooting over to have a peek.

'Pig?' said Dad. 'Or duck. Could be a duck.'

'Ducks don't have bristle, they have beaks,' opined Brenda, handing back the pâté. 'And I think it smells funny. I'm not sure we should eat that.'

'Don't be silly!' chuckled Dad. 'It'll be lovely.'

'Well you can, but I'm not. I don't want brains pâté with bristle,' declared my mother.

'Nor me,' I said and went back to my comic.

'Fine,' said Tony, chucking the bag on top of the dashboard. 'All the more for me!'

Three hours later and Dad was being sick in the bucket. Bent over and in agony, he was in a physical torment so intense that between vomiting he was prostrate on the tent floor and weeping. My mother was torn. While my father's immediate welfare was at the forefront of her mind, she was also aware that the heady aroma of pig brain's puke in the confines of hot canvas was a smell so special that we were all at risk of chucking up our guts. Not only that, but she had seen this coming from several miles off, a fact that was taking the edge off her predilection for caring. The man was warned, and that was that. Unable to cope with the sticky stench for one more minute, Brenda had made sure Tony was past the worst, put a plastic cup of water in his hand and escaped with me to the Land Rover. As we sat, she shook her head a lot and said, 'I told him. Didn't I tell him? Who eats puréed brains? An idiot, that's who. Well at least we're getting our holiday disaster out of the way. Better to have it now and have done with it. At least this way we can just get on and enjoy the rest of the holiday.'

Thankfully, by morning Tony was much better. The tent stank but that was to be expected: the bucket, almost brimful with sick, had been malevolently fermenting overnight. We stood and watched as he hobbled over to a hedge and emptied it, the early-morning sun rendering it an almost bucolic scene. The horror was over for now, and Dad, weakened but still determined, had an itinerary to stick to and stick to it he would.

'Are you sure you're well enough to drive?' asked Mum, staring at my father's paler than normal face. 'We can always stay here another day.'

'I would rather cut off my cock,' said my dad in a low mumble and, with that, he shifted Bessy into first gear and put his foot down.

Orléans was to be our next stop, a visit rather than a stay, and was on the itinerary for cultural edification alone. We had parked near to the cathedral and walked with heads pointing upwards, startled by the splendid Gothic twin towers that dominated the skyline and humbled all before them. A triumvirate of rose windows lay beneath the towers, perched above not one but five doors, each window framed between two octagonal columns. As I gazed up, it was impossible not to be struck with a sense of religious awe. 'This was where

Joan of Arc used to come for mass,' said my mother, ever ready to enrich my breadth of knowledge. 'Do you know who she is?'

I shook my head. I'd never heard of her.

'Joan of Arc was an exceptionally brave woman,' explained my mother. 'She led the French against the English. And had a very bad haircut.'

'According to my book,' said Dad, having a quick read of his well-thumbed guidebook, 'she was only seventeen when she was in charge of the French army. Imagine that? Seventeen and commanding an army. You'd think she'd be interested in other things. And she was always moaning on about visions from God. You wouldn't want to be stuck next to her at dinner, would you?'

My mother, ignoring my father, carried on. 'And Orléans was under siege from the English and no one had been able to lift it until Joan of Arc came along. She got things done, like most women do. Half the wars in history would have been solved if everyone put a woman in charge. And what thanks did she get for solving everything? They burnt her at the stake. Tied her to a big pole and set fire to her.'

'It wasn't the French who did that,' interjected Dad. 'That was the English. They said she was a heretic.'

'What's a *heretic*?' I asked.

'Someone who holds an opposite view to everyone else,' explained Dad. 'In short, Protestants. And your mother.'

'Did they burn her here?' I asked, looking about. I had the same feeling as when we'd been to the Tower of London and had got to stand on the spot where Anne Boleyn had been beheaded. There was something ghoulishly fascinating about being in the precise location of a momentous killing and I wanted to stand in the long-gone footprints of Joan of Arc and imagine the blazing faggots.

'Doesn't say,' mumbled Dad, poring over his guidebook. 'But it does say that when she was being burnt, she asked for a priest to hold up a crucifix for her to look at. And then, when she was dead, the English burnt her again, twice, to make sure the job was done. And then they swept her up and chucked her in the Seine. So maybe it wasn't here because the river here is the Loire. The Seine's up in Paris. Poor old Joan of Arc. Being killed three times. That's rotten.'

The journey on from Orléans to our next campsite in Argentat passed without incident. My mother would occasionally wave at me to look at a particularly spectacular château perched in the distance or point out buzzards drifting in wide loops over fields but, other than that, we were all in a quiet mood. The further south we travelled, the more rugged and picturesque the landscape became: flat arable land turned gradually into dense, forested hills as we dropped down through the valleys of the Dordogne. The weather was exceptional, cloudless skies with an endless chorus of grasshoppers that greeted us every time we made a stop. Sitting by the side of the road, perched on one of Bessy's side plates and with peach juice running down my chin, I had to acknowledge that road trips weren't that bad after all. Our second campsite, at Argentat, was amazing: set on a plateau that fell away from a thick incline of fir trees and splayed across the banks of the Dordogne, it was a picture postcard of perfection. The site was bordered by water on three sides. On the river, a few speedboats were skimming across the surface while quieter, bobbing dinghies dipped back and forth in the light breeze. Towards the back of the campsite, in the top right-hand corner, sat a magnificent château, towering over all it surveyed with a glorious beneficence. It was an almost impossible concept, but we seemed to have found ourselves on a posh campsite.

'Look at that caravan,' said Brenda, pointing a finger towards the plot opposite ours. 'They've got lace curtains! Look! And that one over there, the other French one, it's got an awning over the back window. Look at that. Goodness. This is very upmarket, isn't it?'

We were constantly in awe of people with caravans. They were five-star hotels as far as we were concerned. People with caravans got to sleep on decent beds and sit on a proper toilet, not hover over a stinking bucket that you'd then be forced to share space with for hours on end. We noticed that some caravans even had televisions, a mind-blowing concept. My only experience of in-tent entertainment was the occasional bad-tempered card game and the evening avoid-the-moth hop, a game of agility and bravery that involved sitting as near to the gas lamp as you dared before running off screaming as a flapping behemoth clattered into your eyeballs. That was it. The only other thing available to us was sitting and watching everyone else as they wandered about with their better equipment and amazing dinners. 'Roast chicken,' Dad would say under his breath, giving one of us a nudge. And Mum and I would sit, in silence, quietly salivating and wondering why it was that all these beautiful treats were passing us by. It was agony. But this year, the pain was bearable. We were on our way to a holiday village where lace curtains and awnings would be immaterial. Triumph was ours for the taking.

The holiday complex at La Presqu'île was, to our untrained eye, nothing short of wondrous. 'Oh my!' declared Brenda, as we stepped into our apartment for the first time. 'Well this is very nice!' She had done it at last. She had got us out of the tent and inside four walls. She was triumphant.

In real terms, the small studio apartment was basic. There was a small toilet and a shower, a tiny kitchen with a two-ring cooker and a sofa that opened out to turn itself into the most uncomfortable bed my father would ever sleep on. 'This is sixpence up from camping,' Tony had moaned when my mother was out of earshot, but for Brenda our little studio flat, complete with balcony that looked out over a salt lake stretching away to the Pyrenees, was a palace. 'I'm glad we brought some smart clothes,' she reasoned as she stood, chin in hand, gazing out over the view. 'I think everyone should dress up to watch sunsets from balconies. Don't you?' Dad and I looked at each other and said nothing.

Immediately below our apartment sat another studio flat that, instead of a balcony, had a deck-like platform stretching out to a jetty at the end of which were moored a string of small boats. There was a light breeze blowing across the lake and a gentle *tinka-tinka-tink* was humming through the air as the ropes running up the boats' metal masts rattled in the wind. 'Can you see those mountains in the distance?' asked Dad, pointing towards the Pyrenees range on the horizon. 'That's Spain. That's a whole different country.' I was impressed. Standing in one country, gazing out at another: I was beginning to feel like a proper traveller. As we stood, staring out and marvelling as to how we had found ourselves in a proper apartment with a proper balcony and a proper view, there was a bubble of noise from below us. We all looked down as a meshed and heavy-looking bag was tossed out from under the rim of the jetty followed by a large tanned hand attached to a bulbous gentleman in a snorkel. He hauled himself out of the water, a small plume of water snorting out from the top of his breathing pipe. As he stood, dripping water on to the bone-dry deck and pulling off his mask, I was struck by how very round and brown his tummy was. It was in total disproportion to the rest of his body. His legs were sinewy and toned, his arms muscular, yet his gut was a balloon. It was like staring at a pregnant man. 'I wonder what he's caught,' murmured Dad, leaning over the balcony for a better look.

'Maybe they're crabs,' suggested Brenda. 'Or pilchards.'

'Pilchards aren't a fish,' said Tony with a small frown. 'They just come in a tin.'

'Of course pilchards are a fish,' said my mother, shooting Dad a confused glance. 'Don't be mad.'

'Are you sure?' he asked. 'Aren't pilchards like kippers? Kippers aren't a fish. You can't catch a kipper. A kipper is really a herring that's been smoked. I thought a pilchard was a sardine, which is a fish.'

Hearing the chatter above him, the man below looked up. '*Bonjour!*' he shouted, with a wave. I waved back at him.

'*Excusez-moi, mais nous ne parlons pas Français!*' Dad yelled back.

'English?' he shouted back, smiling.

'Yes!' my mother shouted down. 'We were just wondering what you had caught in your bag? Your bag. From the sea. *Wooosh wooosh.*'

'It's OK,' he said, putting his hands on his hips. 'I speak English quite well. I've been collecting mussels.'

'Ohhhhhhhhhhhhh,' the three of us said in unison.

'Would you like to come down and watch me clean them? Perhaps your daughter would enjoy?'

I nodded. This sounded like fun.

'Yes, thank you! She'd love that. You go with her, Tony. I'll stay here and unpack,' said Brenda, beaming. 'How lovely. What a nice man. You don't get this on campsites.'

Our downstairs neighbour was called Monsieur Caen who, it turned out, was renting the apartment for the whole of August with his wife and ten-year-old daughter, Rejane. As Dad and I came down, Madame Caen was uncorking a bottle of wine while Rejane, a tubby child spilling out over the top of her bikini bottoms, was carrying a bucket of fresh water out to the back deck for her father. Madame Caen did not speak English and so we stood for a while as various requests were barked back and forth in French. 'Come, come,' gestured Monsieur Caen towards the deck and handed my father a small tumbler of wine as they went. I followed on, smiling at Rejane as we passed each other, noting with slight consternation that my smile was not returned.

'I fish every day,' Monsieur Caen was explaining. 'While we are here, we eat nothing else. We never have to go to the shop. Everything we need comes from the lake. So!' declared Monsieur Caen, raising his glass. '*Salut!* We shall drink. And then we shall eat, yes?'

'Eat what?' I asked, staring at his belly.

'The mussels!' announced the monsieur, tapping his netted bag. 'We shall eat the mussels! We like to eat them raw. This is the best way. With a touch of cider vinegar.'

'*Raw?*' asked Tony, looking a little worried. 'I didn't know you could eat mussels if they weren't cooked.'

'Of course!' pouted Monsieur Caen. 'They are much nicer. You will love them. I prepare one for you. You will try it.'

'Because I don't know if I really like mussels...' said Dad, staring at the bag of crusted molluscs.

'These you will like,' guffawed the Frenchman, slapping Dad on the shoulder. 'They are the best. I make one.'

Tony was looking a little uncomfortable, sensing that he'd got himself into a culinary cul-de-sac from which there was no chance of escape. The monsieur had tipped the contents of his fishing bag into the bucket and was stirring the mussels through the water with his forearm. Taking a small pocket knife, he then cut out one super-large mussel that, as he put it in his hand, stretched the length of his palm. 'That's a very big mussel,' said Tony, scratching his cheek and shifting awkwardly. The monsieur grinned. Sticking the point of the knife into the bottom of the mussel, the Frenchman prised the shell open to reveal an enormous, gold-fleshed monstrosity.

'*Et voilà!*' said Monsieur Caen with a flourish. 'Now I take away the hair, which you cannot eat. Cut it here so that it slips out. And then we splash on the vinegar. So! And now you eat!' The mussel, still in its shell and wincing, was thrust under my father's nose. Looking at him, I knew he would have done anything in that moment not to have eaten that mussel, but with glass of wine in hand and a just-arrived gratitude for some immediate neighbourly hospitality, he realised he had no choice.

Taking the mussel between his thumb and forefinger, Tony's face had sunken into an anagram of despair. Raising the mussel to his lips, he stopped short of taking the plunge and sniffed it instead. 'I can smell the vinegar,' he said, as if that would postpone the inevitable. The monsieur nodded and gestured with his hand for my father to eat. Dad, staring at the Frenchman, opened his mouth but then closed it again in a textbook display of prevarication.

'*Mangez! Mangez!*' urged Monsieur Caen, impatient for my father to get on with it.

Dad, heaving a terrible and heartfelt sigh, shot one last miserable glance in my direction. As he tipped the shell towards him and the large, raw mollusc slid into his mouth, his face con torted. The mussel sat, unswallowed, on his tongue; his face was a mixture of fear and disgust. Terrified, he found himself unable to dispatch the thing in one, horrified that getting rid of it was now going to involve chewing. Tony puffed his cheeks out in an attempt to roll the mussel into a place in his mouth where neither the texture nor the taste would be quite so offensive but, sadly, there was no respite. Wherever it sat, its thick, unpalatable mass groaned back at him. The fact that he had a captive audience made matters worse. Monsieur Caen was continuing to shout encouragement while I was staring with my mouth open, transfixed that someone could have been made to eat something so very awful. Tony's first bite into the mussel was accompanied by a distinct and pained whimper. Closing his eyes, my father lurched forwards a little, his body reacting instantly to the repulsive requirements of consuming a raw mussel. He had put down his glass of wine, bent forward and begun clinging to the edge of the table, moaning every time he bit down. Every now and again he would stand suddenly, turn away and commit to an upper torso body heave while clamping a hand to his mouth. His eyes were watering and he was breathing heavily through his nose. By my reckoning, he was ever so slightly sick into the back of his mouth at least five times. Finally, after an eternity of trying, he got it down. Panting, he reached for his glass of wine and downed it in one.

'Another?' said Monsieur Caen, a question that was greeted with the sort of deadly silence it deserved.

'Not again!' said my mother thirty minutes later, as my father lay on the bathroom floor being sick into the toilet. 'You ate a raw mussel? Are you mad?'

'It tasted like a dog turd!' wailed my father, throwing up at the very thought. 'It was the single worst thing I have ever tasted in my natural born life. Honestly. It was like a spoonful of shit! Oh! I'm going to be sick again! Oh!'

My father threw up for the next two hours. But it wasn't all bad. At least it was into something that had a flush.

The holiday village was, to my eye, an impressive complex. From the front door of our apartment block I could look out over a long row of tall bamboo. Beyond that there was a pool, basic and empty, but with the lake and the sea only a mile away, it was virtually redundant. Behind the pool, over to the right, there was a white building with a red tile roof that housed a village shop with a range so extensive my father was convinced it was a supermarket. 'There's an aisle, Brenda,' he said, astonished, 'that's just wine!' Behind the shop, in the centre of the complex, was a large, domed building inside of which were two restaurants: one, a general family eatery that promised a two-course meal for ten francs a head, the other a grander à la carte affair catering for the posher end of the market with an obligatory five-course menu. My parents had stared at the menus for both and decided that, given we'd come all this way, we could factor in an extra-special one-visit-only to the à la carte restaurant. 'It'll be the meal of our lives!' cried my father, rubbing his hands together. We thought we were in the lap of luxury. In reality, we were staying in a sticky-back-plastic compound that was about as posh as a fish finger masquerading as a salmon.

The shop was a point in question. Just because it sold rotisserie chickens, my parents treated it with the reverence due to Harrods. Only one thing marred my father's enjoy-ment of the onsite market and that was the girl who worked in it. Never had a face been blessed with a more surly lip. '*Vous avez rapporté des bouteilles?*' she would ask, arms crossed.

Dad, whose job it was to limp us through any lingual shenanigans, would stare at her for a bit and then ask, '*Quoi?*' At which she would stare back at him a bit harder, say noth-ing and then blow a strawberry-smelling bubble out of her mouth. It went without saying that we were desperate to try one of the rotisserie chickens that were bursting with bronzed juices and smelt of herbs I hadn't even heard of. In the 1970s, I thought there was only one herb: parsley. And that only came on top of scrambled egg at weddings. Things like tarragon, sage or thyme were the things of myth and legend. It was inconceivable that herbs were actually used to flavour things, especially meat, but here we were, staring at a cooked chicken that had green bits stuffed under its breast skin. It was like something from another world.

'Ask her if we can have one,' said Brenda, staring in at the slowly turning chickens and salivating. 'They look lovely.'

'*Excusez-moi*,' began Tony, clearing his throat. '*Je voudrais un poulet. S'il vous plaît.*'

'*Non*,' muttered the girl, not moving a muscle.

My father, thinking that perhaps the problem was a lack of understanding, repeated the request, but this time a bit louder. '*Excusez-MOI. Je VOUDRAIS le POULET. Le POULET. Voilà. POULET.*'

'*Non*,' said the girl again.

'She says we can't have one,' said my dad, turning to look at us.

'But there's five in there,' complained my mother, tapping the rotisserie glass with her finger. 'Five! *Cinq le poulet! Cinq!*'

'*Oui!*' nodded Tony, turning back to chivvy the shop girl. '*Cinq poulet. Là! Mais nous* only want *un poulet. Un!*'

'*Non*,' said the girl, pulling a strand of bubble gum out of her mouth and wrapping it round her finger.

'This is outrageous,' snapped my mother. 'Why won't she let us have one? It's because we're English, Tony! She's saving them for the French! But we're here first! Tell her that, Tony! We're here first!'

'*Nous sommes ici première!*' translated my father. '*Pour le poulet!*'

The girl, who was as immovable as the Alps, looked at us and, in indecipherable, very quick French, mumbled, '*Si vous voulez un poulet, il faut le commander. On les cuit sur commande. C'est pour ça que vous ne pouvez pas en avoir un. Ils sont tous commandés. Si vous voulez en commander un, c'est possible, mais vous ne l'aurez pas avant demain. Alors, si vous voulez un poulet pour demain, il faut me le dire maintenant. Vous voulez commander un poulet, oui ou non?'*

'What did she say?' asked my mother.

'Something about chicken,' said my dad, looking a bit cross-eyed. 'But I'm not sure what.'

Behind us, a woman had wandered in, creeping past my mother to the counter. '*Je suis venue chercher les poulets que j'ai commandés,*' she said, lifting up a large string bag in front of the girl. Without hesitating, the girl threw the woman a nod and then, looking directly at us, reached into the rotisserie cabinet, took out two, wrapped them in foil and handed them to the lady.

'*Mais...*' began my father, whose finger was following the chickens as they left the shop. '*Nous sommes ici...première...*'

'And this is the thanks we get for saving them from the Germans!' muttered Brenda, who had been momentarily rendered speechless. We couldn't get over it. Even I was appalled. As we shuffled away from the shop, carrying nothing more exciting than a couple of tins of mackerel fillets, it was as if we'd just witnessed a mass atrocity. 'There were five chickens in that cupboard, Tony. Five!' whined my mother, grappling to make sense of it. 'Appalling behaviour. Absolutely appalling. Mark my words! There'll be a letter sent to the management when we get home! Never in my life! That's racism! Racism!'

My father, quiet and brooding, stopped in his tracks. Looking back towards the shop, he set his jaw and whispered, 'I'm going to get us a chicken if it's the last thing I do.'

The great chicken war had begun.

*

Dad was having a difficult time. He'd had two bouts of food poisoning, was at loggerheads with the girl in the shop and was now having to avoid Monsieur Caen at every turn. The rotund Frenchman, who was never not in his tiny swimming trunks, had taken it upon himself to track down my father at every opportunity to cajole him into going mussel fishing with him. 'They are only five metres down!' he would shout, waving a small, white sailing cap in the air.

My father, who had a morbid fear of the water at the best of times, was in no mood to be diving five centimetres, let alone five metres, and even if he waited till the end of eternity to put another mussel in his mouth it would be too soon. He had no intention of going out with Monsieur Caen but because he didn't want to appear rude, he decided that the best course of action was to hide whenever we saw him coming. We hid behind the bamboo, at the back of some bins, we even crouched behind parked cars, but the only fail-safe way to avoid the monsieur was simply to leave the complex. The beach to the south of La Presqu'île was an exposed spot and, with no dunes or trees to provide shelter, our bolt-hole was a wasteland to the elements. An almost vicious wind wailed across the peninsula, picking up sand that bit into every soft surface that crossed its path. There were only two places we were safe from the blasting: in the sea and behind our windbreak. The windbreak had been a recent addition to our family camping experience and had proved a great success. It provided shelter and, when required, shade but, because of its natural brilliance, it made us dangerously complacent to the weather. In the quiet shadow of the windbreak, everything was calm and so when my father turned to us, hands on hips and said, 'I think I'll inflate the lilo!', neither myself nor my mother batted an eyelid.

My swimming career thus far had not been outstanding. My mother couldn't swim and my father chose not to and so it was in keeping with my family's natural loathing of water that I possessed no aquatic skills whatsoever. I was yet to learn to swim properly and so whenever I was within ten feet of water I was kitted out with two water wings so enormous that, when full-blown, meant I ran about the beach with my arms at virtual right angles. My mother and I had sprinted as fast as we could to the water's edge, not because we were overwhelmed with a rush to throw ourselves into the deep blue, but because the whipping sand was so intense it was practically drawing blood. Dad was somewhere behind us battling with the lilo but we weren't paying any attention to him. Instead, my mother launched herself into the warm water and assumed her usual tactic: bending down so that she was up to her shoulders in water and then pretending to do the breaststroke when, in fact, she was just walking along the sea bottom. Because I was also unable to swim I was under strict instructions not to go out of my depth, a request I was happy to oblige. Two men of Moroccan appearance were standing knee deep to our left, chatting with their arms crossed in that way men do when they're overcompensating for the fact that they're only really wearing a pair of pants. As my mother bobbed past them, one of them, the heavier of the two and with a moustache as thick as a garden hedge, shouted out some encouragement, 'Swim, swim!', gesturing with his arms. 'Kick with feet! This is not the way. You must swim!'

Brenda, a little overwhelmed with the sudden attention, smiled weakly in his direction and muttered something about being quite fine as she was but the man was having none of it. 'Come!' shouted the man, wading towards my mother. 'This is not swim! You must kick! Kick with the legs!' Before my mother could respond or get away she found herself being grabbed around the waist, like when marine biologists are trying to re-home dolphins. She gave out a little squeal but it was to no avail. 'Come now!' shouted the man, heaving my mother upwards as he grinned through his mass of facial hair. 'Now you kick with legs! Kick with legs! And then you swim!' Too startled to even speak, Brenda, in uncharacteristic compliance, did exactly what she was told. She kicked with her legs. As the water around her feet whipped itself into white peaks, the man released her and for six strokes only my mother swam for the first time in her life.

I was livid. One of the constants of my life was that my mother was more hopeless than me yet here she was, actually swimming, while I was still in arm bands. Determined not to be outdone and to restore the natural balance, I ripped off the heavy, bloated bands around my upper arms, threw them into the surf and tossed myself forward, kicking madly as I went. 'Look!' shouted the mustachioed man's companion, who was much younger and athletic-looking. 'Now she swim! She swim too!' I may have only managed ten strokes but it was four more than my mother and that was good enough for me.

While this small family drama was unfolding, Dad was enduring a battle of his own. The lilo, which had seemed like such a good idea at the time, was proving to be a living, breathing nightmare. He had already lost grip of it twice, only to watch it bounce away across the beach to be caught by one gentleman in a dubious all-in-one swimming costume which made my father feel confused and an ancient woman, dressed head to toe in black. She was wearing tights on the beach, Tony noticed, which made him even more confused. He had eventually managed to get the thing down to the shoreline and was looking forward to throwing me on to it and having some fun but as he skimmed it across the surf, the wind, which was voracious, caught a corner and flipped it into the air where an accompanying eddy blew it a good twenty feet out to sea. My dad, who hated swimming with a passion, realised that if we were to have any chance of retrieving it, he would have to make a manly leap in its direction and swim after it. With my mother's cries of 'Be careful, Tony!' ringing in his ears, my father, who didn't want to look as if he couldn't handle things in front of two Mediterranean gentlemen, tossed himself into the waves. My mother and I stopped what we were doing to watch the commotion unfold. Even from behind, Dad looked in trouble. Every time he took a stroke towards the lilo, it floated further away, and in the short time in which it had been loose, it had drifted another twenty yards.

'He will not make this,' said the mustachioed man, shaking his head. 'It goes further away. It will be all the way to Africa before he catches it.'

'Tony!' yelled my mother, cupping her mouth with her hand. 'Just leave it! Come back!'

'I try!' declared the younger man. 'I will catch it!' And with that, he dived into the water. Being a good swimmer, he passed my father, floundering and gasping, in a matter of moments. Seeing the younger man pass him, Tony stopped where he was and tried to tread water but he too was now drifting. If he was going to make it back to shore, he was going to have to swim against the current. As he turned and headed back towards us, defeated, I could just make out his face, which was wearing an expression so wracked and broken it was a wonder he didn't give himself up to Davy Jones there and then. The younger man, a good fifty feet out from the shore, had not, despite his best efforts, managed to catch the lilo and had turned back. Adding insult to injury, he then passed my father again, even stopping to offer to help him. By the time my father got back to the shore, he was exhausted, and as he lay on his back in the breaking surf, panting and unable to speak, he had the look of a dying crab.

'What were you thinking, Tony?' asked my mother, who was standing over him and staring down. 'I mean, honestly?'

An hour later and we were back at the complex shop. '*Un poulet*,' said my father, hunched over the counter, hair full of sand and skin crusted with salt.

'*Non*,' said the girl and went back to reading her magazine.

We had been trying for three days to get a chicken but with no success. We had still failed to grasp the basic pre-ordering requirement and had instead convinced ourselves that it was a deliberate attempt by the French to deny us the good shit. 'Like the Italians are about first press olive oil,' opined my mother. Unable to see any way round the shop girl's intransigence and realising that my father needed something to lift his spirits, Brenda decided that it was time for us to play the à la carte card. We would spruce ourselves into our finest togs and dine like kings. At twenty pounds a head, it was going to be the most expensive meal of our lives to date but, as my mother pointed out, it would be 'a splash out and we'll remember it for ever'.

Glowing with a just-scrubbed cleanliness, I was in no doubt of the enormity of the occasion. I had been bathed, hair primped and was wearing my long black dress with floral trim, a party frock of considerable import. My mother had even insisted that we pose for official pre-supper photos on the balcony during which I was under strict instructions 'not to pull any stupid faces'. This meal was going to be serious.

The interior of the restaurant must have seemed quite grand to my eight-year-old eyes. As a family we were relative novices when it came to dining out. It was only the second time I'd been in a restaurant. My first trip had not been a great success: we'd gone to an Indian restaurant where I had puked lentil dahl all over the table to the considerable distress of my parents and the man dining alone opposite. We hadn't been in a restaurant since. As a result, I was easily impressed and the presence of plastic lobsters stuck on the walls was something to marvel at, as was the fact that we were presented with a whole basket of bread, for free, which seemed to be an astonishing luxury. 'We don't have to pay for this,' said my dad, tucking into his third slice of French bread. 'Amazing!'

Because we were having the five-course à la carte menu, we had no idea what we were getting. There was a copy of the menu at the restaurant entrance but we had decided not to look at it because we wanted the frisson of surprise and, in any event, Dad wouldn't have understood it. Our meal was a leap into the unknown and for us, whose holiday staples were tinned meat, ratatouille and nothing else, the prospect of a decent meal was intoxicating.

We began well: langoustines in garlic butter. I liked them so much I borrowed a pencil from the waiter and, much to the amusement of my parents, wrote an instant thank you note to the chef on my napkin. 'Dear chef,' it read. 'The big prawns were really nice. I liked the butter best.' I finished the note off with a small drawing of a prawn looking sad, because it was about to be eaten, and handed it to the waiter to be dispatched to the kitchen. Posh restaurants were brilliant, I concluded. Bring on the next course.

Course number two wasn't quite the same success. In fact, it was unidentifiable. It looked like soup, had the texture of soup but was cold, green and very, very greasy. Brenda, taking a sip and swilling it about a bit, had a stab at guessing what it was, 'Is it that famous cold soup? The one that's leek and potato?'

'Vichysoisse?' suggested Tony, who was clacking the soup between his lips.

'Although it doesn't taste anything like leek or potato. And it's got a strange, oily quality that I'm not sure I'm fond of.'

'I don't like it,' I said, having had a dip and deciding it

was revolting. There was no way the chef was getting a thank-you note for this one. It was utterly disgusting.

'*Excusez-moi*,' asked my father, finger aloft as our waiter bustled past our table. '*Qu'est-ce que ç'est le soup?*'

'*Avocado, monsieur*,' said our waiter, who I noticed had a cigarette in one hand.

'Avocado soup?' quizzed Brenda, staring down into her bowl. 'What?'

'It's a bit like eating liquid snot,' suggested my father, battling on with another spoonful.

'Well I suppose we had to expect one course we didn't like,' said my mother, keeping things upbeat. 'But then that's the gamble. It's an adventure, isn't it, Emma?'

'S'pose,' I said, pushing my spoon through the rapidly congealing folds of soup.

My parents had both just about managed to finish their avocado soups but given the amount of money they would be shelling out for this meal they would have eaten an unskinned squirrel if it had been put in front of them. I, however, had no such obligations. If it was disgusting, it wasn't going in my mouth. As the waiter took my bowl away I sat with my arms folded and gave him a hard stare: he could take that back to the kitchen this time, I thought.

'Two down, three to go!' said my dad, leaning back into his chair. 'Wonder what we'll get next?'

'That soup's made me feel a bit ill,' said my mother, pulling a face. 'It was very greasy, wasn't it?'

'Hello!' said my dad, sitting up and looking over at our waiter, who was striding towards us with an enormous round platter on his shoulder. 'Here it comes! Whatever it is, it's big! What do you think it is? Some pork? Some roast chickens?'

'We're not allowed roast chickens,' I pointed out, a comment which induced a small, crushed groan from my mother. All eyes were on our waiter. The memory of the langoustines lingered, the soup could be dismissed. Here, surely, was a treat of some magnitude. Nothing repulsive could possibly be delivered on such a majestic plate.

'*Et voilà!*' announced the waiter with a flourish. '*Fruits de mer!*' And with that, he placed the large silver platter in the centre of the table. We all looked at it.

'Oh no,' whispered my father. 'No. Oh God, no.' It was a veritable scrum of shellfish: clams, oysters, winkles, scallops and the dreaded mussels. And all of it was raw.

'I'm not eating any of it,' declared Tony, with a definitive shake of the head. 'No way. Forget it. Not if I was starving.'

'But we can't eat this all on our own!' said Brenda, over-whelmed. 'You'll have to have some of it! If you just avoid the mussels, you'll be fine. You just got unlucky. You just had a bad one.'

'I'm not joking,' said Tony, sweeping a dismissive hand across the iced platter. 'I'm not putting one single thing in my mouth. Not one!'

'Mummy,' I said, peering into the heap of shells. 'That one just moved.'

'That's because it's still alive,' explained my mother, with a touch of the Dunkirk spirit about her. 'That's how they like to eat things in France. It's the French way.'

'Can't we eat them the English way?' I asked, feeling a little uneasy. 'Do we have to eat them like the French?'

'Yes,' said my mother, picking up a clam. 'I'm afraid we do. Although I wonder if we should just pretend to eat it? Maybe if we just eat one of the scallops and then make it look as if we're eating the rest? Perhaps that's for the best? If we scoop everything out from their shells and then put them in a napkin and then Daddy can put them in his pocket? Perhaps we should do that? What do you think, Tony?'

'My position on this matter is clear,' he said, arms folded. 'I'm not putting one solitary living creature in my mouth ever again. Ever again, Brenda. Not even if my life depended on it. Or yours, for that matter. Or Emma's. I would happily let you both die before eating another mussel. Or a scallop. Or an oyster. Or whatever other sea shit they've got on that plate. Actually die. Do you understand?'

'Look,' said my mother, in negotiating mood, 'if we all eat one scallop then we've shown willing. Scallops are barely cooked anyway. They'll be fine. We can just say they're underdone.'

'Underdone?' squealed my father, shoving a scallop with a forefinger. 'That's not underdone. That's very much in the land of the living.'

'Tony!' snapped my mother, leaning low across the table. 'Just eat one scallop. That's all I'm asking. I'm going to eat one. Emma's going to eat one.'

'Do I have to?' I asked, staring at the pale rubber-like mass in front of me.

'Yes,' insisted my mother. 'I'll cut yours up, Tony. Squeeze some lemon on it. It'll be fine. And then put everything else in your pocket. That way we won't look weird.'

In order to get my scallop down, I had had to cut it into tiny slivers and smother it in vinegar and lemon juice. Immersed in sharp fluid, the scallop was like eating tangy gristle. My dad, who had somehow acquiesced to my mother's demands, was physically crying as he sat, fork in one hand, head in the other, heaving the tiny shards of scallop into his mouth as if he'd been asked to suck dynamite. Mum had been bold and downed hers in one and then set about methodically removing everything else from its shell and arranging it into a melted blancmange-like heap to be wrapped in a napkin and dealt with. For some reason the thought of just sending the whole thing back wasn't to be contemplated: our inability to consume high-end cuisine was to be our dirty secret.

'Right,' whispered my mother, as she tied a knot in the top of the mollusc-laden napkin. 'Take that, Tony. Quickly! Before the waiter sees you! And stick it in your pocket. And next time you go to the toilet, just get rid of it. Flush it down the toilet or something.'

'The napkin's seeping,' moaned Dad, taking it in his hand. 'This isn't right. These people are animals, Brenda. Who eats something when it's still alive?'

'Ssssshhhhhhh,' whispered my mother, bending low across the table. 'Just pretend you liked it. We'll have meat next. It'll be fine.'

Dad, because the shellfish in his pocket was seeping an unspecified juice down his leg, slumped off in the direction of the toilets. He looked more miserable than I had ever seen him. 'Daddy doesn't like this meal much, does he?' I commented, before adding, 'But it is pretty horrible. Do you think the next thing will be a bit nicer?'

'Absolutely!' said my mother with a firm nod. 'The next course will be lovely!'

But it wasn't. It was roast pigeon sitting in a pool of blood. 'What's the matter with just cooking something?' wailed my father, as he cut into his pigeon breast only to reveal a ruby red interior. 'They've just shown this to an oven! They've stood with it five feet from a hot surface, waved it in its direction and then put it on a plate. That's what they've done. This isn't a restaurant, it's a butcher's counter! We've paid good money for this, Brenda! Sixty quid this is costing us. *Sixty quid!* I've eaten two prawns and a potato. That's it!'

Sadly, we weren't able to put three pigeon carcasses into my father's pockets, so this time, my mother came up with the cunning wheeze of cutting the meat off the bones and then just arranging it into indiscriminate shapes around the plate. 'When we have Spam fritters at school,' I offered in an attempt to help, 'I squash the fritter as much as I can and shove it inside a bread roll and then throw the bread roll on the floor. Shall I do that now?'

'No,' said my mother, even though she was sorely tempted. 'But you can drop some under the table. They won't know till we've gone. And if it's under your chair then they'll just think you were a bit naughty. I can live with that.'

'Can you take some of mine?' Dad asked, shoving a fork load of bleeding pigeon in my direction.

The meal had been a total disaster. Even the presence of a reasonable chocolate mousse to finish had done nothing to abate the deep-felt sorrow that flowed through us all. We had come in the expectation of gastronomic heaven and been served a casserole of hell. As we walked back to our apartment, my parents were so downcast that they might as well have been told I was dead. 'That was the worst meal of my life,' whimpered my father. 'Sixty quid. Sixty bloody quid.'

'I'm just shocked at the soup,' added Brenda. 'No one makes soup out of avocados. Nobody. That's like making soup with a banana. It's not right. Let's just try and forget about it and put this sorry mess behind us.'

But we couldn't forget about it because four hours later the meal delivered its final twist. I had woken, consumed with an overwhelming sense that something was about to explode out of me. 'Daddy,' I managed to snivel in the direction of my parents' bed. 'I think I'm going to be sick.'

'Now or at some point in the future?' he asked.

'Now,' I said, feeling a deep and terrible gastric churning. My father, leaping from his bed, scooped me out of mine and ran, holding me aloft, towards the bathroom. But my mouth was already open, and as we galloped towards the toilet, I sprayed a stinking line of vomit across the entire length of the apartment walls. As we got into the bathroom, I threw up again, this time aiming towards the toilet but missing and hitting the bottom of the shower instead. Then I lifted my head to take a breath, and something in my bowel gave way as hot, liquid shit shot out, filling my pants and dripping down my leg. Crying and horrified I then sat, shitting and puking, sometimes simultaneously, for the next thirty minutes. Just as I was reaching my most desiccated, my mother stumbled into the bathroom and threw up into the sink, a sight so revolting that I threw up again, this time into the shower. When my dad's turn came to throw up, he didn't have anywhere to go other than the shower because every other receptacle was taken. It was Armageddon and the irony was, the culprit was the prawns.

I had sick in my hair, sick on my hands and all three of us were in tears. 'And the chef got a thank-you note!' sobbed my father, who was now on his third brush with illness in a fortnight. 'It's not right! Not right!' We had had obstacles thrown at us left, right and centre but this was the lowest of blows. We stayed in bed for the next forty-eight hours. And no, we didn't get a chicken.

Weakened and jaded by our terrible brush with food poisoning, it was with nothing but relief that we left the La Presqu'île complex. We just wanted to go home and so my parents decided that what should have been a leisurely drive back up through Southern France was, instead, to be a sprint back to Calais. The plan, therefore, was to press all the way to Paris, stay in the Bois de Bologne campsite, spend a few days seeing the French capital and then return to Britain.

The Bois de Bologne was not unlike a refugee camp. Set in the outskirts of Paris, it was jam-packed with the flotsam and jetsam of itinerant travellers and had the feel of an out-of-town migrant encampment rather than anything to do with holidays. There were very few families but instead an abundance of men in their twenties who looked a little roughshod and desperate. They hung about in small groups, smoking miserably and talking in hushed tones, their dishevelled hair and perma-stained clothes adding to the air of melancholy.

My mother, not quite herself after the attack of the giant prawns, still managed to muster up some enthusiasm, even if all about her were exuding ennui. Our presence in the French capital was a cause for celebration: this was the height of chic, the pinnacle of style. Somehow, in a suitcase filled with dirty, two-week-old clothes, she had rustled up outfits that cut a dash. She was in a natty shirt and tank top, I was giving it double denim. We may have been broken, we may have even been a little beaten, but my mother was determined that we would stride down the Champs-Élysées looking damned fine.

Paris, the city of effortless panache, palatial at every turn, was elegant in scale and grandeur. The city of pavement cafés, where well-groomed ladies clipped along the pavements like prize ponies, wrapped in cashmere and dressed to kill. Above all, Paris felt lofty. It was uplifting and my mother was in raptures. 'I think this might be the most beautiful place on Earth,' she eulogised, wafting a hand in the direction of the Eiffel Tower. 'I mean, look at that. How can something so ugly be so incredible? Only in Paris, Tony. Only in Paris.'

My father, whose brief love affair with France was well and truly over, could only stand, hand in pockets, and grunt. If ever a man was sick with his holiday, it was him. If our holiday were a dog, he would have taken it to some scrub-land and shot it. Not even the divine transcendence of the Mona Lisa could lift his spirits: 'Small, isn't it?' his only comment. He shrugged his shoulders at Napoleon's tomb, was indifferent to Notre-Dame and dismissed the Arc de Triomphe as 'pointless'. Nothing could lighten his mood. Brenda, who wasn't prepared to give up until the last filthy sock was in the washing machine back home, decided that, in one last attempt to engage her husband in the joys of the

French capital, we would walk to Montmartre, the area of the city where writers and artists clustered in one creative lump. Tony, she reasoned, would like it there because he taught art and was quite good at sculpture.

In contrast to the impressive, open vistas of the Champs-Élysées and the Place de la Concorde, Montmartre was a maze of crushed buildings and shadowy corners: cheese shops and charcuteries wafted heady, thick aromas through alleyways; men in scuffed sandals and cheesecloth flares sat in front of slatted shutters, red wine in hand and a floating fog of Gallic cigarette smoke dappled through the sunlight. As always, my mother had been providing a running commentary about how Montmartre was the stomping ground of the great French Impressionists like Toulouse-Lautrec, 'you know, the artist who painted the cancan' and how great writers throughout history had hung out there for inspiration. 'Does it make you feel inspired, Tony?' she had turned to ask. But my father didn't reply. He had stopped in his tracks and was staring with a look of total disbelief. Standing, leaning up against a shabby brick wall, was a man with a thick, black muddle of hair, a blue shirt that was slightly torn on one sleeve and a half-drunk bottle of wine in his left hand. He had splashes of wine on his chin and a look in his eye that suggested the bottle was not his first that day. At first glance, he just seemed the sort of usual drunk you could find in any dark corner of any city. But then I looked a bit closer. His penis was hanging out of his trousers. Not only that, but there was a cigarette inserted into the end of it. And not only *that*, but the cigarette was lit. My father, realising that I had seen this confusing display, cleared his throat a little and took it upon himself to explain the disarray. 'You see, the thing is, Em,' he began, putting a hand round my shoulder and leading me away. 'The French are mad on smoking.'

Five minutes later, and we were still discussing it. 'I mean, can you smoke a cigarette through your penis?' my mother asked with a muddled expression. 'Is that actually possible?'

'I have no way of knowing, Brenda,' replied my father, before adding, 'Only in Paris, Brenda. Only in Paris.'

In order to eradicate the slightly grubby memory of a man's smoking genitals, Brenda decided we would make our way up the steep Montmartre hill to the tremendous three-domed Basilica of Sacré-Cœur. If anything was going to transcend the earthy disappointments of man's lower impulses, it was the splendid opulence of the ivory-white cathedral. It was a considerable climb from the base of Montmartre hill and the steps were strewn with people resting, sketching or just admiring the view. We had been walking all day and my legs, already tired, burnt as we slowly trudged upwards. From the halfway point I was so worn out that I held on to the back of my dad's trousers, hoping that I would be pulled along in his slipstream, but it made little difference. At eight years old, I was now too big for piggybacks and carrying; I had to fend for myself.

As we reached the top, we were all panting. It was a particularly hot day and my double denim was doing me no favours. My mother, pulling off her tank top and tucking it into the back of her trousers, turned to us and said, 'Let's sit down before we go inside. Cool down and enjoy the view. Look, there's a statue there with a low plinth. Let's sit on that.'

'I'll get some water,' said Dad, who had spotted a small vending trolley and wandered off towards it. Mum and I parked ourselves on the plinth, sweaty and done in. I couldn't really be bothered with traipsing round another cathedral. We'd already done Notre-Dame, which had been the same inside as Orléans, which, I was sure, was going to be the same as Sacré-Cœur. My parents were obsessed with the inside of cathedrals, and we weren't even religious. As I sat contemplating this anomaly, a woman entered my frame of vision. She was wearing a patchwork smock and walked with a slight hunch of the shoulders as if she couldn't quite be bothered to stand up. She had light brown hair that hung in lifeless strands to just below her ears and her face was scrunched and angry, her eyes trapped behind tight eyelids. I wouldn't have paid her any attention except for the fact that she was muttering quite loudly to herself.

'Here,' said Dad, handing me a small bulb-shaped bottle, 'I got you an Orangina.' I loved Orangina. It was the one brilliant thing France had to offer: a delicious, fizzy drink with bits of orange in it. Delighted that I'd been treated, I shook the bottle so that the orange bits were swirling round the bottle, took the top off and drank. On a hot day and after the climb we'd had, it was nothing short of nectar. Dad had sat down on the plinth between Mum and me and was sharing a large bottle of water with her. We sat drinking, not saying anything but looking out over the spectacular views of Paris. It should have been a quiet, reflective moment where we contemplated greatness and whether or not, one day, we could ever have a holiday where something didn't go wrong, but the woman in the patchwork dress had other ideas. Having wandered to and fro in front of us, muttering, she came a little closer, ranted something incomprehensible in French, gestured violently towards the sky and then, no more than two feet away from my father, yanked up her patchwork dress and, knickerless, produced a piss that would put a shire horse to shame. For the second time in an hour we had been treated to some French genitals.

'I have that woman's piss up my trouser leg,' said my father in a dead, flattened tone. 'I'd like to go home now, please. I don't want to be here any more.'

It was the final straw. Even my mother knew that enough was enough. We looked at my father. France had broken him.

Chapter Seven

Riders on the Storm

'Oh God!' moaned my mother, throwing herself into a chair. 'It's SO hot!'

We were in the clutch of a mass wilting. Britain was in the grip of a heat wave and June had been one of the warmest on record with temperatures soaring to an incredible ninety-five degrees. No one knew how to cope or what to do: if British summers weren't drenched in drizzle and permanently overcast, everyone just stood about looking frightened and perplexed. Dad had made a half-hearted attempt to counter the heat by buying a small, round paddling pool, which we all took it in turns to sit in. It provided a few brief moments of wet bliss, but other than that we could do nothing except lie around listless and gently sweating.

Our new neighbours were a childless couple who, much to my mother's amusement, seemed to always be wearing the same clothes. 'They're like Tweedledum and Tweedledee!' she would giggle, catching a glimpse of them in yet another matching outfit. They had introduced themselves pretty quickly, mostly because they were enraged by what they perceived to be the 'greatest swindle of the century' perpetrated on them by the previous owner, a quiet, elderly lady who you couldn't imagine coming up with anything more dishonest than using margarine instead of butter. When they came to view the property, our ex-neighbour had wafted a hand into the back garden to reveal what appeared to be an impressive collection of trees. In fact, what the lady had done was break branches off her one and only tree, stick them in the ground, and create the illusion of a blooming orchard. In the scorching early summer heat, the branches had withered and died and all our neighbours were left with was an empty vista of dried-up sticks. They were livid.

'I mean it's just incredibly dishonest,' moaned Tweedledee, folding her arms and shaking her head.

'Although she was quite old,' added Tweedledum with the saddest of nods. 'Perhaps she was just confused? Although I have to say, I was very disappointed.'

All this, of course, was being conducted over the garden fence. It was so hot that my mother was wearing a bikini, an item of clothing I only associated with being on holiday. As first encounters go, it felt incredibly daring to be so scantily clad but the weather was so draining, everyone was past caring. 'I see you've got a paddling pool,' noted Tweedledee with a jerk of her chin. 'We've got a hose. I got so hot yesterday I must have stood under it for ten minutes. And he did. Didn't you? So hot.'

'So hot,' agreed Tweedledum as they indulged in a little synchronised head shaking.

'And you've got a hutch,' said Tweedledee, poking her head over the fence to have a good look down our garden. 'You got a rabbit? Bet he's hot with all that fur. Oh! It's times like this when I'm SO glad I'm not an animal. Aren't you?'

'So glad,' nodded her husband.

It was true. I now had a rabbit called Mork, whom I spent every available minute with. Mork didn't seem to be like other rabbits and had grown so massive my mother wasn't entirely convinced he even *was* a rabbit. 'Are you SURE it's not a dog?' asked my mother, staring at him, a question that gave me the brilliant idea of taking him for walks on a lead. On would go his collar and off Mork and I would hop: he would terrorise any dog that came within sniffing distance and I would shrug off the stares and the pointing. It was a match made in heaven.

Leaping on our neighbour's interest like a ferret on a rat, my mother, shooting the hutch a fast glance, turned back to seize the opportunity: 'I don't suppose you'd like to look after Emma's rabbit, would you?' she asked. 'It's just that we're going to go on holiday in a couple of weeks and we need someone to feed it.' It was a masterstroke. They were brand-new neighbours and she was wearing a bikini. It was impossible to say no.

As a family, we were still in tense negotiations as to where we would be going on our summer holiday. My parents were planning to move house in the following year and so had decided that, because they were saving, we were only going to go away for a week and, wherever it was, it was going to have to be cheap. My dad, treating the thought of any holiday with nothing but suspicion, had been holding out for somewhere in Britain but because it was so hot and unbearable, my mother had begun lobbying for the family *bête noire*: France. 'The thing is,' she argued, 'it's hot there too, but it's a different sort of hot. It's a dry hot. Whereas here it's a wet hot. So if we went there it'd be much nicer.'

'It will still be hot,' said my dad.

'But a nice hot, Tony, a nice hot.'

'I don't care whether it's a nice hot. It'll still be France, Brenda!' wailed my father. 'I'm not going there! You're not making me! No! Never again! No!'

I didn't know what the difference was between a nice hot

and a wet hot; all I knew was that a few days later, my father was sitting at the bottom of the stairs, head in hands and downing a large tumbler of whisky. 'What's the matter?' I had asked, as I scampered past him to fetch Mork's lead.

'We're going to France,' he said, with a touch of the suicidal. 'I don't want to talk about it.'

Somehow, Brenda had done it. To this day I have no idea how. Maybe it was the bikini. Whatever it was, we were heading back over the channel but this time, she had promised, Dad would not be made to eat anything that hadn't come out of a tin. We were back on basic rations.

'You know,' said my mother who, as far as I could tell, was the only person delighted to be back in France, 'we should treat this holiday as the occasion it is. There's no point in being miserable. Holidays are what you make them.'

Had my mother learnt nothing? Holidays were *not* what you made them. Holidays were in the hands of malevolent forces hell-bent on wreaking chaos at every turn. Holidays were assault courses of the mind and body, endurance tests designed to break spirits and shatter spleens. In my nine years on the planet I had learnt one thing: going on holiday was awful. It was a small crumb of comfort to me that my father was now coming round to my way of thinking and as we sat, chugging along down the now familiar poplar-lined roads, sunflowers in the fields on either side of us, I thought, 'Yes, it IS nice to look at. But in the same way cheese looks nice in a mousetrap.'

We had taken the ferry all the way to Cherbourg and from there, we had driven across the peninsula and back to Argentat, the campsite we had enjoyed so much the previous year. As is often the way when you revisit somewhere you've been before, the allure was not quite as sparkling. The table tennis hut, once such an astonishment of riches, was now a bit battered round the edges, the pool a little more dull. Even my mother, who was like a blinkered horse when it came to acknowledging any idea she'd had might be just shy of perfect, was forced to concede that the place had lost its gloss. 'This isn't quite as nice as I remember it,' she said, hands on hips. 'Still, at least it's cooler than England. What a relief!'

'Storm clouds gathering over there,' said Dad, looking up to the west. 'That'll explain the drop in temperature. Still. I'll get the tent up.'

Our pitch backed on to a thin line of trees that acted as a windbreak between us and the river. My parents were busying themselves with the tent and the stove and so I wandered off, tiptoeing through the branches to stand at the water's edge. The low evening sun was casting a pink tinge across the water, dragonflies were hovering and the steady, soporific chirrups of cicadas underscored the moment. Picking up a round, flat stone I skimmed it across the surface of the lake and watched with satisfaction as it bounced away. Sometimes, it was the simplest things that provided the greatest pleasure and as I stood, throwing stone after stone, I felt real contentment as if I were actually enjoying myself.

I had returned to our pitch, having been called to supper by my mother. She was sitting in a chair reading while Dad was making tuna-stuffed tomatoes, a Delia Smith favourite so tried and tested he could have made it in his sleep. He had stopped what he was doing and was staring skywards. 'Those clouds are shifting,' he said, tin opener in hand. 'We might get some rain after all.'

'I can't remember the last time I saw rain,' answered my mother, looking up and letting her book fall closed. 'Must be well over a month. It'll be nice. Clear the air.'

My father nodded, then slapped himself on the arm with

a sudden violence. 'God!' he exclaimed. 'I'm being eaten alive! Awful midges!'

'It's because we're so close to the lake. And because it's been so hot,' explained my mother, returning to her book. 'Still, if it rains, then they'll clear away. So let's hope it does. Oh, Emma! Why don't you get out the cards? They're in the activity box. We can have a game after supper.'

The grandly named activity box was actually just a cardboard box that didn't contain any essential camping equipment. It was for odds and sods: the occasional book, a couple of magazines, a scattering of pens and pencils and our only form of in-tent entertainment, a pack of cards. It had also, over the years, gathered an assortment of corks, a few pamphlets (in French) on tourist attractions we hadn't been to or were anywhere near and, for a reason that was never explained, a Slinky. 'They're not in here,' I said after a thorough rummage. 'I can't find them.'

'They must be there,' said my mother, allowing herself a small frown. 'Have another look.'

'They're not,' I said again.

My father wiped his hands and bundled over. 'Right,' he said, determined, 'let me have a go.' Diving into the box with both hands, he tossed the contents as he would a salad before stopping and upending the box so that everything lay spread out on the tent floor. 'I don't believe it,' he said, looking up, ashen. 'We've forgotten the cards.' The news was treated with the same solemnity and despair as if we'd just found out that Britain had exploded in an unexplained industrial accident. No cards? This was a disaster. Now what were we going to argue about?

'But didn't you pack them?' wailed my mother, getting up to stare at the card-less mess. 'I told you to pack them!'

'No you didn't,' complained my father, in protest. 'I

thought you were packing them. Non-essential equipment is your responsibility. Not mine.'

'No, Tony,' said my mother, hands moving to her hips. 'Non-essential equipment is clothes. Not the activity box. The activity box comes under tent stuff. Not clothes stuff. The cards were your job.'

This was serious. No rummy, no whist, no beggar my neighbour. We were skating into a catastrophe. Now all we had to look forward to was sitting around and staring at each other. 'Perhaps,' I chipped in, in an effort to help, 'we could invent a new game using all those corks?' My parents turned and stared at me. 'And we've still got the Slinky...' Quite what we were going to do with the Slinky in a tent with no stairs was another matter but before that conundrum could be unravelled, a fat, splashing raindrop landed square on my father's forehead.

'Rain!' he said, wiping the wet from his eyebrow. 'Let's get the table and chairs inside before it really comes down. Emma, you get the cups and plates. And be careful, Brenda. Don't upend the tomatoes. All the tuna will fall out.'

There was a squall of activity all over the campsite as the sky darkened and the rain began to fall in thick, steady drops. Caravan awnings were being winched in, windows slammed shut, towels were being hastily gathered and everywhere, families were retreating to the inside of their tents. Because the ground was so dry, the patter of rain on the hard earth sounded almost metallic and each raindrop sparked up a plume of dust so fine it looked like steam, making the soil look as if it were boiling. In the distance, a low rumble of thunder began rolling towards us, the starter flag for any decent storms, and the rain which had an individual and random quality, became more pack-like, shifting shapes like a flock of starlings.

We sat, eating our tuna tomatoes with the door to the tent tied back to one side, staring out at the unbroken flow of rain with the same dulled interest as if we'd been eating a TV dinner. Dad, having finished his supper, stood up and popped his head out to stare up at the sky. 'It looks set in,' he said, peering upwards. 'Sky's very dark. This might last for hours.'

'You have remembered to put the ground sheet under the sleeping compartment, haven't you?' asked Brenda, recalling that previous basic error. 'Because we don't want that mistake again.'

'Yes, Brenda,' replied my dad in a defensive tone. 'I have remembered to put the ground sheet under the sleeping compartment. And the tent is waterproofed. Although, Emma – you should never touch canvas when it's wet because it lets the water come in. So when it's raining, don't touch the inside of the tent.'

'OK,' I said, moving my chair a little further into the centre of the tent. 'Are we just going to sit here for the rest of the night then?'

'I think we'll have to,' said Dad, gazing out. 'Can't do anything in this. Shame we haven't got the cards.'

'Yes,' added my mother sharply. 'Isn't it?'

'We could play I-Spy!' suggested Dad, shifting focus. 'I'll start. I spy with my little eye, something beginning with R!'

'Toilet roll?' I asked.

'That's a T,' answered Tony with a shake of his head. 'Not an R.'

'Rope?' said Mum.

'No,' said Dad, grinning. 'You'll never guess it. Not in a million years.'

'Rain!' said Mum in a flash, shooting my father a triumphant glance.

'Oh,' said Tony, a little deflated. 'I didn't think you'd get that.'

'Right,' said Brenda, sitting up taller in her chair. 'My turn. I spy with my little eye, something beginning with T!'

'Tent!' shouted Dad.

'Yes!' yelled Mum, thumping her hand down on the table. 'Damn!'

'My turn!' said Dad, giving a little jump. 'I spy with my little eye, something beginning with B!'

'Bucket,' I said, cheek slumped into my hand. 'And I need to go. So everyone can go outside or something.'

'We can't go outside, Em,' said my dad, shovelling a thumb in the direction of the tent door. 'It's tipping it down. We'll have to stand with our backs turned.'

'It'll be like that time we first went camping,' laughed my mother. 'Do you remember? When Emma fell in the bucket?'

'Oh God, yes!' laughed my dad and then they both stood, howling with laughter while I sat and stared at them. We were stuck inside the tent with nothing to do. It was going to be a very long night.

The storm picked up pace at around midnight. That first, distant thunder had failed to make good on its promise and so we had gone to bed thinking we were going to avoid it. But the storm had merely circled the area before clattering in to do its worst. I was woken by an enormous, ear-splitting crack that juddered through the tent. My parents were already awake: Dad was sitting up, torch in hand, pointing it at the edges of the tent ceiling, while Mum was busy putting any stray clothes back inside the suitcase. 'I'm sure we'll be fine,' she said, her voice strained. 'But just in case.'

The rain was now slashing down, the relentless battering against the tent canvas loud and frightening. All about us, lightning was striking, its fall so intense that every time it hit, we were briefly illuminated. 'It must be hitting no more than feet away, Brenda!' shouted my father above the din. 'Do you think we should get in the Land Rover?'

My mother shook her head. 'We can't go out in it, Tony!' she said. 'It's landing so close and so often we could be hit before we got to the car. We can't risk it. We'll have to stay here.'

Despite all my father's best efforts to waterproof the tent and lay the ground sheet properly, water was starting to seep up into the tent. The ground, dry from so many weeks without moisture, couldn't cope with the sudden onslaught and the campsite was rapidly turned into a series of streaming rivers. Not wanting to get our bedding wet, we bundled our sleeping bags together, placing them on top of the camping table just outside the sleeping compartment. With nothing to sleep in, and water ever rising, Dad placed my air bed on top of their air bed and we sat, huddled together, knees up against our chests. The thunder and lightning were almost indistinguishable, the air crackling with so much electricity that hairs were visibly standing on end with the static. As the storm fractured the skies, we clung together, terrified, as the lightning fizzed and scratched the ground around us.

Brenda, historically the more hysterical parent, was displaying an uncharacteristic calm that was verging on unnerving. In normal circumstances I would have expected her to be praying to the Virgin Mary for deliverance but, instead, she was silent, her face flashing in and out of darkness, wearing an expression so serene it was as if she'd already been taken by the angels. My father, on the other hand, was wild-eyed and swearing. With every clap of thunder, he physically jumped; at every lightning strike, he winced. He had been muttering about our proximity to the treeline and had worked himself into a skidding mess. Berating himself for having pitched the tent in such a precarious spot, all he kept saying, over and over, was that if we were killed, it would be all his fault. In normal circumstances my mother would have put his mind at ease but because she was in a semi-catatonic state, my father's blusters went unanswered. I was somewhere in between. Despite a small but intense gnawing in my chest, there was something deliciously spine-tingling about being trapped inside the tent while Hell rained itself down around me.

The campsite the following morning looked like a shanty town. Heads were poking out of tents surveying the damage: chairs tipped over, branches down, the place looked bruised. The storm had passed but the rain proved to be lingering, which meant there would be no chance of getting anything dry. I had gone with Dad to the camp shop to fetch croissants, hopping over puddles and marvelling at a tree that had been struck in the night. It was split right through its centre, scorch marks flailing down one side, burning into a blackened pool at its base. Luckily, the tree had not come down but that didn't stop my father wagging a finger in its direction and declaring that he had been perfectly within his rights to be so anxious. 'You see!' he said, tapping at the air. 'Trees and storms don't mix. This campsite's a death trap. Mark my words.'

The weather was in no mood for shifting: a dense, low sky smothered the horizon, dull monotone grey for as far as the eye could see. The rain, reduced to a thin but persistent mist, was still falling, meaning our options were severely reduced. 'I suppose we could go for a drive,' said Mum with a shrug. 'I'll bring the camera. We could find some old French village and have a wander.'

So that's what we did. Brenda had recently discovered photography and had bought a Minolta Hi-Matic 7S 35mm camera, which, she kept telling me, was 'state of the art'. 'You won't find another lens like this one!' she would say with an emphatic nod. 'If I knew how to work all the F stops properly, every picture would be a work of art!'

In short, my mother had a flashy camera, knew just about how to get it in focus and that was it. It was like giving a Ferrari to a learner driver. She took pictures of flowers, trees, walls, stones, doors, windows, roofs, vines, benches; if it didn't move, it got snapped. Her face would scrunch itself into a fist of concentration, tongue poking out, and she would twist the lens in and out of focus until finally, she thought she had it, although we would discover, when the photos came back, she invariably hadn't.

We had stopped in a small village, about half an hour from the campsite, and Brenda was hard at it, taking pictures of vine-covered walls, a row of pots and a towel that was slung over the lower half of a swing door. The drizzle was refusing to let up and I trudged behind, head sunk into the back of my anorak hood and hands deep in pockets. As my mother cooed over the gabled rooftops and a particularly ornate wooden balcony dripping with honeysuckle, I noticed that there was an old couple standing outside the neighbouring house under a striped but battered awning. The woman was dressed head to toe in black and was carrying a limp cotton bag out of which poked a length of baguettes. The man standing next to her was in a heavy overcoat and cap and had the stub end of a cigarette glued to the corner of his mouth. Brenda, who had finished agonising over her angles for the balcony turned and saw them. 'What fabulous faces!' she said and, without thinking, lifted her camera and took a picture of them.

'*Mais non, qu'est-ce que vous faites?*' yelled the woman, gesturing angrily towards my mother, her voice shrill and piercing. '*Vous n'avez pas le droit de prendre notre photo. Qui vous a dit que vous pouviez le faire? Mais non, de quel droit!*'

Startled and not quite understanding what was happening, my mother took a step back and mumbled something indistinct.

'*Vous vous prenez pour qui?*' screamed the woman, pulling one of the baguettes out of her bag and waving it at us. '*On n'est pas des animaux dans un zoo! Est-ce que je viendrais chez vous, moi, prendre des photos de vous? On n'est pas des sauvages! Donnez-moi cet appareil-photo! Donnez-le moi!*'

At this point the woman, brandishing the baguette, lunged towards my mother and made a grab for the camera. My mother, letting out a small scream, clutched the camera to her, all the while being beaten over the shoulder with the baguette. '*Donnez-moi l'appareil-photo!*' yelled the woman. '*Comment osez-vous! Sortez de ce village! Sortez d'ici!*'

Dad, who had been strolling nonchalantly in the distance admiring the simple charms of rustic French architecture, looked up to see his wife being battered with some bread. My father had a proper problem on his hands. The assailant bearing down on my mother was a woman who looked as if she wasn't a day under ninety. This was going to require a delicate touch. My father's first course of action was to appeal to the woman's husband. '*Monsieur! S'il vous plaît!*' pleaded my father, as if a simple man-to-man gesture might do the trick, but the man, who had failed to move one facial muscle during the entire escapade, a small detail that led me to believe this must be a regular occurrence, simply shrugged his shoulders and took another puff on his cigarette. Dad, realising that no help was going to be forthcoming, then placed himself between my mother and the woman. '*Madame!*' he kept shouting, holding out his arms, '*Pas de pain! Pas de pain!*'

'*Fichez-moi le camp!*' screamed the woman, in a voice that sounded like an eagle being strangled. '*Fichez-moi!*'

The baguette, which seemed to be made of wood it had lasted so long, was finally giving way and was now bent at a right angle in the middle. My father, sensing an opportunity, grabbed the end of it and gave it a tug, wrenching away the top half with his hand. He then used his half of the baguette to parry away the blows of the old woman's half baguette in a bizarre bread-based fencing match while shoving my mother behind him and shouting, 'Run! Come on! Get out!' Chased out of a village by an old woman and a baguette, my mother covered in crumbs, not one of us batted an eyelid. It was just another day at the office for my family on holiday. We got back in the Land Rover, said nothing and drove back to the campsite.

'The bloke in the camp shop says it's going to rain for days,' said Dad, throwing a tin of mackerel on to a chair. 'I'm thinking we should move south. Have lunch and then go. What do you think?'

'Everything is so wet,' said Brenda, casting a sorry look around us. 'And if it's not going to get dry today...'

'Or tomorrow,' added Dad, with a definitive suck of the cheeks.

'Then you're probably right. Do you mean leave now? After we've had lunch?'

'Well there's no point hanging about, is there?' asked Dad. 'And to be honest, we are very close to these trees. I just think we should leave, Brenda. Don't want to spend all week sitting in the rain, do we?'

After a quick consultation of the map, it was decided that we would drive down to Aix en Provence, a town north of Marseilles. The campsite was just shy of the dramatic Mont Saint-Victoire mountain where Aix's most famous resident, the artist Paul Cézanne, produced much of his work. That alone was the selling point for Brenda. 'I'll get some lovely pictures of that!' she declared, beaming. The drive was long but worth it. After three hours of driving a small patch of blue sky appeared over some hills, the sight of which prompted a rousing burst of 'Here Comes the Sun', a song that was adopted there and then as that year's holiday theme. By the time we arrived in Aix, the skies were blazing: summer had returned.

Aix hadn't seen rain for weeks and, to our bone-dry neighbours, the sight of our sad and soggy tent was worthy of note. As Dad dragged and heaved at the damp canvas and Mum hung out the towels and clothes that had got wet, a man so hairy he looked as if he was wearing a wetsuit wandered over. 'Where've you lot come from?' he asked, folding his arms and spreading his legs a little.

'Argentat,' answered Dad, assuming the same pose. 'Terrible storm last night. Tree got struck by lightning. Right by us.'

'Well, it wasn't right by us. It was the other side of the campsite,' interjected Brenda.

'It was pretty close,' continued my dad. 'And the weather had set in so we thought, head south.'

'Good move,' said the hairy man. 'They haven't had rain here in six, seven weeks, apparently. Weather's been glorious. I don't think I've seen a cloud since I've been here. Couple over there now. But that's the first I've seen. Tree came down, you say?'

'It was split, it didn't come down,' explained my mother.

'Good as,' added Dad, pushing out his bottom lip. 'I mean, it'll have to come down. Totally struck in two. Burnt bits on the ground. The lot.'

'Wow!' said the man, shifting a little. My dad nodded silently and stared at his feet. My mother rolled her eyes in my direction. 'Well! Let's hope you haven't brought the

weather with you!' continued the man, raising his considerable eyebrows.

We were such an oddity on the campsite that no less than
five people approached us to ask why all our stuff was so wet.
One woman even came over to offer us a couple of sleeping
bags her family weren't using 'on account of it being so hot',
but was politely declined by my mother who was in no mood
to be the resident refugee. I had no interest in hanging
about to be stared at so casually wandered off to explore the
campsite. It was the usual fare: a concrete shower block up a
dusty path, a pool cased inside a wire-mesh fence where
scrawny boys with shoulder-length hair took it in turns to
dive in and a long, low hut that sold food and milky lollipops.
Dotted throughout the site were occasional standpipes, all of
which had small queues of children carrying pans or bottles,
dispatched by their parents to fetch water for that night's
supper. I'd be joining them shortly: it was always my job to
fill the water container, even if I could never manage to carry
it if it was more than a quarter full. Still, it was better than
having to empty the bucket.

The grass all about me was bleached to the colour of
straw and tall, wizened patches dotted the edges of plots,
hiding fat cicadas that were just beginning their early-evening
symphony. A wind was creeping in with the twilight, tiny dust
balls blew along the pathway in front of me, while overhead
a small flurry of bumping clouds tumbled over each other as
if on the run. But from what? I stood for a moment and
looked up and around. Cézanne's mountain, which rose away
from the site with a sense of drama, had taken on a deep
almost blue tinge, casting a strange light on everything below
it. The weather was changing. And then I heard it: low, quiet
and prowling like a tiger. Somewhere, behind the mountain,
there was thunder.

'Did you hear it?' I asked, running back to our plot. My mother nodded. My father was chewing his lip.

'I'm sure it's miles away,' said Brenda, waving a dismissive hand into the air. 'Probably just bouncing off the mountain. You know, like radar.'

'You don't think we're too close to that tree, do you?' asked Tony, staring at a large plane about twenty metres from our plot.

'Tony,' said my mother with a sigh. 'It was just a bit of thunder. A long way away. It doesn't mean we're going to have a storm. It's just the air settling after a hot day. And, no, we're not too near that tree.'

'And it's not raining, Daddy,' I added. 'So that's good.'

During supper you could cut the tension with a knife. We sat in front of a still-drying tent, our air beds, yet to be inflated, laid out to the left of us and surrounded by a wash house scene of hanging clothes and blankets. We spoke very little, my father's ear turned towards the mountain, listening out for every thunderous growl. 'I think that one was further away,' he would mutter, a lump of courgette hanging in mid-air. 'Yeah! That was definitely moving away.'

After we'd eaten, I was given the plates to wash under the standpipe and, as I stood in line waiting, I could see my father striding back and forth, face upturned, straining to get a better view of what might be going on behind the mountain. The wind had thickened and the tops of the trees around the site were beginning to bend. A large, empty crisp packet rolled past me and I watched as it darted from left to right bouncing like a clumsy lamb. Something warm and wicked was rolling in: we were in for a bumpy night.

By dusk, the robust breeze had turned into a bluster, squalls of dust whistling around our ankles. Somehow, our beds had managed to dry off and Dad was hard at work, pumping away with his foot to get them inflated. 'You know, it might just be windy,' said my mother, ever hopeful. 'It hasn't thundered for a while. It's probably that famous wind. What's it called...mistral? That's what it is. It'll just blow about for a bit and that will be that, I expect. Although knowing our luck it'll probably turn into a hurricane. Or a tornado. What's the difference between a hurricane and a tornado? Aren't they the same thing?'

'A hurricane is a storm system,' muttered my father, pumping furiously. 'A tornado is the one with the funnel. Like in *The Wizard of Oz*.'

'Brilliant!' I said, livening up. 'Will we get lifted in the air and everything?'

'There's nothing brilliant about a tornado, Emma,' said my father, head down. 'They're very dangerous things. I still think we're too close to that tree.'

'Tony, stop panicking,' said my mother, getting up and having a stretch. As she stood, the wind caught her camping chair and blew it over. 'Blimey,' she added, bending over to catch it. 'It is windy, isn't it?'

Despite the wind, it was incredibly hot and we all lay on top of our beds wearing nothing more than our pants. I had borrowed the torch so I could read *Fattipuffs and Thinifers*, a book about a pair of brothers, one thin, one fat, who find themselves in parallel worlds of obesity and abstinence. I didn't really know what the moral of the story was: I just liked the pictures of the fat trains. The tent was being battered and the wind was now so strong that the side walls were banging back and forth. Dad had gone very quiet but I could hear him shifting every time a particularly violent gust cuffed the side of the tent. To make matters worse, it had started raining and as if *that* wasn't bad enough, the thunder was back. 'I think that's a lot nearer now,' I mumbled, as a loud clap devastated the air above us.

'Pass me the torch, Emma,' said Dad, sitting up and holding out his hand. 'You'd better stop reading now.'

The storm, not yet at full strength, was cranking up a notch. Rain was pelting against the canvas and the wind, already intense and brutal, deepened as it hammered the tent from side to side. The noise, just as it had been the night before, was incredible. Underpinned with the steady crash of rain, thunder and lightning took it in turns to punctuate the storm and over it all, a dread, pained howling as the wind screamed around the campsite. 'I think this might be worse than last night,' whispered my mother.

The tent, now being thumped from all sides, began to visibly strain from the assault. The poles, creaking and whining, began to slowly vibrate as if trying to shake themselves loose from the canvas. My dad, pointing the torch into one corner, followed the length of the back right-hand pole from ground to ceiling. It was shuddering violently and, as we watched, with one ferocious jerk it snapped in two. 'Christ!' yelled my dad, throwing down the torch and leaping up. 'The bloody tent's coming down!'

Scrabbling through the inner tent door into the main compartment, my father reached up and grabbed the overhead pole that ran down the centre of the tent. The tent frame, wanting to take off into the storm, was bucking and struggling to break free and my father had to use all his strength to wrestle it back to the floor. As the tent tried to wrench itself out of his grip, he yelled with exertion, arms widespread, muscles at breaking point. Water was pouring down on top of him as his fingers, crashing against the top canvas, created breakthrough points for the rain water that had gathered in a huge pool on the tent roof. As I looked at him, in a pair of green underpants, eyes closed and screaming, it was like the Incredible Hulk had gone on a camping trip and found himself upset with the facilities. For two hours my poor father held down the tent, storm raging around him, my mother and I on our knees holding on to corner poles in an effort to spread the burden. As the wind died down, the centre pole was completely buckled, so hard had my father had to pull on it. We were wet, sweating and exhausted. Two nights, two storms. The Holiday Gods were turning nasty.

'Turns out you did bring the weather with you!' shouted the hair-suit man from the day before as he wandered past us in a cagoule the next morning. Yet again, the rain had lingered and the glorious drought that Aix had been enjoying was at a dripping end. We stood staring at our now wonky tent. The top was sunken, the back right side collapsed and, yet again, everything was drenched. 'It's going to be like this for the rest of the week according to the paper,' he continued. 'Come down from the North. You should have stayed where you were! It's lovely up there now!'

'I can't go through another night like that, Brenda,' said my dad in a solemn hush. 'I know it's mad. But let's get out of here. Let's go back. We can go somewhere different but let's go where it's warm. Let's go back North. I just don't want another storm. The tent's in a state. I don't think it could stand another night like that. I'm serious. Please.'

And so we packed our saturated belongings into the back of the Land Rover and staggered back from whence we had come. We would outrun this storm if it was the last thing we did.

My father was determined not to stop until we had blue skies overhead. With my mother singing, '"Here Comes the Sun"...PLEASE!' and me staring out the window for any chink of hope in the leaden sky, we negotiated our way out of darkness and into the light. We didn't quite achieve blanket blue but in our tired and frazzled state, a mottled sky was on the brink of acceptable and, besides, we were running out of time: we needed a few hours to get our stuff dry.

We had stopped at a campsite just outside Luant. Set on the fringes of a forest, the four-acre campsite had a long line of empty caravans dotted along the treeline while tents were encouraged to enter the forest. 'Why do they always make the tents go by the trees?' complained my father, throwing a desperate arm in their direction. 'Why do they do that?' The spot we'd been directed to felt isolated and, taking a quick panoramic glance, we weren't immediately near anyone. A hundred metres to our left, however, we could see three much smaller caravans and a tent that showed some signs of life: there was a large wooden chair sitting by the door and a pile of pans scattered on the floor. My father, who was still twitchy, waited until the camp owner was out of sight. 'I'm not pitching here,' he said, shaking his head. 'Let's move closer to that lot.'

Our tent was so wet it was impossible to get it up and, with considerable effort, we helped Dad spread it across Bessy's bonnet to let it dry. In any event, the tent frame needed some repair work and Dad set about trying to hammer the central pole back into something approaching a straight line. I was given the role of worker's mate, a vital contribution that involved holding anything my father might care to hand me before then handing it back. The upright pole that had snapped the previous night was of particular concern and, in the absence of anything space age, like gaffer tape, my father was forced to attempt a patch up with nothing more than a ball of string. Mum, meanwhile, had gone for a short walk to check the lay of the land. There was something not quite right about this campsite and she wanted to put her finger on it.

Dad, having managed to get the tent frame up against all odds, stood back and had a look at it. It wasn't pretty and had the air of a just-run-over bicycle. To make sure it was safe, he got me to go round and shake the corner poles: if it didn't fall down then we were in business. 'I think we might get away with this, Em,' he said with a half-pleased nod. Mum, who was wandering back through the trees towards us, had picked up a lengthy stick and was using it to swish at the ground in front of her. She was frowning and kept looking back over her shoulder.

'There's nothing here, Tony,' she said, meandering up. 'It's all a bit weird. I can't find any toilets. Or a wash block. And there doesn't seem to be anyone around. Apart from one man I saw crouching behind a tree and digging at the floor. Which didn't strike me as being particularly normal.'

'What was he digging up?' asked Dad, giving a corner pole a little shake.

'I couldn't see,' answered Mum, looking up at the tent frame. 'He was too far away.'

'He could have been burying something,' I said, even if no one had asked for my opinion. 'He might not have been digging up. He could have been digging down.'

My mother turned and looked at me, thought about that and dismissed whatever awful thought she was having as excessive. 'Are you sure the frame's going to hold the tent?' she asked, moving her attention to the more immediate problem. 'It looks a bit...incapable.'

'If it stays up when we put the canvas on then we're in business,' answered Dad, having a feel of the tent to see if it had dried off. 'In fact, I think that'll do. It's not quite there, but it's dry enough. Let's give it a go. Come on.'

The three of us hauled the tent from the front of the Land Rover and lifted it, with a reverence reserved for the Turin

Shroud, on to the main frame. Mum and I stood back and could do nothing more than hold our breath as Dad hoisted the legs into the upright. Saving the snapped pole till last, Dad took hold of it and, with a shrug and a quick, 'Here goes nothing!', he launched it upwards. The tent swayed a little as the poles shifted in what seemed to be nothing more than a precarious balancing act, before settling and coming to an uneasy rest. No one said anything. The tent did not fall down. 'Well then,' said Dad, after what seemed to be a healthy gap. 'It hasn't collapsed. Good. Right then, Emma. Water, please!'

Dispatched with the large plastic water container dragging behind me, I couldn't immediately find a standpipe from which I could draw our night-time liquid requirements. With the sound of my father hammering in pegs behind me, I walked deeper into the forest, casting around for any signs of a tap. Mum had been right, this wasn't like a normal campsite: there was something unnerving about the obvious absence of large numbers of people, the lack of any noticeable facilities and the forest itself, while not dense, was still thick enough to generate an air of spooky unease. Realising that I had overshot what I could only assume was the main part of the campsite, I turned back on myself. I could see our tent ahead to the right and the three small caravans and the other tent to the left. Other than that, I could see nothing. The floor was strewn with dead pinecones and with only a thin pair of flip-flops on my feet, walking through them was problematic and uncomfortable. As I stared down, concentrating on where I was placing my feet, I heard an unfamiliar noise off to my left. I looked up and, with a considerable gasp, came to a shocked and astonished stop. I was staring at a large, hairy pig with tusks, trotting behind which were three smaller pigs, all equally hairy. They were snaffling down on what appeared to be a heap of vegetable peelings, next to which, I noticed with a start, was a standpipe that was leaking water. One of the smaller pigs was drinking from the pool that had gathered at its base. I threw a quick glance over in the direction of my parents but they were too far away for me to attract their attention without startling the creatures. With genuinely no idea of what I was looking at, I was at a loss as to how to proceed. I would have to remain, still and quiet like a sapling, until they were done.

I arranged myself into as silent and inconspicuous a position as I could muster. I had placed the water container in front of me, to act as a barrier should any untoward charging kick off, and had arranged my hands with the palms facing down so that, in the event of a pig-based explosion, I would be able to push away the water container and create a diversion. The creatures, it had to be said, were paying little if no attention to me but I could hear them snorting and snuffling as they demolished the mystery meal that had been left out for them. Just as I was wondering who it was who had left out the potato-and-carrot-based debris, I had my answer. A man, brandishing a large and dirty pan, galumphed into view. He was extremely thin and was wearing nothing but a pair of rancid-looking grey shorts and a pair of canvas plimsolls which had lost their laces. His face was a concertina of brown, weathered lines, his hair a crow's nest of mess and his mouth seemed to be packed out with not just his own teeth but a few extra from who knows where that jutted out at random angles. If ever there was a physical breed standard for a mad man, he was it.

Waving the pan above his head, he let out a strangled 'Baroooooo!', hopped about on the spot and waited until the hairy pigs, which had now devoured their free evening supper, were giving him their undivided attention. 'Barooooo!' he howled again, this time banging at the pan with a flat wooden spoon. A little alarmed by the strangeness of it all, I edged away and stood behind a tree where he couldn't see me, heart thumping in my chest. Banging and baying, I could only assume that he was leading the animals away, an arrangement that suited me down to the ground, and so I stood, patient and silent, until my immediate vicinity fell quiet. Poking my head from around the tree, I watched as the man bounced off towards the tent to the left, the strange creature and its young trotting along behind. As soon as they were sufficiently far away, I grabbed the water container and filled it as best I could before heaving it back to my parents.

'Mum! Mum!' I gushed, abandoning the container as I reached the edge of our pitch. 'I saw these pigs! But they weren't pigs! They were really hairy and had tusks! Like they were prehistoric or something! And I am not making this up. I swear it!'

'That sounds like wild boar!' said my mother with a small frown. 'Surely not?'

'Honest, there was a big one and three little ones. And they were eating peel and stuff. And then this man came over and did a dance and they went off with him.'

'A man did a dance for the boar?' asked my mother. 'What did he look like?'

'Like a tramp on holiday,' I said, thinking quickly. 'He wasn't wearing much. Just some shorts. And he had too many teeth.'

'That's the bloke I saw digging up earlier!' exclaimed my mother, eyes widening. 'Tony! Emma saw that man. And he's got wild boar. There are wild boar on the campsite!'

'Hang on,' said Dad, who was just positioning the last peg to be hammered in. 'Wild boar? Don't talk soft.'

'There was, Dad,' I squealed. 'I didn't even know what they were! I thought they were pigs gone wrong.'

'Can boars attack humans?' asked my mother, hand rising to her throat. 'Wasn't there that woman who was killed by a boar? And if it's a mother with babies, then that makes it double dangerous. That's a fact. Right. Emma, don't go wandering off again. Stay where I can see you.'

Dad, who was looking up at us, incredulous that wild boar were roaming about, shook his head and raised the mallet to bang in the last peg. As he drove the hooked metal into the earth, he stood up and wiped his forehead with the back of his hand. 'Right then,' he said, tossing down the mallet. 'That's that. Now then. What's this about wild boar?'

And as the words left his lips, somewhere, creeping in from the south, there was the sound of thunder.

'Oh no,' whispered my mother, heaving a considerable sigh. 'Not again.'

My father's head slumped towards his chest, as if something small and indefinable had just shattered inside him. Putting his hands on his hips, he stared down at the ground and chewed his lip. A moment passed and then, with a sharp kick of a pinecone, he raised his head and declared with some vehemence, 'That thunder isn't coming here. It's just not.'

'Oh my God,' said my mother suddenly, her eyeline drawn off to the left. 'There they are! Look at that! It's wild boar! Wild boar!'

The boar had appeared from behind the caravan nearest to us, no more than ten feet away. The larger boar was snorting into the air while the piglets were rooting around in the pinecones with their snouts. We stood, transfixed and slightly terrified. 'Look at the tusks, Tony!' whispered my mother from the corner of her mouth. 'If we startle it, it'll come at us. Like a rhino.'

'Do you think I should shoo them off?' my dad whispered back. 'They might try and get into the tent. Eat our food.'

'Can they open tins?' I asked, wide-eyed.

Before my father could do anything, the crazy man popped up from behind the boar. He was still waving the pan in the air and pounding on it with his spoon. Seeing us, he stopped, stared at us for a moment and then gestured towards the boar with a demented grin that displayed his gravestone teeth to considerable advantage. He shouted something at us but, not being able to speak French, we were unable to make head nor tail of it. '*Le cochon*,' braved my father, pointing towards the animals. '*Ils sont OK? Pas dangereux?*'

'*Dangereux!*' yelled the mad man, waving his arms in the air. '*Dangereux!* Ha hahah hahah haa haaaa haaaa haaa haaa ha ha ha haha haaaa haaaa!'

'OK,' said my father very quietly. 'Everyone into the tent.'

'What are we going to do?' whispered my mother, as we all stood inside the firmly zipped-up tent. 'He's a maniac. We're in a forest with a maniac and some wild boar!' Overhead, low rolling thunder grumbled in our direction. 'And there's another storm coming!'

'No, Brenda,' insisted my father, peeping out of the tent's side window. 'The storm is not coming. Let's pile up the chairs and the table against the door. Just in case. Emma, you keep an eye out. Tell us if he does anything strange or comes too close. I've got the mallet. We'll be fine.'

Posted as look-out, I took it upon myself to report absolutely everything I could see. 'He is banging his pan...Now he is waving his spoon like a wand...He's waving it over the pigs...The pigs are running around...Now he is shaking a caravan...and laughing. Oh, and it's started to rain.'

Any way you mixed it, the situation was not ideal: as twilight set in, so the storm took hold. My father, in deep denial, sat in the sleeping compartment, his back turned to my mother and me who were taking it in turns to crouch under the small gap in the window and check what was going on. The rain was whipping up again, just as it had before, and while the thunder had drifted off, we were in no doubt that it would make a pounding return. The man was still outside and seemed in no hurry to take shelter. If anything, he was revelling in the storm, dancing around and laughing, all the while banging on his filthy pot. As the rain lashed in at an angle, we could just make him out, darting in and out of the little light there was. 'There's something about this that's a bit *Texas Chainsaw Massacre*,' said my mother suddenly, before stopping and adding, 'I wish I hadn't said that. I think we should get in bed.'

The thunder returned with a vengeance an hour later, accompanied, as ever, by cracks of lightning that snapped into the ground, taking swiping bites like a massive aerial Tyrannosaurus Rex. My father, still sitting upright and clinging to the torch, was taciturn, and in the flimsy light looked drawn and anxious. My mother, to take her mind off having to contemplate yet another potentially disastrous night, was also sitting up but had chosen to sing some Bob Dylan songs which were fine until she got to 'Blowin' in the Wind' which, at the very least, was about as inappropriate for the circumstances as you could get. Every now and again, we could hear the crazy man laughing his head off, which elicited disconcerted glances from my mother followed by a steely resolve to just sing a bit louder. As Brenda was launching into a particularly gutsy rendition of 'Hey Mr Tambourine Man', my father, without warning, stood up and, without looking at either myself or my mother, said 'I'm just going to the car', whereupon he unzipped the tent and left.

My mother and I looked at each other. This was a puzzle. What had he gone to do? Or get? 'Perhaps', began my mother, looking a little bewildered, 'he's gone to get more pegs?'

'Or the Slinky?' I suggested, because anything was possible.

'Hmmm,' said my mother, ignoring my last remark. 'I'll just go and check.' Getting out of her sleeping bag, Brenda tiptoed out to the main tent compartment, held back the already flapping door and peered out into the slashing rain. 'Tony!' she shouted out over the din of the storm. 'What are you doing?' As far as I could tell, she got no reply. 'What is he doing?' my mother muttered to herself. 'He's just sitting there in the front seat, gripping the steering wheel. Tony! Tony! He won't even look at me! Well!' She turned and poked her head back into the sleeping compartment. 'Your father has abandoned us, Emma. Let this be a lesson. All men will walk out on you eventually. We're not staying here. Grab your things. We're going to the Land Rover.'

Bundling up my sleeping bag as best I could, I ran, tightly gripping my mother's hand, over to Bessy. Thunder splintered the clouds above us, rain ripped into our eyes and as we opened the back door to leap in, a sheet of lightning lit up the night sky. I looked over my shoulder and saw the mad man, briefly illuminated, laughing in our direction, a sight that sent chills rushing through me. 'Well thank you very much, Tony!' shouted my mother, shoving my father in the shoulder. 'Just leave us to the mercies of the night! What the hell are you thinking of? She's only nine! *Nine!*'

'It's dangerous in the tent,' mumbled Dad, who was still staring straight ahead and holding on to the steering wheel not unlike someone approaching a full mental breakdown at considerable speed. Before my mother had a chance to respond, another bolt of lightning snapped through the air. My father flinched and reached for the ignition keys. 'That's it,' he said, shaking his head. 'I'm not staying in the middle of these trees. I'm not.' Shoving Bessy into first gear, he screeched away from the tent, out of the forest and into the middle of an adjacent field where we came to a heaving stop. We sat, staring back at our pitch as the wind howled past us, and watched with almost clinical interest as the tent, battered from side to side, very slowly just crumpled in on itself.

'There's that man again,' I said, noticing the resident crazy dancing round our flattened tent. 'I think he's in the nude now.'

My parents said nothing. They were too busy holding their heads in their hands and wondering what they had ever done to deserve this.

We had given up. The tent needed a new frame, the weather was stalking us and we had no cards. What was the point? We drove back to Calais the following morning, the back of the Land Rover stinking of damp canvas, and arrived home in the early evening. We were shattered and beaten. We had been home barely fifteen minutes when the doorbell sounded. It was Tweedledum and Tweedledee.

'Did you have a lovely time?' asked Tweedledee, wringing her hands together. 'Did you have a dry hot?'

'No,' said my father. 'It was a wet hot. A very wet hot. In fact, it was just wet. Oh, never mind.'

'The thing is,' said Tweedledum, taking over. 'It's about Emma's rabbit, Mork.' My chest turned to ice. 'I'm afraid he's died.'

Fuck you, Holiday Gods. Fuck you very much.

Chapter Eight

Things that go *Bump* in the *Night*

I had never seen anything like it. From the sweeping opening sequence as the Imperial Starfleet cruiser filled the screen to the moment the Death Star exploded, I don't think I blinked once. *Star Wars* had arrived and I was obsessed with it. I'd queued up eleven times at my local cinema, collected the bubblegum cards, stared at the plastic dolls in the toy shop and used up every single penny of my piggy bank money on an amazing lightsaber. I say amazing, but it was just a torch with a length of red tubing that only worked if you stood in the pitch dark. Still, I didn't care. I had a lightsaber: I was a Jedi. Dad was more than happy to indulge my new passion and delighted in creeping up behind me, talking deep into a glass tumbler and rumbling, 'Now *I* am the master!' followed by an uncanny impression of the Darth Vader breath rattle. Simon, who was now my official boyfriend because I'd sent him a large padded Valentine card and he'd sent me an empty box of After Eight mints with a plastic ring in it, spent every waking hour with me running around killing Stormtroopers and pretending that we really did have the gift of the Force, a mystical concept that had managed to touch me in a way that no organised religion could ever hope to. *Star Wars* had taken over my life. I was so consumed with it that nothing else mattered. 'Emma,' said my mum in one of her sterner tones, 'can you clean your room, please?' In the three weeks since joining the Rebel Alliance from my base just south of the bunk beds, my room had assumed the appearance of a municipal tip.

'You don't need me to clean my room,' I said with a gentle sweep of my hand through the air.

My mother stared at me. 'Yes,' she said, eyebrows rising, 'I do need you to clean your room.'

'No,' I said again with another sweep of my hand. 'You do not need me to clean my room.'

'What are you doing?' asked my mother. 'What's the arm thing about?'

'I'm using Jedi mind tricks on you,' I explained, a bit gutted that my Force skills were not what they might be.

'Well go and use your Jedi mind tricks on picking up all the stuff on your bedroom floor. Thank you.'

1977 was turning out to be a momentous year. Not only had I found my purpose in life, we had moved to the house where I would spend the rest of my childhood. It had been found one spring evening while out walking, my parents having chanced upon a rough-looking track that ran off the main road from Hitchin to Codicote. Curiosity aroused, they had wandered up it. Lined with horse chestnut trees and covered in gravel, it was as out of place as the black squirrels sitting in the branches. 'Look at that!' my father had squealed. 'A black squirrel, Brenda! It's black!'

At the top of the track there were two cottages to the right and then, just beyond them, a five-bar gate that led off to another, slightly larger house. Opposite the cottages there was a dilapidated tennis court, net sunken and forlorn, weeds fighting up through the tarmac. The cottage on the left showed signs of life but the one to the right had no curtains and appeared empty. 'Let's have a look,' whispered my mother, giving my dad a nudge. Checking that no one was around, my mother darted through a gap in the large hedge that fringed the front of the cottage. A small path led down to a gate, which my mother, bold as brass, unlatched and crept through. 'Brenda!' hissed my father, who was gesticulating as wildly as he could. 'Don't go in! There might be someone there!' But my mother was undeterred: before her lay the most magnificent garden, and open-mouthed she stepped into it as if into Wonderland. The garden was over an acre in size and had a large main lawn, punctuated by a voluminous rose bush in the middle. To the left there was a smaller garden, bursting with fat, vermilion poppies, all manner of wild flowers and a raised mound smothered in borage. 'What's this?' gasped my mother, realising that behind the mound there was a neat flight of stairs. With a quick look over her shoulder, she skipped down the steps to find a large, heavy door. 'It's an air-raid shelter!' she said, astonished. 'It's got bunk beds in it!' Towards the bottom of the garden, beyond the rose bush, there was an orchard packed with apple trees, pear trees, plum and peach, and with the ground covered in fallen fruit, a slightly fermented smell filled the air. 'Isn't this wonderful?' sighed my mother. 'What a beautiful garden.'

'Right,' said my dad, who hadn't stopped looking back up towards the house. 'Let's leave. Come on. Before we get into trouble.'

Fate, as I knew all too well, had crushed our family but, for once, we had been thrown a bone. The very next day, as my parents walked past an estate agent's office, they saw it. The house was up for sale. Uninhabited for two years, divine intervention had sent us to breathe life back into it. It took every single penny my parents had and then some, but it was worth it. We had found our home.

The nutty problem of where we were going to go on holiday that year was, as ever, unresolved. It was Jubilee year and everyone except my mother was in the grip of a national fervour. I'd been given a large commemorative coin by the government, which was all very well but it would have been better if I could have spent it. If it had been legal tender I could have bought a small plastic Luke Skywalker, a Hans Solo AND a Princess Leia. Brenda, dismissive of the monarchy and all it stood for, had stared at the coin with disdain before chucking it into the back of the cutlery drawer. 'What an utter waste of money!' she declared, all fired up. 'Bloody Queen! Why are we being forced to celebrate someone whose entire life has been paid for by us? We should be like the French! Cut all their heads off! And boil them down into soap!'

'That's horses,' interjected my father, reaching for something in the fridge. 'Not aristocracy.'

'Anyway, talking of France...' she continued, ignoring my father. 'What about a nice trip into the mountains? We haven't been there.'

'No,' said my father, who then set about smashing some lamb with a tenderiser just so no one could be in any doubt as to his feelings on the matter.

'Well I'm not staying here,' answered Brenda, folding her arms and leaning against the back door. 'Everywhere you look there's bunting and saucers with the Queen on. I saw a chicken and ham pie in Halseys last week and the crust was in the shape of the Queen's face. Absolutely ridiculous.'

'Was it really?' I asked, lowering my lightsaber, because I wished I'd seen that.

'And it'll only be worse in seaside towns and villages,' added my mother, rattling on. 'You know how patriotic they are the closer you get to the sea. It's because they're all permanently terrified of invasion.'

'Brenda,' said my father, giving the lamb a particularly emphatic thump, 'I am not going to France.'

'What about if we go to France but not in the tent?' asked my mother, letting her head fall to one side. 'Does that make it any better?'

'I am not going to France,' repeated Tony.

'What if we leave the tent, let's forget the tent,' Brenda battled, 'and stay in one of those house things. What are they called? Where you sort of stay in someone's house except it's not their house and they're not living in it, it's like the French version of bed and breakfast except you don't get breakfast and there isn't a landlady. It's more self-catering. But in villages and places like that. What about that?'

'They're called *gîtes*,' mumbled my dad, still not looking up. 'And I'm not going.'

'Because we really don't need to take the tent this year,' added my mum, shaking her head. 'And it would be different. We've never stayed in a *gîte* before, have we, Em? It would be an authentic rustic experience!'

'Will there be *Star Wars* in France?' I asked, because at that precise moment, that was my primary concern.

'They've got *Star Wars* everywhere,' said my mother. 'Although it will be in French. And we don't really go to the cinema when we're on holiday, do we?'

'I think we should probably stay at home then,' I said, letting that last statement sink in. 'I don't want to go to France either.'

'Right then,' jumped in Dad. 'That's two against one. We're not going to France.'

'No!' protested my mother, waving her hands in the air. 'Hang on a minute. Let's not be hasty. I think we should do this properly and pull a destination out of a hat. How's that? We all write somewhere on a piece of paper and put it in a hat and then pull one out. But we all have to agree to abide by the decision. Yes?'

Dad and I looked at each other. There were two of us and there was one of her. The odds were stacked in our favour. 'No funny business,' said Dad, shooting my mother a sharp stare. 'Fair and square?'

'Fair and square!' declared my mother with a firm nod.

'And I get to pull it out?' continued Tony, eyes alight with the possibility that this year, for once, he might not have to cross the channel.

'Yes, you can pull it out,' replied my mother.

You could have cut the atmosphere with a knife. We all sat round the dining room table, pens in hand, scribbling our preferred destination on pieces of paper. 'Make sure you fold it up good and tight!' said my mother who, despite the fact she was now the underdog, was displaying no signs of nerves whatsoever. We had thrown our scrunched-up holiday nominations into a navy-blue bobble hat worn by my father when gardening on chilly mornings. Taking it, my mother gave it a shake and then stood on a chair with her arm out. 'Go on then,' she said, giving the bobble hat another rattle. 'Pull one out. Tell us where we're going.'

My father took a deep breath, stood up and reached into the bobble hat. Pulling out one piece of paper, he gave a small, almost anxious smile and unfolded it. Reading it, he blinked sharply and looked up. 'Tatooine?' he said, staring at me. 'Tatooine?'

'That was my choice,' I explained, smiling. 'It's the planet Luke Skywalker's from.'

'Why didn't you write England?' my father wailed, throwing the piece of paper down to the floor. 'Why didn't you do that?'

'Because I wanted to go to Tatooine,' I said, realising that I might have sealed our family's fate for the worst.

'Pull again, Tony,' said my mother, beaming.

With the odds now shortened to an even 50-50 chance, Dad reached back into the bobble hat, frowned, closed his eyes and pulled. 'Here,' he said, handing me the piece of paper. 'I can't do it.'

I stared at the piece of paper. I looked up at my parents. My mother was grinning and nodding at me to open it. My father looked as if he were staring at a corpse. I unfolded the paper. 'France,' I said, in a whisper.

My father spent the next hour down the bottom of the orchard swearing.

It wasn't all bad. Mum had stuck by her word and agreed that this year the tent would not be coming. It was a small crumb of comfort to my poor father whose shoulders had descended so low he was starting to look as if he was growing a hump. It felt strange to be going anywhere without the tent and I wondered if we were committing an unspeakable treachery: punishment was never far away where our holidays were concerned and by abandoning the tent to a dark corner in the garage there was a sense that we were dancing with the devil. 'I feel a bit sad we won't be in the tent this year,' said my mother, as we drove off the ferry into Calais.

'I don't,' said Dad, slapping a small hand-drawn 'DRIVE ON THE RIGHT' sticker on the inside of the windscreen. 'I hate the bloody thing.'

Because we had a lot less to carry, I was, for the first time ever, sitting upright in the second row of seats behind my parents instead of lying on my belly in the back. Given that I was a Jedi in waiting, my more dignified travel arrangements suited me down to the ground. 'Don't wave the lightsaber in the back of the car please, Emma,' said my mother, as I was engaging in a particularly intricate manoeuvre. I had had to negotiate long and hard to bring my Jedi weapon on holi-day: stuffed into an old leather belt my dad had given me, I went nowhere without it. Around the house I had even taken to wearing an old dressing gown because it was the nearest thing I could find to a Jedi outfit. I had to be stopped once from wearing it to school. At the time I was in tears, but now, with a sense of detached reflection, I can't thank my mother enough.

The holiday had been murderous in the organising. If you were planning to stay in a *gîte*, you couldn't just write off to the owner and check availability, you had to write first to the relevant tourist office in the appropriate governmental depart-ment for the area you were proposing to stay in, engage in a little to-ing and fro-ing with them and then, and only then, were you allowed to approach the owner. My mother had decided we would head for the Cantal, a mountainous region in the Auvergne, where we would be staying in a small village called Bourriergues. It was all part of her plan to fulfil her promise of an 'authentic French rustic experience'.

Even I who, like my father, was reluctant to be there, had to concede that the drive through the Auvergne was spectac-ular: forested hillsides, lakes, craggy volcanic peaks in the distance, an unspoilt terrain with villages and towns sparsely distributed. The few houses we did pass had battered, worn-down fasciae and an idiosyncratic feature of the region that I had never seen before: hay lofts set under the eaves. Each house had the usual peaked roof but in the centre of each peak there was an open doorway bursting with hay as if they were outsized nests for giant birds. As we approached villages, stacks of logs would appear along the roadside, often creeping for miles, fuel for the harsh winter months ahead, and outside every house, heaped cages that on closer inspec-tion were full of rabbits. 'Why have they got so many pets?'

I asked, staring at them. 'Are they breeding them for pet shops? Can I get one and call it Mork Two?'

'I don't think they're pets,' my father explained, trying to be as sensitive as he could. 'I think they're for food.'

'Pardon?' I said, looking up at him in disbelief. 'They eat rabbits?'

'And horses,' piped up my mother. 'They'll eat anything, the French.'

'Even Darth Vader wouldn't eat a horse,' I said, shocked to my core. 'That's just evil.'

'I don't think they've got horses in space, Em,' opined my dad. 'Mind you, he's pretty evil. He'd probably eat one given half the chance.'

Mum hadn't been lying when she said we were going to 'immerse ourselves in remote French culture'. As we pulled into the tiny village of Bourriergues, I was shocked by just how remote it was: there were no shops, a handful of houses, some of which were already crumbling into ruins, and very few signs of life. Our first problem was how to work out where we were staying. There was a villager we could ask but, ominously, she was dressed all in black and carrying a scythe over her shoulder. 'Who knew the Grim Reaper was a woman?' mumbled my father, a comment that ended with a sharp nudge from my mother.

All we had to go on was a handwritten letter in French that looked as if a tarantula had been dipped in ink and left to run riot. Waving it out of the window at the passing villager, my father called out, '*Excusez-moi, Madame! Où est l'homme ici?*' Staring at her from the side window, I was struck with the thought that it wasn't possible to look older without actually being a skeleton. Her skin was wrinkled in on itself, like a crushed fleshy fan, and was so thin I wouldn't have been surprised if a sudden gust of wind had blown her face off. Her hand, as she reached for the letter, was split and swollen at the joints, her purple bruised knuckles the badges of a long, hard life. She peered at the paper through watery eyes, one of which was such a pale blue that it was almost certainly blind. Everything about her seemed fragile and delicate so when she looked up at my father and answered in the loudest, raspiest, bowel-shaking voice I had ever heard, we all jumped. '*Il habite dans la maison au bout du chemin!*' she yelled, words firing like bullets. '*Au bout du chemin! Continuez! Continuez! Au bout du chemin! La dernière maison! C'est là qu'il habite!*'

My father, whose French had not improved, had his usual problem: he was fine if he was trying to converse with slow-speaking French people with no discernible accent but when it came to tackling the quicker and rougher end of the guttural market, he was at sixes and sevens. 'Pardon?' he said, shaking his head a little.

'*Au bout du chemin!*' she yelled again, gesturing with her finger. '*La dernière maison. Il y a un tonneau dehors. C'est la maison que vous cherchez. Combien de fois faut-il que je vous le dise? J'ai du travail, moi. Le gazon ne va pas se tondre tout seul. La dernière maison. C'est là qu'il habite! La dernière maison. Cette maison-là. Là! Celle-là!*'

My father stared at her and swallowed. 'Sorry... I...Pardon?' he said again.

The woman, who was now staring back at my father, and not with a look I would have enjoyed being at the end of, threw an arm into the air. '*Mais qu'est-ce qu'il y a? Je ne peux pas vous l'expliquer plus simplement. La maison DU BOUT. Là. De ce côté. Un, deux, trois et puis quatre! C'est celle-là que vous cherchez. Numéro quatre! Quatre! Même un enfant pourrait comprendre. Mais vous apparemment vous ne comprenez pas. Alors je vous souhaite une bonne journée messieurs-dames.*'

Voilà. Ça y est. Il faut que je tonde le gazon. Que je tonde le gazon! Numéro quatre! Quatre!'

'What did she say?' asked my mother, scrunching up her face.

'I haven't got a clue,' my dad said, sounding a little crushed.

'She was talking like that bounty hunter in the Mos Eisley cantina,' I said, wanting to show solidarity. 'You know, the green one that Han Solo shoots. I don't think she was even speaking French, Dad. Honestly.'

'She kept saying one word over and over, though. Wasn't it a number? Do you think she meant the number of a house?'

'Seriously, she's probably not even a human,' I said, putting a hand on my dad's shoulder.

'Oh, I don't know,' said my father, defeated from the off. 'Let's just sit here until someone normal notices us.'

'Give me the letter,' said Mum, flapping her fingers together. 'I'll just go and knock on some doors. Someone will be able to speak English.'

'They won't, Mum,' I said, shaking my head. 'This is worse than outer space.' My mother turned and gave me a sharp look before getting out of the car. We watched her wander off towards the dilapidated houses on our right. There was a moment of quiet in the Land Rover. 'Dad,' I said, leaning forward to get a good look at his face. 'We're not really staying here, are we?'

'Tatooine,' mumbled my father. 'We could be sitting in a nice guesthouse in Norfolk. We could be eating scones with cream and jam. But no. You had to write Tatooine.' And as I watched my mother peering into empty buildings and turning to us and shrugging, I knew he was right.

*

Eventually we found him. Or rather, he found us. He crept up on us from behind, slouching up from the bottom of the village with a sack on his back. Monsieur Durand was a tall, gaunt-looking man with something of the rat about him. He had a heavy, waxy coat that had seen better days, his trousers, thick brown cotton, were a few inches too short and, on his head, the ubiquitous French cap perched at a tilt. He was unshaven, had deep gouges around his mouth, the hairiest eyebrows I had ever seen and his eyes were as black as treacle. I gripped my lightsaber a little tighter. I didn't trust him.

'*C'est vous les Anglais qui logez chez moi?*' he asked, putting an elbow on my dad's front window and leaning in to get a good look at us. His voice was so deep and incomprehensible, it was like thunder made flesh.

My father, not having understood, battled on regardless. 'Monsieur Durand?' he asked, lifting the letter and pointing at it.

'*Oui, oui,*' said the fellow, nodding. '*Bonjour. Vous êtes que trois? Et dans une si grande bagnole. Suivez-moi et je vous accompagne à la maison. Elle est pas loin. Juste après ces maisons, à gauche. Venez. Suivez-moi.*'

Monsieur Durand then went to the front of the Land Rover and started walking off. 'Where's he going?' asked my mother. 'Was he speaking in Spanish?'

'I think we're supposed to follow him,' began my father, turning the ignition on. 'Yes. There you go. Look, he's waving at us.'

As we drove slowly past the other properties in the village, I was filled with a small but significant sense of dread. Everything had a look of the graveyard about it, crumbling and covered in lichen, so as we arrived at what was going to be our home for the next week, I was pleasantly surprised to see what appeared to be a charming country cottage. Painted white and with a large, sloping stone tile roof, it was on the verge of looking as if it had been scraped off a chocolate box. Wooden shutters framed the windows, an old stone well sat on the front lawn and pots of red carnations provided a splash of colour stretching all along the front wall and up a small flight of steps to the front door. My mother, sensing that all was about to come good, turned and beamed, 'There,' she said, with a satisfied nod. 'Now isn't THIS lovely?'

Monsieur Durand, who had dumped his anonymous sack over the railings at the top of the steps, had opened the door and was gesturing for us to come inside. There was something fractious in his manner, as if we were an inconvenience he could do without. There was no hallway: instead the door opened into one main room that incorporated the kitchen, the dining room and the sitting room in one. It was rather gloomy: one long trestle table, covered in red plastic gingham, dominated the central space, while to the left was a large fireplace, trimmed with matching gingham and decorated with an assortment of inexplicable knick-knacks; a pinecone, a candleholder in the shape of a platform boot and a small, porcelain Minnie Mouse. Over to the right there was an unmemorable but functioning cooker and pushed up against the walls towards the back of the room were two battered and tatty leather chairs. On the wall, just behind the front door, there was a small television set sitting on a purpose-made ledge and just below that, in the murk of the corner, there seemed to be a black cupboard-shaped object but, at that moment, I wasn't quite able to make out what it was. There would be time to investigate later: the monsieur was in full flow.

'*Alors ici, dans la cheminée, vous verrez les tuyaux. Les tuyaux qui montent au mur, ici, et les tuyaux au-dessous, à l'horizontale. Bon, ces tuyaux chauffent toute la maison, donc quand vous faites le feu, faites-le ici, sur les tuyaux horizon-taux, et voilà comment fonctionne le chauffage. C'est clair?*

We all just stared at him.

'*Alors, là-bas on a la cuisinière. C'est une cuisinière à gaz. Vous appuyez sur le bouton et après vous l'allumez avec des allumettes. Je crois qu'il y en a là-bas. Par ici: la salle de bains, les toilettes. Et puis dans ce couloir, il y a une chambre à gauche et au bout du couloir il y a une autre porte mais qui est verrouillée. Vous voyez? Elle est fermée à clé,*' he said, pointing at a door at the end of the corridor. He walked towards it and jiggled the handle a little while shaking his head. '*Vous avez pas le droit d'y entrer. C'est une pièce qui sert de garde-meuble, donc vous n'avez pas le droit d'y entrer. Vous comprenez?*' He stopped and looked at us, waiting for a response.

My dad blinked, shook his head and then said, '*Oui!*' before turning to us and saying, 'I think he's telling us that that door is locked and that his brother lives in that part of the house. That's why we can't go in there.'

'His brother?' said my mother, frowning a little. 'So we're sharing?'

'Looks like it,' said Dad with a shrug.

'*Alors en haut,*' continued the monsieur, grabbing hold of the banister, '*il y a deux chambres. La première sert aussi de garde-meuble, comme vous pouvez le voir.*' He swept an arm into a huge barn-like room with open beams running along the ceiling. It had six empty beds in it, no mattresses, just metal frames and springs all heaped up against each other on one side of the room, while on the other there was a pile of planks and bags of plaster. '*Et à côté, il y a l'autre chambre. Elle est loin d'être gaie mais le lit est assez confortable.*'

'Blimey,' I said, noticing the total lack of any furniture other than the bed.

'Nice view though, Em,' said my mother, maintaining a relentless cheeriness. 'Look at that. Field of cows. A shed.'

'Got quite a strong smell of manure,' noted my father, biting his bottom lip.

'Well it's the genuine rustic experience, isn't it,' added my mother quickly. 'Like I said.'

'*Je vais ouvrir cette fenêtre. Elle est un peu dure quelquefois,*' said Monsieur Durand, moving towards the large dormer window. Using both hands, he gave the whole thing a shove and, with a loud scrape, the lower section moved upwards. Within what seemed like seconds, the room was full of flies: fat, filthy-looking flies gorged on cow shit. Noticing our instant repulsion, the monsieur flapped one hand through the air and said, '*On en à cette époque de l'année. Vous avez qu'à les tuer s'ils vous dérangent. Et des fourmis. Nous avons un petit problème de fourmis en bas, mais l'homme qui nous en débarrasse, eh bien sa mère vient de mourir, alors il n'est pas là en ce moment. Vous n'avez qu'à ne pas vous en approcher et il ne vous arrivera rien.*'

'What's he saying?' asked my mother, flapping a hand across her face.

'No idea,' said Dad, spitting something foreign out of his mouth.

'*Bon, je crois que c'est tout. Je vais vous laisser déballer vos affaires, et vous installer. Ah, oui, il y a un homme dans le village qui est un peu simplet. Il n'est pas bien méchant, mais il est un peu demeuré. Il aime bien errer dans le village. Vous le verrez donc sûrement. Mais comme je vous l'ai dit, il n'est pas du tout méchant. Bon. Bon séjour. Et si vous avez besoin de quelque chose, vous n'avez qu'à me le dire. Madame, Monsieur.*'

As he left, there was a strange, metallic scraping noise that seemed to be coming from behind the house. 'What's that?' asked my mother, straining to recognise it.

'Probably the brother,' said my dad. 'I think.'

But it wasn't the brother. There was no brother. The holiday had begun.

'Is it my imagination,' said my mother, as we sat round the trestle table, having unpacked. 'Or is that small cupboard over there moving?'

I looked up. The black mass I'd spotted earlier and assumed was a cabinet was indeed appearing to shift its shape. The three of us sat, transfixed, as the early-evening sun brought a small, pale spotlight to the darkened corner. The surface was moving. 'What the hell?' said my father, moving slowly towards it. 'Oh my God!' he yelled as he got close enough to see what it was. 'It's not a cupboard! It's an ants' nest!'

'What?' screamed my mother, leaping up from the bench. 'Don't be ridiculous. It's massive!'

'I'm not joking!' said my father, examining it further. 'It's a bloody ants' nest. The whole thing is an ants' nest! Some of them have got wings, Brenda! They're everywhere!'

'Well pour boiling water on it or something!' wailed my mother, who had edged herself to the far wall. 'Or salt. Or whatever it is that kills ants! Just do something!'

'Boiling water isn't going to do it,' said my father, shaking his head. 'This needs an exterminator. This is an infestation. What are we going to do?'

'Can we set fire to it?' asked my mother. 'Cover it in lighter fluid and burn it?'

'We're indoors, Brenda!' my father pointed out, sweeping a hand through the air. 'There's wood everywhere. We'd burn the house down.'

'Do you want to use my lightsaber?' I offered, turning it on and holding it out.

'Not now, Emma,' snapped my mother. 'Tony, we can't

just leave it there. Let's pour some hot water on it and see what happens. At least that way we'll get rid of some of them.'

'Well I can try,' replied my father with a shake of his head. 'But it's only going to scratch the surface. This needs special equipment. I've never seen anything like it.'

A large, copper-coloured pan was swiftly filled with water and left to boil. Feeling bold, I sidled my way towards the dark, seething mound of insects. The nest looked solid, its shape not unlike an extra-large rucksack. Every millimetre of it was moving, a constant, swirling mass of activity. Dad had gone outside to find a stick and then, standing behind me, he leant forward and very gently used it to probe into the outer layer. Large, angry ants swarmed the stick in an instant, scrambling up its length to attack the perpetrator. 'Bloody hell,' said Dad, withdrawing and throwing the stick out the front door. 'They mean business.'

'Can't we just move it outside?' I said, giving the whole thing a once over. 'You know, just pick it up and chuck it out?'

'Yes, Tony!' said my mother, from the safety of the other side of the room. 'Why don't you do that? Maybe it's too big for hot water? I just want it out of the house!'

'What am I going to pick it up with?' complained my dad, looking at both of us. 'I'll be bitten to death!'

'You could use one of those bags in that room upstairs. That would be big enough,' I said, intoxicated by my rush of good ideas.

'The bags that had plaster in them? There were a couple of empty ones, you're right,' said Dad, thinking that through.

I beamed and nodded. I was displaying the sort of skills that would make me a Jedi yet.

Mum hatched a plan: Dad would wear a long-sleeved shirt back to front to protect his arms, oven gloves on his hands (she had found a slightly burnt pair on the floor next to the cooker) and her own voluminous Brigitte Bardot-style sunglasses to fend off any attacks to the eyes. Suitably armoured, he would, in what we hoped would be one deft movement, slip the plaster bag over the top of the ants' nest, scoop it up and dump it down the well. At least that was the idea. 'Right,' said Dad, pulling on the last oven glove. 'Let's discuss this before anyone does anything. Emma, you stand well back. Brenda, you're going to pass me the bag but pass it to me with the top open. Hold it out. So the top is as wide as possible. Then I'm going to turn the bag over and then, Brenda, are you listening?'

My mother nodded.

'Then I want you to hold the bottom end of the bag as wide as you can so that I don't have to pull the bag over the nest. I just want it to drop down over it easily. OK? Then when I've done that, I'll get the open end of the bag and pull the ends together in an upward scooping movement which should pick up the nest in one, I'll clamp the top shut, Bob's your uncle. Does everyone know what they're doing?'

It all started very well. My mother handed my father the bag exactly as he had wanted. Crouching slightly and with a quick grit of the teeth, Tony positioned the open end of the bag immediately above the ants' nest, stretching it between his oven glove as a woman would roll knitting wool. 'Right, Brenda,' he said, letting his weight fall forward on to his front foot. 'Get a hold of the bottom. Ready?' She nodded. With one quick dive to his knees, the bag fell to the floor. Grabbing its edges as best he could, he gathered them together and gave the whole thing an upwards yank, but it wouldn't come away. Somewhere it was attached. 'Where the bloody hell...?' yelled Dad, scrabbling to see what was keeping the nest tethered. Ants were already pouring out of the bag and covering the oven gloves. 'Oh no!' shouted Dad, 'it's attached to this beam! Quick! Get me something I can hit it with! Quick!'

Sensing that my moment of destiny had come, I turned on my lightsaber and strode forward, plastic tube aloft, and started bashing at the back of the sack with everything I had. What I had failed to realise was that, unlike a proper lightsaber, my souped-up torch had no cutting power whatso-ever and, unlike a real Jedi, my aim was not what it might be. Instead of cutting the nest free and becoming the hero of the hour, I just managed to hit the sack repeatedly, sending more ants spilling out and up on to my father. 'No!' he shouted, in a squeal reserved for disastrous occasions. 'No, Emma! Don't do that! Oh God! Brenda! Get me a knife or something!' My mother, now running round the room in frenetic splendour, came back brandishing nothing sharper than a log. Dad, real-ising that still holding the bag was pointless, let go, took the log and used it to smash at the back of the nest. That didn't work, so instead, he set at it with his foot, stamping away at it and letting out a strange, primeval scream as he did. His shoe, which was a soft brown suede, had, I noticed, turned black with ants which were now running up his trouser leg. Desperate to get this whole sorry incident over with, Dad then just grabbed at the nest with the oven gloves and pulled at it until, with one sharp snap, the whole thing came away. Scrambling to get a hold of the bag ends and scooping as many ants into it as he could, Dad then picked up the whole thing and ran, still screaming, into the garden, where the whole lot was thrown, with some venom, down the well.

There were ants everywhere. We were shell-shocked.

'There's that noise again…' said my mother, punctuating the panting silence, as the steady *scraaaaaape, scraaaaaaaape, scraaaaaaaaape* of metal began for the second time that night.

*

'Oh, Tony!' said my mother, pouring more camomile lotion on to a cloth. 'You've been bitten everywhere.' My father's leg was in a terrible state, a join-the-dots mass of red, raised welts that ran from his ankle all the way to his groin. As my mother dabbed on the thick, creamy analgesic, my father, sitting in his pants on the edge of the bath, looked the picture of misery: his head was in one hand, his eyes devoid of life. Ants were still running riot and every now and again he would open an eye, see one and stamp on it in an act of quiet yet determined revenge. I had stood in the doorway watching for a while but had wandered off to stare down the well thinking that I might be able to see the dispatched nest. The courtyard in front of the house was covered in gravel and, as I crunched my way towards the well, I glanced over to my left to follow the trailing crimson clouds that fell away behind the rooftop. I stopped what I was doing. There was a man standing by the Land Rover. He was grinning at me. Perhaps it was because I hadn't been expecting to see anyone, perhaps it was because the buttons on his cardigan were done up wrong, but I turned on my heels and ran back into the house.

'Mum!' I shouted, dashing into the bathroom. 'There's a weirdo outside the house.' My mother, mid-dab, stopped and looked up at me.

'What sort of weirdo?' she asked, a weary edge colouring her voice.

'I dunno,' I said, 'he's just standing by the Land Rover.'

'It's probably the brother,' said Dad. 'I'll go and check, though. Just to be sure.' Wrapping a towel around his waist, my dad hobbled to the front door, Mum and I not far behind. The man was still standing outside but had now moved to the well, where he was just loitering and doing nothing except staring towards the house. His face was slightly sunken as if someone had forgotten to put all the bones in and his general demeanour was of someone who wasn't quite sure where he was. '*Bonjour!*' shouted out my father then, turning to us, whispered, 'I'll just ask him if he's the brother and if he lives here.' Clearing his throat a little, my dad then shouted out '*Vous êtes le frère? De Monsieur Durand? Vous habitez ici?*'

The man looked back at us blankly. '*Non,*' he said and then turned and looked off in the direction of the cows.

My father, momentarily flummoxed, turned back to us and whispered, 'He said no, he's not.'

'Yes, I gathered that,' my mother whispered back. 'Ask him what he wants.'

'*Monsieur!*' shouted out my father again. '*Qu'est-ce que vous voulez?*'

The man looked back. '*Rien,*' he said and then slunk off across the front courtyard and disappeared into an outhouse.

'I told you he was a weirdo,' I said, poking my head between my parents.

'Maybe he's a friend of the brother?' suggested Dad. 'Perhaps he's come to borrow a hoe or something?'

'I don't like this, Tony,' said my mother, pulling us all back inside and shutting the door. 'I don't like it one bit. People can't just come in and wander about as they please. And what about that locked door? Just because we can't open it, it doesn't mean the brother can't open it. He could come in during the night. What's to stop him doing that?'

'All right,' said my dad, holding up a calming hand. 'I'll move those leather chairs and push them up against the locked door. What a start to the holiday, I don't know…' And with one very sorry sigh, he trailed off.

The noise started as soon as we'd gone to bed. *Tkk tkk tkk tkk tkk tkk tkk bonk, tkk tkk tkk tkk tkk tkk tkk bonk.* Something was on the roof. With the wooden shutters on the windows closed, my bedroom was a black so deep and complete that I couldn't even see my hand in front of my face. In the pitch darkness the noise was exaggerated and startling. *Tkk tkk tkk tkk tkk tkk bonk!* I was already having trouble sleeping because the mattress on my bed was so uncomfortable: every time I moved it gave out arthritic groans and felt so filled with lumps and bumps that it was like trying to sleep on a sack of turnips. My parents, who were in the room on the ground floor, were having an even worse night of it. Not only were they having to put up with the sporadic and mysterious *tkk tkk tkk tkk tkk tkk tkk bonk*, but they were also battling with a strange fizz emanating from the fridge and a puzzling crackle popping from the turned-off television set. 'But it's turned OFF, Tony,' I kept hearing my mother complaining. 'How can a television make a noise when it's turned OFF?'

The *tkk tkk tkk tkk tkk bonk* was relentless. Worse still, there was no discernible pattern to it, which meant I lay awake waiting for it to sound again. Occasionally, there was a lull in the proceedings and I would heave a sigh, decide that, perhaps, that was that, allow myself to attempt a shabby but none-the-less welcome drift back into sleep only to be spiked awake by another rattling *bonk*! 'Can you hear that noise?' asked my dad, poking his head round my door. 'Can you hear it up here?'

'Yes,' I said, face glued to my pillow in eternal hope. 'What is it?'

'I don't know,' said Dad. 'Can I borrow your lightsaber?'

I got out of bed and felt around in the dark. I had placed it immediately under the bed but, because it had rolled a little towards the centre, I had to get down on my knees and reach. Finding the handle, I pulled it towards me and flicked it on. I gasped a little: in the treacle-black of the bedroom, my lightsaber looked magnificent.

I had never seen it burn so sharp or so brilliant. Taking the lightsaber from me, my father unlatched the shutters, opened the window and, leaning out as far as he dared, tried to stare up at the roof. 'Can't see anything,' he said with a grimace. Below him, suddenly, there was the sound of rushed steps on gravel. 'What the...?' said my dad, turning round sharply, but he was too late. Whoever or whatever it was had gone. 'Right,' he said, shutting the window back up with some force. 'That's it. We're all sleeping in the same room from now on.'

There were three in the bed and the little one said, 'Why do I have to go in the middle?' No one replied. *Tkk tkk tkk tkk tkk tkk tkk bonk.*

We had not slept well. I had woken up with my father's elbow in my eye, my mother was complaining that her back might actually be broken and Dad had lain awake for most of the night with a log in his hand. We had wandered downstairs to find that the remaining, scattered ants had regrouped and were enjoying the croissants we had left out for breakfast. They had also, inexplicably, managed to get inside a jar of hot chocolate and, hell-bent on ruining anything we might be able to consume first thing in the morning, were making light work of a couple of peaches. As if that wasn't enough to contend with, there were now so many flies in the house that it was verging on a pestilence. I looked at my mother and gave serious thought to asking her whether this was what an authentic rustic experience holiday was supposed to be like but thought better of it. We would have plenty of time to turn on each other. I could wait.

'What are we going to eat for breakfast?' asked Brenda, carrying the blackened, crawling croissants at arm's length in the direction of a bin.

'The nearest shops are seven miles away,' commented Tony, scratching at his leg. 'I could always go out and see if I can find some mushrooms. Have a look round the fields. Probably be loads.'

'Are you sure about picking mushrooms?' asked my mother, throwing my dad a small frown. 'How will you know if they're edible?'

'I've picked mushrooms loads of times!' protested my father. 'Back in Wales.'

'But Welsh mushrooms are less exotic than French mushrooms,' argued Mum, brushing a fly out of her nostril. 'Although I *am* starving. Well, if you're sure. Just don't pick anything poisonous. In fact, we'll all go. That way I can keep an eye on things.'

The field immediately opposite rolled away from the house down towards the edge of a brook lined with beech trees. It was still early and the dew had made the hedgerows a glistening mass of spiders' webs. Towards the bottom of the field there was a donkey who displayed no interest in us whatsoever and off in the distance we could just make out the hazy outline of the Puy Mary, the tallest peak in the region's volcanic park. The mushrooms were plentiful and my job was to tag behind my parents with a tea towel and collect everything picked. We had found a mass of mushrooms growing at the bases of the beech trees, thick stalks with round caps the colour of just-baked bread. Dad had brought a knife with him and, cutting one of the mushrooms lengthways, he said, 'There you go,', showing my mother and me the dissected mushroom in the flat of his hand. 'All white on the inside, top's a bit spongy, looks like a bun. That's a cep. Totally edible.'

'I'm impressed,' said my mother. 'Look at us!' she added, 'Living the wild life! It's good, isn't it?'

'Hang on,' said my dad, sweeping away an area of long-dried leaves. 'What's this?' Poking up through the vegetation was the biggest mushroom I'd ever seen. A pale, velvety cap that must have been ten inches across sitting on a blood-red stalk. The underside of the mushroom was a deep crimson and there was a faint odour coming off it that wasn't altogether pleasant. 'Sometimes,' said my dad, cutting through the base with his knife, 'the ones that look like they're going to kill you are perfectly all right and vice versa. In fact, the most danger-ous mushroom in the world looks totally harmless.'

'Are you quite sure, Tony?' asked Brenda, squinting at it in the tea towel. 'It's red and it smells bad. It smells like a dead crow. What are you saying? It's teasing us?'

'I bet you that mushroom is completely delicious,' said my dad, waving his knife in its direction. 'I'll bet you a quid.'

'Tony,' said my mother, pursing her lips. 'This isn't a mushroom version of Russian roulette. Put it back, please. Just leave it here.'

'You're being panicky,' said my father. 'It'll be fine.'

Before a full-blown fungus-based argument could take flight, a gentle tinkling of bells began to cascade down from the top of the field. Looking up, I could see a herd of large, red-brown cows with enormous Viking-style horns sloping down towards us. With them was a woman, stocky, pink-cheeked, with big arms and wearing a wrap-around apron and Wellingtons. She was carrying a long wooden staff in one hand and a bucket in the other. Seeing us, she called out in thick, impenetrable French. 'Come on,' said my mother, 'we better go. She's probably telling us to piss off out the field. These are probably her mushrooms.' But the woman was smiling and it became clear as she waved at us and pointed towards the cows, specifically their udders, that she wanted us to meet her herd.

They were Salers cows, common to the Auvergne, and as we strolled up the field towards them, my mother, as ever, decided to regale me with some cow-based facts. 'Did you know a cow has four stomachs?' she told me. 'And in India, cows are treated better than people. They think they're really holy. They can do what they like.'

'Actually,' said my dad, tossing a mushroom into the air and catching it. 'It's not true that cows have four stomachs. They have one stomach with four compartments.'

'And technically, only a female cow is a cow,' ploughed on Brenda, ignoring that last remark. 'The males should be called bulls.'

My father, I noticed, then mouthed the phrase, 'males should be called bulls' while pulling a face at my mother behind her back.

The woman, who was nodding at us and growling something along the lines of '*Bonjour*', was already hunched down by a set of udders. She was using her staff for balance while tugging away with her right hand, the steady jet of milk splashing into the tin bucket. She talked at us in a continual stream of chatter that, to my ear, just sounded like a cross between a broken engine and several pairs of shoes in a tumble drier. Still, it was wonderful to be watching a cow actually being milked. Seeing that I was fascinated, she beckoned me to come and have a go. I knelt down, the still dewy grass wet through my trousers, and reached for the udder nearest to me.

'Go on, Em,' said Dad, who was standing behind me. 'Give it a squeeze. Don't yank it. Just squeeze it.' At first, nothing came out and, as I squeezed hopelessly on the soft, leathery udder, I felt a little frustrated. The woman had managed to fill quarter of a bucket in no time and here I was, struggling to get even a drop but then, without warning, a splash of milk shot out between my fingers. I turned and grinned at everyone. It felt amazing. The woman let me carry on milking for a few more minutes and then, tapping me on the shoulder, stopped me and reached for the bucket. She lifted the bucket to her lips, took a swig and then passed it to me, gesturing at me to drink. Not wanting to be impolite, I lifted the bucket to my lips. The tin rim was a bit muddy and smelt like cheese that had gone off. I didn't really like milk: I had been forced to drink it at school every day at 10.30 when a crate would be brought round and we'd all have to stand, sharp little blue straws pierced through the lids and sucked till the bottle was dry. Without fail, I was always the last man standing. The milk from the bucket was thick and warm, much warmer than I was expecting, and as I swallowed I had to struggle not to yak it back out my nostrils.

'Hang on. Is that unpasteurised milk?' asked my mother, staring into the bucket. 'Should you be drinking that?'

'What?' I asked, rubbing the residue away from my mouth as fast as I could.

My mother looked at me. 'Never mind,' she said with a shake of her head. 'I'm sure you'll be fine.'

I had wandered back to the house listening to my parents bickering in front of me and wondering what my mother had meant. What was unpasteurised milk? And why was it bad for you? I had inadvertently had a bigger swig of milk than I had intended, but it was impossible not to, given that I was drinking from a bucket. 'Right!' snapped my mother as we came in through the front door. 'I am positive that I saw a book in the bedroom that had a mushroom on the cover. Emma, go in the downstairs bedroom and have a look for it, will you? There's a line of books in the alcove.' I did as I was told. When my parents were on the cusp of a full-blown row it was best to keep my head down. She was right. Third book along: *Champignons de France* with a cover illustration of a map of France with various mushrooms dotted all over it. There was a lot resting on this. Whoever had got it wrong about that large red mushroom was going to be in miserable torment for the rest of the day. I handed it to my mother, who, sitting forcibly down on the bench at the dining room table, opened it with a flourish. 'There!' she declared after a ten-minute scan. 'That's it there! *Cèpe Diabolique! Satanus Boletus!* Well that does it. I was right. It's clearly poisonous.'

'It doesn't say it's poisonous!' cried out my dad, grabbing the book and looking at it. 'Where does it say you can't eat it? Nowhere!'

'Tony,' shouted my mother with a sense of the triumphant. 'I might be going out on a limb here but anything that's got the word Satan in its name isn't going to be harmless! Look! It's called *Cèpe Diabolique*! It's literally a diabolical mushroom.'

'There's that man again!' I cried out, noticing the strange man from the night before slinking past our front window.

'Right,' said my dad, who needed to vent his anger on something. 'I've had enough of this.'

'Be careful, Tony!' called out my mother. 'He might be a mad man!' But it was too late. My father had left the building. He was gone for twenty minutes. Mum and I sat on the trestle bench with our arms round each other. Argument or no argument, we both still liked Dad more than a strange man with a hollowed-in face so when he returned there was a palpable sense of relief. 'What happened?' asked my mother urgently. 'Did you talk to him?'

'I couldn't find him,' muttered my father, looking down and scowling. 'He just vanished.'

'Strange men, weird noises, mushrooms made by Satan...what IS this place?' wailed my mother.

'And that woman with the scythe,' I added. 'Don't forget her.' So we all sat and thought about that. And then sort of wished we hadn't.

*

By nightfall we were in a state. Brenda had convinced herself that the man we kept seeing was a malignant spirit who had been killed and eaten by the villagers and that, if we didn't keep our wits about us, then we were all going the same way. 'Don't be ridiculous,' said my father. 'There's no such thing as ghosts and the French aren't cannibals.'

'But they eat horses,' I said, because I was inclined to believe my mother. 'And rabbits.'

'They're insatiable when it comes to meat, Tony,' reasoned my mother. 'And who knows? It's like tigers. Once they've got a taste for man flesh they can't get enough of it.'

'Right,' said my father, standing up and holding out his hand. 'That's enough! Stop it, Brenda! You're just giving everyone the heebie-jeebies. We are not being haunted by a man who was eaten by his neighbours and neither are his neighbours trying to eat us!'

Scraaaaape. Scraaaaaaaape. The grinding, metallic moan began again. 'Oh Jesus,' whispered my mother, grabbing my hand. 'Jesus, Mary and Joseph.'

'What is that noise?' I asked, looking up at my father.

'Don't go out there, Tony!' yelled my mother, as Dad walked towards the door. 'That's the first rule of horror films! Don't split up. And don't go outside! The first person who goes outside always gets killed!'

My dad, rubbing a hand down his face, turned and looked at us. 'Brenda,' he began, with a weary sigh. 'There will be a perfectly logical explanation for that noise. There will be an explanation for the sound on the roof. There will also be an explanation for the man who seems to want to wander around this house at all hours of the night and day. Let's all stay calm.'

Scrrraaaaaaape.

'Please don't go outside, Daddy,' I said in a dread hush. The combination of strange surroundings, the slightly timeless nature of the village and the lack of sleep had nurtured a micro-climate of panic. We were terrified.

The scraping, sounding increasingly like the sharpening of the largest knife known to man, had thankfully diminished, only to be replaced as the sun tucked itself behind the hills with our old friend the *tkk tkk tkk tkk tkk tkk tkk bonk!* As we lay, squashed together in the upstairs bedroom, our imaginations were running riot. 'Do you think someone's on the roof?' whispered Brenda, staring up at the ceiling.

'No, Brenda,' said Tony, trying to keep his sanity. 'Unless it's the tiniest man known to living science. It'll be an animal, like a rat. In fact, I'm going to put a stop to this. Pass me your lightsaber, Emma, and turn the lamp off. I'm going to have another look.'

For the second time my father approached the shuttered windows. Very gently and quietly, he pulled them open and with the softest of touches, pushed open the windows. *Tkk tkk tkk tkk tkk tkk bonk!* Grabbing hold of the windowframe, he turned so that he could sit on the windowledge, legs facing into the room, and lean back so as to get a good look at the roof. My mother, concerned that he was going to hurt himself, held on to his legs and said, 'Don't fall out, Tony. If you do, I'll kill you.' I remained in the centre of the bed, clutching on to the blankets. My lightsaber fizzed into action.

'Still can't see anything,' whispered Dad, his face drifting in and out of the red light. 'Wait a minute! Something's moving...what the? Jesus!'

Something darted across the beam of light. Whatever it was, it was now in the room and moving fast. My mother, feeling something spit past her, decided that now was as good a time as any to start screaming. Dad had jumped back off the windowledge into the room and was desperately swinging the lightsaber around in order to catch a glimpse of whatever it was. 'Put the light on!' he yelled in my direction. 'Put the light on!'

Terrified, I reached over to the lamp and found its switch. I was also now screaming and, as the light snapped on and my father shouted, 'It's a bat! It's a bloody bat!', my mother and I screamed again and continued to scream as my father, using the lightsaber, tried to chase it out the window. The bat darted and swerved, every twist met with another fresh scream from either me or Mum, who was now running round the room in a bent-over hunch with both her arms over her head. My father, both hands on the lightsaber, was swiping at the air, ducking and spinning in turns, desperate to get the bat out of the room. I stared at him, glued into this unfolding horror, and realised what my father had to do.

'Use the Force, Dad!' I yelled. 'Use the Force!' The bat, flapping its blackened wings, dived, just skimming the surface of the bed, rose, circled the top of the room and then, as my father made one enormous sweep into the air, shot, like a bullet from a gun, out the open window. It was over. My father ran to the shutters and slammed them shut. My mother was on her knees and panting. I was peering over the top of the blankets. 'Do you know what, Dad?' I said, as my parents both got back into bed. 'You ARE the Master.'

'Thanks,' said my dad, hitting his pillow with his hand. 'Now let's just try and get some sleep.'

But we couldn't. The footsteps were back.

Another night lying awake in abject terror had not helped matters. Forbidden from investigating the strange footsteps, my father had lain, both eyes open and unblinking, acutely attuned to every bump, scuff and groan that the night had to offer. By dawn, he was mentally and emotionally exhausted. I had managed to get a few hours' sleep but had woken with severe lower abdominal pain, for which I almost certainly had the *lait cru* to blame. As a result, I was grumbling and unresponsive. My mother, whose fervour for the 'authentic rustic experience' was waning with every passing minute, was also feeling unwell: her period had started and so, giving Tony something of a shove, she demanded that we drive to the nearest pharmacy and get painkillers for her and milk of magnesia for me. My mother's periods were always a family affair in our household and we seemed to be either preparing for it ('Don't do that, my period is due!'), dealing with it ('Don't annoy me, I've got my period!'), or coping with the aftermath ('I can't lift anything, I've just finished my period!'). What this meant was that my mother was totally period-free for only two days every month. In the 1970s, feminine hygiene was a lumpy affair. I wasn't even aware that tampons existed: my mother didn't trust them and so my abiding memory of what it meant to be a woman was of sanitary towels the size of small bricks with loops at the ends that had to be attached to pants with safety pins. This was what I had to look forward to. The reason I mention this is because it always fell to either me or my father to carry them. My mother, who never had a handbag, seemed to own clothes that were constantly devoid of pockets and so her sanitary towels were forever being foisted on us. 'Here,' she said, handing my father a fat, white rectangle as we climbed into Bessy. 'Take this.' Without a second thought, he took it, folded it in half and shoved it into the back pocket of his jeans. I glanced at him in the rear view mirror and was almost shocked by how tired he looked. But I had more pressing problems to deal with. My lower abdominal pain was getting worse.

The nearest village with a pharmacy was a twenty-minute drive. Perched on the edge of a large volcanic lake, it was a dark, gloomy place, the ambience not improved by a thick-set fog that seemed to have come from nowhere. It was an odd place: the deserted streets, the narrow, granite houses pressed together in oppressive proximity and the crumbling turreted towers. 'Do you know,' said my mother, looking around her as we trudged our way upwards, 'I wouldn't bat an eyelid if Dracula came running out. This is like walking round the set of a 1930s horror film.'

'Please stop going on about horror films,' muttered my father, who was almost cross-eyed he was so shattered.

'*Apothecarie*,' said my mother, pointing towards a small shop front and reading its sign. 'There we go. Hang on a minute. What the hell is that?' Sitting in the front window was a large glass bottle in the shape of a decanter, inside of which was a massive, coiled snake in liquid. Next to it was a faded newspaper article in a frame that read '*L'Eau de Vie de Serpent*'. We all stared at it. 'Do you think they drink that?' asked my mother, gesturing towards the grim, yellowish waters. 'God, this place is weird.' She pushed open the door and a small, tinny bell jangled above us. The shop was as dismal as the day and looked as if all it sold over the counter was melancholy and evil. Every corner was a deep molasses of dark brown clutter: indiscriminate boxes and bottles covered with a thick film of dust. The shopkeeper, who had the aura of an old gardening glove, was standing behind a grey counter, a pair of scales in front of him, on to which he was measuring out an unidentifiable black shredded mass.

'*Bonjour monsieur*,' said my father, clearing his throat for the ordeal to come. '*Je voudrais le medicine pour le mal tête et le mal...what's stomach? Le mal gastronomique. La burble burble burble!* Oooh. Pain. Here.'

The man, who was wearing half-moon spectacles, stared over them and, without speaking, reached underneath the counter to produce a small, grey box and a blue tinted bottle. '*Dix-huit francs*,' he rattled in a voice that sounded as if it was coming from under water.

'Sorry,' said Dad, leaning forward, '*Dix* what? What was it?'

'*Huit*,' burbled the shopkeeper again. '*Dix-huit.*'

My father, who was so tired his brain had switched everything off except the one small standard lamp that kept him upright, swayed a little on the spot and heaved a terrible sigh. 'Sorry,' he repeated, closing his eyes and trying to think. 'And *dix-huit* is...ummm.'

'Eighteen,' said the shopkeeper with utter disdain.

'Yes. Eighteeen. *Dix-huit*. Yes,' retorted my father, reaching into his back pocket for his wallet. 'Yes. I knew that. I just...'

The shopkeeper was now looking at my father as if he were a dreadful smell. But then, he did have good reason. 'Dad,' I said quietly, putting a hand on my father's forearm. 'You're trying to pay with Mum's sanitary towel.'

My poor father, in his near-comatose state, had inadvertently pulled out my mother's hefty cotton sanitary towel and, without looking down, had tried to thumb through it looking for money. My dad stared down into his hands and swallowed. '*C'est pour ma femme*,' he whispered, head hanging low on to his chest. '*Pour ma femme.*'

I don't think we'd ever left a shop quicker.

I was feeling wretched. My guts were on fire and a cold, clammy sweat had begun to gather at my hairline. Deep, stabbing cramps churned through my abdomen, leaving me dizzy and breathless. It would be twenty minutes before we were back at the house and I had an awful truth to face: I wasn't going to make it. 'Mum,' I said, 'I really need to go to the toilet.'

'Can you hang on?' she asked, turning to look at my ever-greying face. 'We're not far now. Only about ten minutes.'

I shook my head. Ten minutes may as well have been ten hours. I was at the point of explosive no return. 'Seriously,' I said, eyes tightening with the pain. 'I need to go now. Like right now. Dad, stop the car. I mean it.'

Sadly, my father, who was still reliving the awful, ghastly moment with the shopkeeper, had failed to hear me. The roads up through the hills of the Auvergne were crater-filled and winding and, as we came round a particularly sharp bend, we hit a sizeable pothole that sent a sudden, violent jolt through the car. The effect on my bowel was catastrophic: with no power left in me to hold back the inevitable tide of effluent waiting to burst its banks, I filled my shorts. The stench was immediate and malevolent. Having not soiled myself since I was a baby, and old enough to feel the embrace of shame, I burst into tears. The sensation was horrendous, like sitting in pants made of thick, warm soup. If this was an authentic rustic experience then my mother could shove it where the sun had no hope of shining. I was upset, angry and despairing and, worst of all, I knew there was more coming. 'Stop the car!' I shouted, thumping at my dad's shoulder. 'I've got to get out!'

'God!' said my mother suddenly. 'What's that smell? It's AWFUL!'

'It's me!' I wailed. 'Please let me out! I've got to get out!'

Dad, jolted from his stupor, swerved the car on to a grass verge. I had already got the door open and, as Bessy came to a halt, I leapt out, slumped into a crouching position and, still crying, entered into a pit of degradation that no one should have to endure. 'Oh, you poor thing,' I could hear my mother saying as she got out of the car to see what she could do. There was very little she could do. Hot liquid shit was jetting out of me in considerable volumes and I was smothered in my own muck. It was like waiting for an oil rig to stop blowing. Mentally, I had journeyed to a place that was past caring. I was in so much pain I didn't care that my father was having to scrape me down with dock leaves, nor that my shorts and pants were being removed with the end of a long stick to be thrown behind a bush, nor that my left shoe, which had sadly borne the brunt of one particularly voluminous emission, was being dangled into a nearby brook in an attempt to save it from an otherwise inevitable demise. All I could do was lie on the floor and gently weep. This was my holiday: a time for recreation and fun, a time of peaceful rest and relaxation. Not for us, it wasn't. Our holidays were a hand-picked tour of anguish and torment. I hated holidays. Hated them. And as far as I was concerned, it was all my parents' fault.

'Are you all right now?' asked my mother, wrapping my father's T-shirt round my waist.

I only had one thing to say. I didn't look at her. 'I hate you,' I whispered. And I meant it.

Everyone was in a stinking mood. I hated everybody and everything, my mother was sick of it always being her fault and my father had entered into a zombie-like state from which there was little hope of recovering. None of us were speaking so we'd all gone to bed early, crammed into the upstairs bed in grumbling proximity. The house was awash with aches and pains: the creaks, groans and bonks had begun their night-time refrain, keeping us wide-eyed and twitchy and, to add to the nocturnal wailings, a wind had picked up. We had left the shutters open, at my father's insistence, because the pitch black of the room was more than he could cope with, and, with a full moon casting a considerable light on the front of the house, he was determined to solve the mystery of the late-night footsteps once and for all.

With the entire contents of my lower bowel scattered to the winds, I was feeling a lot better. Even so, the tension, as we lay in bed waiting for the inevitable crunch of foot on gravel, was insufferable. We had seen the mysterious wandering man earlier in the evening standing on a grass verge staring at a pile of logs. As we drove past him, there had not been the slightest flicker acknowledging our presence. It was as if he was in a catatonic reverie, preoccupied with wooden swirls. My mother had shivered. 'Ugh,' she had said, glancing back at him over her shoulder. 'He just gives me the creeps.'

I lay on my back, staring up at the ceiling, the wind outside moaning through the trees. I turned my head to have a quick look at both my parents: Mum was lying on her side, her head facing away from me, but Dad was awake, slightly sitting and staring up into the upper right-hand corner of the room. Something about him looked deeply troubled, as if he couldn't quite believe what he was seeing. I followed his gaze and peered across the moonlit room to the point in the ceiling that was causing such consternation. It was moving. The ceiling was moving. Dad, eyes rigid with fear, slowly leant over me and nudged my mother in the shoulder. 'What?' she mumbled, refusing to turn over.

'Brenda,' said my Dad in an urgent hush, 'the ceiling is pulsating. It's bloody moving.'

'Don't be ridiculous,' she muttered, lifting her head off the pillow. 'Where?'

'Up there,' I chipped in. 'In the corner. It is. It's breathing in and out.'

My mother sat upright and followed my pointing finger. The ceiling was throbbing. Actually throbbing, pulsing in and out as if it was a living organ. It was the single most terrifying thing I had ever seen. 'Jesus Christ!' exclaimed my mother, sitting bolt upright. 'The house is possessed! Possessed!'

I was so frightened that I gave serious thought to wetting myself but, given that I had spent the lion's share of the afternoon already excreting bodily matter in inappropriate places, I managed to hold it in and vented my terror with a rib-cracking scream instead. My parents, edgy and petrified, were visibly shaken. My mother, an ex-Catholic, had pulled the bedding up to her eyes and was whimpering something about Satan and being sorry. My father, on the verge of tears he was so tired and perplexed, had got out of bed and started shouting, 'Come on then!' in the direction of the pumping ceiling. To add to our woes, my mother then heard the telltale sounds of someone, or something, on the gravel below the window.

'Footsteps!' she wailed, hot tears pumping down her cheeks. 'I can hear footsteps. Oh God! Oh God! Help us! We're all going to die!'

My father, who was now in a full fright and flight tailspin, took the log he'd brought to bed with him and threw it in the direction of the pulsating ceiling. There was a tearing noise and a loud clatter as the log fell to the floor. Outside, startled by the cacophony of woes coming from our room, the footsteps scuffed and quickened. My father ran to the window and stared out into the moonlight. 'It's the donkey!' he yelled, turning to us, half-laughing and half-crying. 'The donkey! It's the donkey! Oh, thank you. Thank you! It's the donkey! The donkey from the field!'

'And look!' yelled my mother, pointing at the ceiling, which was now flapping rather than pumping. 'It was plastic! It was a plastic sheet!'

'It must have been the wind!' shouted my father, who had crumpled to the floor like a broken wheel. All three of us were in tears: we were exhausted, relieved and spent. We had wrung ourselves dry and we had only ourselves to blame.

It had all been too much. Spooked by nothing more than our own vivid imaginations, the following morning we decided to call time on our authentic rustic experience and head for home. There had been no brother, the man who wandered about the village was harmless, the footsteps had been made by the donkey and the *tkk tkk tkk tkk tkk bonk* was the sound made by tiny bits of roof tiles crumbling to the floor. Only one mystery remained unsolved: the strange metallic scraping that echoed across the house. We had packed Bessy in silence. Even though we knew that our terror had been entirely self-induced, the house still generated an uncomfortable, back-of-the-neck tingle: we were desperate to get away. As Dad threw in the last of our bags, the familiar and as yet unidentified scraping began again. 'What *is* that?' asked my mother, getting into the front of the Land Rover. 'It's coming from over there. Behind the trees. From the village.'

Dad shook his head. 'I don't care. I don't want to know.'

'For me,' said Mum, putting a hand on his forearm. 'Please. I just want to know what it is.'

The three of us walked up to the top of the driveway and turned left, drifting towards the noise ahead of us. The scraping was rhythmic and unsettling and even though we were sure there was a perfectly innocent explanation, there was an air of dread as we approached the blind corner in the road ahead of us. Apprehensive, I slipped my hand into my father's. We had instinctively arranged ourselves into a tight bundle and, as we came to the point of no return, we huddled to the edge of the corner and peeped round it. There, in front of us, was a group of six people, all of whom were disabled and one of whom was a woman holding herself up on a metal frame. She was wearing massive leather boots which appeared to have horseshoes attached to the bottom. As she pulled herself forward, the metal at the bottom of her shoes was grinding over the tarmac of the road. We had our answer. 'That's it,' said my father, pushing us all back down towards the Land Rover. 'Seen enough. Let's go.'

'I don't think we'll come to France again next year,' said my mother as we sped out of the village.

And for the first time that holiday, we all had something to cheer about.

Chapter Nine

A Taste of Misadventure

The despair had been total. 'Noooooooooooo!' I had wailed, throwing myself face-down on to the floor. 'Noooooooooooo! It's not true! It's not true!'

But it *was* true. Donny Osmond had got married. My life was now officially over. There was only one thing to be done: prostrate myself in front of the record player in the sitting room, play 'Love Me for a Reason' over and over again while gently weeping into the crook of my elbow, cling to the record sleeve and softly moan, 'Donny, oh Donny'. My heart had been shattered.

'Is there any chance you might play a different song?' asked my dad, poking his head round the door with a pained expression on his face. 'You've been playing that one for two hours. What about "Crazy Horses"? That's got a bit of kick to it.'

'Leave me ALONNNNNNNE!' I cried, just managing to lift my head off the carpet. 'You don't UNDERSTANNNND!'

My father had stared at me, shrugged and dispatched the cavalry in the shape of my mother armed with a coconut snowball on a saucer. 'But you couldn't have married Donny Osmond,' said my mother, her arm round me. 'You're only eleven. And he's a Mormon. And I know he's got lovely teeth and wears nice hats but think about it. You'd have to spend Christmas with Jimmy Osmond. And no one wants that.'

It had been an emotional start to the summer. I was leaving my junior school for the last time and had no real sense of what that meant. The boys I'd grown up with would be gone, dispatched to the boys' school, where we wouldn't see them again until we were sixteen and bumping into each other at village discos, feeling awkward. At the beginning of that summer everything felt uncertain and unknown: I would go from being in the oldest year at school to the youngest, to having to wear a uniform, to homework and pecking orders. As I left the gates of my junior school for the last time, I had no idea of what was awaiting me, other than the annual hell of another family holiday. One thing, however, was certain: we weren't going to France. Even my mother, who had a tendency to conveniently forget the events of every preceding summer, had been forced to concede that perhaps it was time for a change. My father, delighted at the very prospect of not having to return to the country that had been his *bête noire*, was in ecstatic mood.

'What about one of the British islands?' he had enthused, pulling down his atlas and flicking to the relevant page. 'There's loads of them. Look. Isle of Man. Guernsey. Jersey. Sark. Skye. Hebrides. Tons to choose from.'

'What about the Isle of Wight?' said Mum, tapping the diamond-shaped island just off the south coast. 'Not too far, big enough to give us plenty to do. And they've got that boat race. The one that's fun to watch.'

'Cowes,' said Dad, nodding.

'They've got cows in boats?' I asked. 'How do they manage that?'

'No,' said Dad, smiling and giving me a small shove.

'That's the town name. It's called Cowes. With an E on the end. There, look.'

I peered over my mother's shoulder to have a look at the map. There it was: the Isle of Wight and its town called Cowes. 'Will it be better than France, Dad?' I asked, because I remained to be convinced that any holiday was worth going on.

'Of course it will be,' nodded Dad. 'Everyone speaks English for a start.'

'Good,' said my mother with a definitive nod. 'Well that's that sorted. The Isle of Wight, it is!'

The Red Funnel ferry from Southampton was a smaller affair than the cross-channel ships we'd been used to; with its flat bed and basic amenities, it was a functional vessel with modest aspirations. There would be no fancy smorgasbord this trip, but it was no matter: it was a beautiful day and, as the ferry slid its way down the Solent Estuary, we sat on a metal bench eating homemade cheese sandwiches wrapped in wax paper. Sometimes, simple things bring simple pleasures and it was as pleasant a lunch as I could remember. The western side of the estuary was dominated by the Fawley Oil Refinery, a growling industrial monster, spewing out smoke, spawning oil tanks and rising up from an intricate network of massive iron pipes and chimneys. It was a significant eyesore along a coast that would otherwise be dominated by nothing more imposing than salt marshes and charming villages. At the mouth of Southampton Water there was a spit, roughly a mile long, at the end of which was Calshot Castle, a squat, rotund structure that had once operated as a fort guarding the waters to Southampton. Perched at the end of the long line of shingle, it had the forlorn aspect of a redundant building: once filled with masculine purpose, now reduced to endless afternoons of tea and scones. As we crossed into the Solent to make the three-mile crossing to East Cowes, I hung on to the ferry railings and marvelled at the swarms of yachts skimming the waters. Suddenly, with the sun shining and multi-coloured sails all around us, it felt as if we were going somewhere buzzing and exotic. I turned and grinned at my parents. They grinned back. 'Look at all the boats!' I said, pointing.

'Good, isn't it?' said Dad, folding his arms with the certainty of a man who knew he was about to be proved right.

'So the Isle of Wight,' began my mother, joining me at the railing, 'was where Queen Victoria used to come for her holidays. And Alfred Lord Tennyson came here as well. He was a poet. Wrote "The Lady of Shallot". And Charles Dickens used to visit. Can you remember what he wrote?'

'*Oliver Twist*,' I said, resting my chin on the back of my hands.

'That's right,' nodded my mother. 'And when you were little, just after you were born, they had some massive music festivals here and Jimi Hendrix played. Just before he died. In fact, I think it was his last concert. Is that right, Tony? Wasn't the Isle of Wight Festival the last time Jimi Hendrix played in public?'

'Don't know,' said Dad, who was now feeling so confident, he'd actually put on some sunglasses. 'Never liked him anyway.'

'Useless,' muttered my mother with a tut. 'Your father has no musical taste whatsoever.'

'I do!' he protested from behind us. 'I like Max Boyce. He's brilliant. Better than that Bob Dylan rubbish you're always listening to. Can't stand him. He just sounds like he needs to blow his nose.'

We were staying on a farm campsite towards the middle of the island. The tent, having not had an airing the previous summer, smelt like compost and the bucket, which had also sat grumbling in a dark corner of the garage with its lid on, was ready to exact a stinking revenge so odious it was like having the insides of your nostrils stripped bare with ammonium. 'Ohhhhh!' cried out my mother, as she took the top off the bucket and was smashed in the face with an eruption of stench.

'Errrrrrrrrr!' I wailed, grabbing my nose to block out the offensive stink.

'Bloody hell!' exclaimed my father, who made a valiant attempt to waft the odour away with a hand.

'Ohhhh!' repeated my mother, scrabbling to get out of the tent. 'That is the smell of despair! Oh, Tony! Do something! We can't live with that! It's toxic!'

'Maybe if I give it a wash out,' said my dad, picking up the bucket at arm's length. 'Keep the lid off for a bit. It might settle down. I can ask the camp owner if he's got any disinfectant.'

'Ask him for sheep dip or something!' yelled my mother, clutching her nose with both hands. 'Proper industrial strength! Ohhh! Emma! Cover your face! Cover it! That smell could melt flesh!'

The bucket had somehow gone into storage not quite empty and had, over the course of two years, been quietly fermenting its own special brew. As smells go, it was the worse thing I'd ever had flood up my nostrils. It was so bad, I was surprised the area wasn't cordoned off by the military and declared unsafe for human habitation: that bucket could have closed the Isle of Wight for ever. Thankfully, Dad was able to lay his hands on a monster bottle of Dettol. He had wrapped a tea towel round his face to shield himself from the worst of the stinking ravages and, as we stood behind the Land Rover and watched from a distance, he poured the entire contents of the disinfectant bottle into the bucket and then slammed the lid back on in the hope that some sort of odour alchemy would weave its magic. It didn't. The stench was in for the long haul. We would just have to get used to it.

The campsite we were staying on had a cobbled-together air, as if it was an afterthought. The owner, who may have been a proper farmer at one point, now looked anything but: long hair, voluminous beard, crazy patchwork bell-bottoms and a knitted waistcoat over a bare and sunken chest. He was a by-product of the infamous Isle of Wight Festival of the late 1960s, during which a drug-induced frenzy had led him to a moment of epiphany from which he'd never quite recovered. He had wandered over to do little other than stare at us and nod his head a lot while sitting on the grass cross-legged and smoking. There was a powerful, sweet smell emanating from the cigarette he was puffing and, though I didn't know it at the time, he was clearly not enjoying the sole pleasures of tobacco. My father, a straight-up-and-down-ale man with an unhealthy regard for authority was disconcerted and so called a hasty family meeting in the inner tent. 'Why is that bloke sitting there and staring at us?' he whispered, jabbing an angry thumb over his shoulder. 'And he's smoking drugs, Brenda. Drugs! Do you think I should tell him to piss off?'

'He's the campsite owner, Tony,' said my mother. 'You can't tell him to piss off. And he's only having a smoke! So what? It's not harming anyone. He hasn't asked you to drop some acid. Just relax. He's harmless.'

'What's he smoking?' I asked, curiosity aroused.

'Never mind,' said Dad, clearly dissatisfied.

'Ugh,' said my mother and wafted a hand in front of her face. 'Let's go out. I can't stay in here. It bloody stinks.'

Driven from the campsite by a mutual revulsion for the bucket, Dad drove us to Alum Bay at the western point of the island with the sole intention of getting our holiday off to an impressive start. 'Who needs France?' he had declared. 'According to what I've heard, you'll never see anything more amazing!' There was always a danger that by overselling our first destination, we would be left with a feeling of inevitable disappointment and, as we wandered down to the bay, I couldn't help thinking that it was no different from any other English beach. The expanse of sand looked normal enough: the odd windbreak, the scattering of families, abandoned sandcastles and the occasional dead crab. So far, so indistinguishable, but it was the cliffs that were the scene stealers: layers of multi-coloured sand creeping upwards as if someone had stolen down one night and striped the place with food dye. Being the late 1970s, when children were constantly being warned about the dangers of throwing frisbees at electricity pylons and the government was hell-bent on making sure every adult knew that rugs on polished floors were death traps, it was baffling that not one warning sign was anywhere to be seen. It was like the Wailing Wall: children hunched up and scraping away, digging out the coloured sands and siphoning the grains into test tubes bought at the small visitor centre at the entrance to the bay. I was quite keen to fill my own test tube with layers of coloured sand but my mother, who had been raised in a bubble of permanent terror, forbade me from going anywhere near the cliff edge on the grounds that the entire rock face could shatter down at any moment. Instead, I was given fifty pence and told I could buy any sand-filled glass ornament as a memento. I chose a small sea horse. It didn't quite plaster up the hole of longing but was the best I was going to get.

'Hey look at that,' said my dad, pointing to a man sitting on a stool with a sign next to him. 'You can take a boat ride out to the Needles. That would be good, wouldn't it?'

'What are the Needles?' I asked my dad, holding my sea horse up to the sky to admire it.

'You can see them there,' he said, nodding in the direction of chalk stacks jutting in a line off the edge of the mainland. 'Over there, with the lighthouse at the end.'

'Why are they called Needles?' I asked, squinting through the sunshine. 'They look like big teeth. They don't look anything like needles.'

'That's because,' said my dad, with the satisfied grin of a man who'd read his guidebook, 'there used to be a needle-shaped chalk column in between the first stack and the second stack. But it collapsed into the sea. And because it looked like a needle, the name stuck. Anyway, do you fancy a boat trip out to look at them? I do.'

'Is it safe, Tony?' asked my mother with a sense of caution.

'Why shouldn't it be?' said Dad with a shrug. 'It's a lovely day. The sea's like a millpond. There are loads of yachts out. It'll be great. See them up close. Brilliant.'

'Yeah, I want to see the Needles,' I said, tucking my sea horse into my pocket. There were only so many times you could look at a bit of shaped glass filled with sand and I had discovered, within the space of five minutes, that saturation point for that particular thrill had already been exceeded. The prospect of actually bumping out over the sea and circumnavigating rocks was much more exciting.

My mother stared out at the sea and sighed. 'Well,' she began, shading her eyes with a hand so as to make a more informed and scientific decision, 'the water does look calm enough. Are there rocks under the water, though? We won't get run aground or anything?'

'Don't be ridiculous,' said my father, puffing out his cheeks.

'And I suppose he's used to driving out to them and back again. I suppose that's all he does. All right then,' said my mother with a reluctant smile. 'But only if we're all wearing life jackets.'

It was complicated from the get go. The man on the stool, it turned out, was merely a conduit for the gig itself. Having paid him the grand sum of two pounds fifty, we were given a piece of coloured paper which we were to present to 'a bloke called Dave' at the harbour in Cowes, who would then direct us to another fellow who actually owned the boat that would take us to the Needles. 'So there's no boat here then?' my mother kept saying, scanning the shoreline for available vessels. There was not. We had been booked on to the five o'clock boat trip, the last of the day and, given that it was just past half past four, we were going to have to get a move on if we were going to make it. My father, absolutely determined that we would be on that boat come hell or high water, sprinted off up the beach, shouting at us to get a move on. I scampered off after him but my mother, who was not blessed in the running department, was lagging behind, struggling through the thick sand. As I cast a glance back at her, she had the pained expression of someone close to collapse and so I ran back, got behind her and shoved. Nothing was going to stop us getting on to that boat.

Out of breath and panting, we had all leapt into Bessy. Dad, on the edge of his seat and leaning over the steering wheel, had screeched out of the car park. I was hanging on to the handrail in front of my seat and Mum, who was still exhausted from her sandy exertions, was slumped in front of me and sliding from left to right like a rag doll tossed on to a see-saw. 'This had better be worth it,' she wheezed, grabbing the door handle and pulling herself upright. 'I think one of my lungs may have exploded.'

Dad, determined that this holiday was going to exceed everyone's expectations, yelled, 'Of course it'll be worth it.

It'll be amazing! Get out of my way! Indicate! Indicate! Stupid idiot! Come on! Into fourth! Let's go!'

I'd never seen my dad like this: shouting at drivers, beeping the horn, cutting corners. This was the man who would mumble the Highway Code in his sleep, who thought nothing of wagging a finger at anyone driving faster than the speed limit. Yet here he was, flouting every known rule, in order to make a point: Britain was brilliant. As we screamed into Cowes Harbour, he was yelling at us to get out of the car before we'd even come to a stop. My mother and I, shocked into submission by this assertive yet desperate man, had jumped out and watched in silent awe as Dad ran helter-skelter shouting, 'Dave! Dave! I'm looking for a man called Dave!' while waving the coloured piece of paper we'd been given in the air.

Dave, it turned out, was surplus to requirements. As we had run past a line of boats, arms in the air and yelling, someone had shouted up at us. 'You want the boat to the Needles?'

Dad, sweating and wide-eyed, had turned on his heels and shouted back, 'Yes! The boat to the Needles! Yes!' A man wearing a battered blue hat had emerged from behind a massive wooden barrel. He had a beaten appearance about the face and a nose so red he could have pulled a sleigh. There was a squint to his eyes that gave him the permanent expression of a man just hit on the head and he was wearing a heavy knit jumper that was stained and full of holes. 'Over here!' he mumbled, gesturing towards a pon toon. 'This way!'

The boat was moored up at the end of a long wooden ramp that wasn't as sturdy as it might have been and my mother, feeling the structure wobble beneath her, grabbed my hand while shouting, 'There are life jackets? Yes? Life jackets to wear?'

The man jumped down into a long narrow boat with an outboard motor and two wooden benches opposite each other and held his hand out to help my mother into the boat, asking, 'Why? Do you want one?'

Brenda, who let out a small, girlish scream as she got into the boat, gathered herself, sat down quickly and, gripping the edge of the bench, said, 'Of course we want life jackets. Life jackets for all of us, please.'

'I'm all right,' said Dad, who was trying to be manly.

'For ALL of us, please,' repeated my mother, giving Tony a stern look. The life jackets were stowed in a metal box in the stern of the boat, tucked under a slatted seat next to the motor. The man, who smelt like seaweed, had pulled it out and tipped the contents out on to the bottom of the boat. I was passed the smallest life jacket from the pile and, as I slipped the heavy, orange waistcoat over my head, I was faintly revolted by a heavy smell of rotten fish. 'Umm,' said my mother, staring at the jacket she'd been handed. 'Sorry, but there appears to be something on this jacket. It looks like blood. Though I'm sure it isn't.'

'No, it is,' said the man with a shrug. 'I keep the fish bait in that box. It's probably guts or something. Just rub it off.' My mother stared upwards and said nothing, but instead allowed an intense grimace to dance on her lips before very slowly scraping the life jacket along the end of the bench to her left.

This was my first time in a small sea vessel and, apart from feeling a vague frisson of excitement, the overwhelming impression was that it stank. It was a combination of fish guts, mouldy seaweed and an undercurrent of non-specific organic matter that may have been left to fester under a damp cloth for anything up to two years. Thank God, then, that we were in the open air. Our skipper, a man not gifted in the art of gentle conversation, had muttered something about it being a bit choppy outside the harbour and then yanked the outboard motor into action. With an unpleasant and ugly sneeze, he then wiped his nose on the end of his sleeve before sitting down to cradle the tiller. 'Cast off,' he said to my dad, nodding towards a rope attached to a pole at the end of the pon toon. Dad started grinning and shot me the sort of beaming glance, eyebrows raised, that went hand in hand with being given a position of responsibility by any man in a hat. He was in his element. My mother, on the other hand, was not. Her left arm had been splattered with nasal juice and she was trying to work out a way of rubbing it off her as quickly as possible without losing her cool. I stared at her as she casually smeared her arm along the top rim of the boat, caught her eye and made a suitably disgusted face that involved turning the corners of my mouth down and sticking my tongue out. She ignored me.

Conditions for a short boat excursion seemed perfect – blue skies, settled waters – and as we pulled away from the pon toon there was no reason to believe that everything was about to go disastrously wrong. We had just passed through the harbour walls. I was staring up, looking at the people dotted along their length, fishing rods and crab lines in hand, buckets by their feet. I was feeling so dandy and on top of things that I threw some enthusiastic waves in their direction. One man in red shorts waved back. Before us were open waters, a few sailboats darting back and forth and, off in the far distance, a large tanker bound for the oil refinery. Above us gulls hung on unseen breezes. This was living. 'Isn't this great!' shouted Dad from his side of the boat. 'Do you think we'll see a seal? Or a shark?'

'Don't be silly,' Mum yelled back. 'We won't see a shark! You don't get sharks off the Isle of Wight!'

'No,' said our skipper, unexpectedly communicative. 'Fellah saw a shark off Yarmouth last week. Don't know what sort of shark, mind. But he saw it.'

'Duuuuh duh, duuuuh duh, duh duh duh duh duh!' sang Dad, mimicking the seminal *Jaws* theme tune. 'And you thought it was safe to go in the water!'

My mother glared at him and then turned to me. 'Don't trail your hand in the water, Emma. Just in case, please.'

'But...' I protested.

'Arm inside, please,' she added, tapping the top of the boat.

Behind us there was a sudden small bang. Startled, we all turned to see a thin plume of black smoke wafting up from the outboard motor. The boat came to a bobbing halt. My mother, watching the smoke snaking a dirty line skywards, was the first to speak. 'Why did it do that?' she asked, tying up the cords on her life jacket. 'Is it broken? Hang on. Is there fuel in that that can explode?'

'Ssssh,' said my father, because that was all he was able to proffer.

'No, seriously,' pressed on my mother. 'What if it explodes? I mean it is full of petrol. And it's smoking.'

'Brenda!' said my dad with a firm tone. 'Just let the man have a look at it. Calm down.'

From the resigned expression on our skipper's face, I suspected that this wasn't the first time the outboard motor had given up the ghost. Having pulled a small toolbox out from under the bench, he rummaged his thick, dirty fingers through a mess of nuts and bolts to pull out a small screwdriver which he was now using to undo the top of the motor unit. In the meantime we were drifting on a current that was slowly dragging us towards a flotilla of dinghies from the local sailing school darting hither and thither as they tried to grasp the basics of seamanship. Distracted by our own problems with the motor, we had failed to notice that we were floating into the paths of learner sailors.

'So do you think you can mend it?' asked my mother,

who had shuffled down the bench to get a closer look at the outboard motor's shattered internal mechanisms. 'What's broken? Maybe we could...Ohhhhhhhhhhhhh!'

There was a massive shunt from behind and as my mother fell forwards on to the floor of the boat there was a loud splash behind her: my father, who had stood up to get an overhead view, had fallen into the water. We had been rammed from the side by a young woman in thick spectacles who, despite her teacher yelling at her, had completely failed to understand the difference between port and starboard and so, instead of steering away, had smashed her dinghy into us. Not only was my father now splashing wildly, we were taking on water.

The boat was going down.

'Start bailing!' shouted the skipper, grabbing the oars in a frantic attempt to get us back into the harbour before we all sank without trace. All I could find to shovel out the water was an RNLI, mug which, in the circumstances, was ironic. My father, now flailing in the Solent, was calling out for someone to help him. 'Never mind him!' yelled the skipper, as my mother leant over the side. 'Let the dinghy get him. No time to stop. Shovel the water! Bail it out!' My mother, torn between saving her husband and saving herself, chose the latter, and I sat watching as the dinghy that had rammed us came alongside my father and hauled him on board. The skipper, who was rowing with fury, shouted at us to bail quicker: the water was squirting in between two planks just below the left-hand bench and my mother, who didn't have anything to bail with other than her hands, decided that the best thing to do was to hold as many life jackets against the splintered wood as she could. Meanwhile, I was bailing like a demon, my small RNLI mug our only hope. Because we had so much to physically do to get us back into the harbour, there was no time to feel afraid. As we approached the harbour walls, I was even able to look up again at the fishers who had gathered to watch us as we limped our way back in. They were shouting encouragement and cheering but the battle was getting the better of us. Water was now up to my ankles and the boat was beginning to tilt and groan. The skipper, sweating with effort, kept looking over his shoulder to see how far we had to go. It was only a matter of yards, but the boat was sinking lower with every stroke. The pon toon was almost in reaching distance and with one heaving pull, the skipper shouted, 'Jump! Jump off!' Throwing the RNLI mug down, I got up on to the bench and threw myself towards the wooden pon toon, landing one leg on and one leg off, trailing in the water. As I pulled myself up, I lay on my side, panting, and turned to watch as my mother, wailing with panic, grabbed hold of the pon toon's end pole and then, very slowly, just slid out of the boat and slipped with a minimum of fuss into the water, where she remained, hanging on for dear life. The boat, with only seconds before it went under, had drifted up against the pon toon. The skipper, whose efforts had been beyond valiant, abandoned his oars and scrambled out. As he ran to the end of the pon toon to pull out my mother, I watched as the greedy harbour waters licked over the top of the boat and sucked the whole thing down. Our ship had sunk.

The three of us sat slumped on the pon toon, heaving for breath and exhausted. Brenda, who was wet from the chest down, only had one thing to say: 'I'd like our money back, please.' (She got it.)

It took Dad about forty minutes to make his way back to us. Naturally, it had all been his fault and my mother took no time in making sure he was aware of it. As we drove back to the campsite, all three of us wearing nothing but our underwear, my parents had a row so blazing that I gave serious thought to asking them to drop me off at the nearest

children's home just so that I could escape the embarrassment. The truth of the matter was that our holiday had, for
the ninth year in a row, got off to yet another dreadful start
and fingers were pointing.

The row grumbled on when we got back to the campsite,
which, for me, was even more embarrassing than having to
endure it in the car. You only had to fart on a campsite and
everyone in the immediate vicinity would know what you'd
had for dinner. The territorial aspect of camping meant my
parents seemed to think that, just because they were inside
the tent with the door zipped up, no one could hear them.
All I could do was sit in the inner tent with a pillowcase over
my head in the blind hope that no one would ever associate
me with my mum or dad ever again.

We had another problem. The campsite owner had taken a
shine to two young women in the tent next to us and had
decided that he would woo them by playing his guitar and
singing Joni Mitchell songs for hours on end. This would have
been fine except that he wasn't that good a guitar player, he
couldn't sing in tune and he didn't really know the words. We
lay in our sleeping bags, the atmosphere still frosty, and
listened to him struggling with his tenth attempt to work out
the chorus of 'Big Yellow Taxi'. 'I paved paradise!' he wailed.
'No. Wait. Wrong chord. Para…no…para…hmm, hmmm,
hmmmm, went to the parking lot! And it was a swinging!
Hot. Spot. No. Hot. Hot. No wait, I can do this. Hot. Spot!'

It was like listening to a badly scratched record being
played at the wrong speed by a man whose throat had been
sealed off by the authorities only to have every sound he
made diverted down one unnaturally tight nasal cavity. After
what felt like an eternity of endless, stumbling wailing, my
dad, who had had enough and just wanted this day to end,

sat up and quite loudly said, 'Utter shit! Your singing is shit!' The guitar playing fell silent.

'Daaaaaad!' I hissed, sitting up to glare at him. 'Ssssssh. They'll hear you!'

'I don't care if they do,' he said with defiance. 'I have not come on holiday to listen to shit for hours on end. Shit! Utter shit!'

Outside I could hear mumbling and giggling. Mortification was coursing through my veins and I threw myself down, burying my head under the pillow. To my abject horror, there was a sudden, loud unzipping of our tent door. This was a first. Even though it was clearly the easiest thing in the world, the unzipping of someone else's tent was an affront so intense as to be on a par with murdering kittens. 'What do you think you're playing at?' I heard my dad shout amid a maelstrom of indiscriminate scrabbling. 'They've undone our zip, Brenda! Look at that! Bloody cheek!'

My mother, for once, was past caring. She'd endured fish guts, snot and gone down with a sinking vessel: a small, retaliatory zip prank was the least of her day's troubles. 'Just come back to bed, Tony,' she said with a heavy sigh. 'And next time keep quiet.'

'This isn't over!' muttered my father, as he yanked himself back into his sleeping bag. 'You mark my words!'

And he was right. It wasn't.

We needed a normal day, one without incident or accident. So my mother decided we would pay an edifying visit to Osbourne House, the former summer residence of Queen Victoria. 'The thing is,' mused my mother, as she thumbed through the guidebook that she'd bought at the entrance, 'I can identify with Queen Victoria because she came on holiday to the Isle of Wight twice as a child and so did I.

Although I suspect her overriding memory wasn't of having all her clothes tucked into her pants and being forced to eat hard-boiled eggs covered in sand.'

It was a conspicuous building, its design plucked from the Italian renaissance and, like that other royal indulgence, the Brighton Pavilion, it looked as if it had landed on the island by accident. Two campanile towers dominated the outline, framing the building like bookends. 'Apparently,' said my mother, nose in guidebook, 'Prince Albert designed it.'

'It looks like an upside-down table,' I said, arms folded. I was not as enamoured of palaces and cathedrals as my parents. For me the inevitable trawl round a large, ostentatious building just meant hours of trudging with the bribe of a cake at the end of it or, if I was very lucky, a trip to the gift shop where sometimes I could come away with something as dazzling as a key ring.

'That's the biggest vase I've ever seen!' said my dad, staring at a vast porcelain monstrosity. 'Look at that, Em! It's massive.'

I shrugged. I couldn't see the point of it. It was just an enormous vase that filled up the room.

'That was given to Queen Victoria by the Russian tsar,' commentated Brenda, flicking to the relevant page. 'They were all murdered, the Russian royals. Killed by the communists.'

'Who cares?' I said with a shrug. 'I don't.' My parents looked at each other. It was going to be a long day.

If there was something I hated more than being dragged round a stately home, it was being dragged round a stately home garden. I couldn't have cared less about ornamental fountains or bushes trimmed into orbs. Neither was I interested in rose trees, lavender or staring into a greenhouse where there might or might not have been a small, wrinkled-looking lemon hanging forlornly on what looked like a desiccated old twig. My parents, in a desperate effort to get me into the spirit of things, had even taken to walking round the gardens pretending to be Queen Victoria and Prince Albert, which would have been embarrassing enough, except that it was my mother pretending to be Prince Albert and my father pretending to be Queen Victoria. 'La dee dah!' trilled Tony, wafting a hand in the air. 'Don't look at table legs!'

'Achtung!' yelled my mother. 'Let's have zum more kinder!'

I hid behind a tree and hoped the pain would stop. Sadly, it did not.

Our return to the campsite was dominated by a desire on my father's part to track down the campsite owner and give him a piece of his mind. 'But you don't know for sure it was him,' reasoned my mother. 'Come on, we've had a nice day. Let's not spoil it.'

'Of course it was him!' remonstrated my father, casting about to see if he could spot his nemesis. 'He unzipped our tent, Brenda! Unzipped it!'

'Yes,' nodded my mother with a sense of defeated rue. 'That was startling.'

Thankfully, the mischievous camp owner was nowhere to be seen and so we drove on to the tent. 'If I was temporarily blinded or had my eyes pecked out by gulls,' my mother noted as we approached our pitch, 'I'd still be able to make my way back to our tent by following the smell. I had hoped it would have improved, but it hasn't. Oh well. We may as well be sleeping in a sewer.'

At that precise moment a small girl with lanky brown hair wandered past. She stopped, gulped and emitted a perfect plume of bright-pink vomit. 'Oh dear,' said my mother, going forward to help her. 'That wasn't the smell of our bucket, was it?'

'Blancmange,' said the girl weakly, eyes watering with tears.

'Thank God for that,' said my mother, giving her a small pat on the back. 'On you go then.'

Because we weren't in France, it was felt, after a minor yet tense discussion, we wouldn't have to spend our holiday eating Spam, nor would we have to live on a nightly misery of over-boiled ratatouille so devoid of taste that just looking at it induced weeping. Instead we could extend our holiday diet to thrilling dishes such as fried eggs and bacon and, if we were really lucky, a boil-in-the-bag beef curry. Supper, which was always conducted on a wobbly table behind the wind-break, was inevitably followed by a game. That year we had splashed out and taken two board games: Mastermind, which involved having to guess the correct combination of black and white markers in a line, and Frustration, which promised 'Fast and furious pop-o-matic family fun!' but instead delivered a mild undercurrent of simmering resentment.

Dad had insisted that, because it was the Football World Cup that year, we should have our own 'International Frustration Tournament', complete with leader board and running commentary. The criteria for calling the tournament 'international' was satisfied, according to Dad, because he was Welsh and my mother 'looked a bit Spanish' and would make up for the woeful fact that England had, for the second World Cup in a row, failed to qualify. The game involved each of us having four coloured pieces (Dad was always red, Mum blue and I was yellow) which would have been straightforward enough, except my father made us give each piece the name of an international footballer, though for some reason his pieces were all named after members of the Welsh rugby team. The game was a straight chase: you had to get your pieces round the board and into a colour-coded safe zone. As you moved, you could land on other players' pieces. sending them back to the start, and to get into the safe zone, you had to get the exact number required – unless we were playing 'family rules' where you could get into the safe zone with any number thrown on the dice irrespective of whether there was a free slot. This was a constant source of tension: invariably, we wouldn't have established whether we were playing 'family rules' from the off. There would be angry exchanges towards the tail end of every game as my mother would happily slot 'Emlyn Hughes' into her safe zone without hitting the exact number required and then shout, 'Family rules! Family rules!' in protest as my father, who was adamant that it absolutely was *not* 'family rules', would move the offending piece back to where it started.

That evening we had gorged ourselves on a starter of Pot Noodles followed by a tinned Chinese takeaway chop suey with chicken, a meal that, to our feeble minds, was verging on space-age technology. 'It's a Chinese takeaway!' my father had squealed. 'But in a tin!'

'Unbelievable!' my mother had said. 'What with that AND digital watches, it's like living on the moon.'

The Frustration board had taken centre stage and Tony unfolded the current score sheet with the solemnity of a monk. 'Three games into the International Frustration Tournament,' he began, speaking into an imaginary microphone, 'and there's everything to play for. Wales in the lead with two wins under his belt, but fast on his heels, it's the young upstart and the Brazilian team…'

'Can't my team be from *Grease?*' I asked, interrupting. 'The film, not the country.'

'No,' said my dad, batting the thought away in an instant. 'The young Brazilian nipping at the lead with the one win and trailing in miserable third with no wins whatsoever, just to repeat, no wins, that's no wins, is Brenda and the England team, who are shit.'

My mother sighed and shook her head.

Before we could get going, however, we heard a voice bouncing over the top of the windbreak. 'So, if you smoke it through a potato, it kind of goes real mellow,' it said. It was the campsite owner. Dad, ears pricking like a wolf, stopped what he was doing and stood up.

'Hey!' he shouted out. 'What do you think you were doing last night with our zip?'

'Tony!' hissed my mother, pulling at the back of his jumper. 'Sit down!'

Sensing a multitude of embarrassments, I slid towards the bottom of my camping chair so that I was practically horizontal under the table. The campsite owner's head appeared just behind the windbreak, a small mischievous smirk hidden behind a plume of smoke curling from his pipe. He was wearing a large floppy hat so that his eyes were barely visible from beneath the brim. Lifting his chin a little, he peered over the top of the windbreak to look down at our table. 'Frustration?' he said, taking the pipe out of his mouth and gesturing towards our board game. 'How apt.'

'Never mind that!' blustered Dad, stepping a little closer. 'What about our zip? You can't go around undoing people's zips!'

'I don't know what you're talking about, man,' said the campsite owner with a lazy shrug. 'Why would I be interested in your zips?'

'Don't muck about!' said my dad, pushing his chest out. 'You undid our zip last night and you know it!'

'Oh God,' mumbled my mother, head falling into her hand.

'I don't think I touched your zip, man,' parried back the campsite owner, stepping a little closer. 'I'm not hung up about zips. I don't have a thing for them. Unlike you. You're uptight about zips. That's fine.'

'I am not uptight about zips!' protested my dad, pointing a finger into the air. 'But you can't go around unzipping people's zips. It's not on.'

'I didn't unzip your zip, man,' drawled the campsite owner, taking a puff on his pipe. 'Chill down. It's just a zip.'

I was watching events unfold through my fingertips. The tension was unbearable, the mortification complete. Nothing was more horrific than a public argument on a campsite, especially if it involved your parents. A couple of people, who had been tucked away behind windbreaks, were now standing so as to get a good look at the unfolding drama. One man, lazily licking an ice cream, had even wandered over to watch. My mother, sensing that things might be about to take a turn, was also now standing and, with one hand on my father's arm, had taken a teacher-like tone in an attempt to calm things down before they escalated. 'Look,' she said, 'let's all relax. We know it was you who undid our zip and we're just saying that that's not really acceptable. So let's draw a line under it and say no more about it.'

'I didn't touch your zip,' said the campsite owner again.

'Look, pal,' said my dad, edging even closer. 'Maybe your wacky baccy has got the better of you, but you know full well that you came over after your shitty singing and undid our tent. That's a fact.'

The campsite owner pushed up the brim of his hat with a finger. 'Shitty singing?' he said, fixing my dad with a considerable glare.

'Well,' said my father, 'it wasn't good. In fact, yes, it was shitty. Your singing is shitty.'

A small, intense silence descended, during which the campsite owner, still staring, nonchalantly reached for my father's sunglasses, took them out of his shirt pocket, snapped them in two and shoved them back into the pocket

from which he had taken them. It was all done with such
alarming speed it was as if the universe had stopped, turned
on its axis and gone into reverse. A small, indistinct noise
piped out of my mother's mouth in protest but any hopes
she had had of preventing a full-on 1970s man fight were
now lost. With a thick, guttural, 'What the bloody…', my
dad grabbed the campsite's owner hat, threw it to the
ground and stamped on it. The campsite owner, not to be
outdone, let out a banshee-like yell and leapt on to my
father's back; he, in turn, spun round in crazy circles while
swinging punches over his shoulder. Unable to dislodge
him, my dad then fell to the ground, where the pair of them
thrashed like eels as they tried to kick each other. Managing
to half get up, my dad reached out to grab hold of the table
but was treated to a crouching leap that sent him, the table
and the Frustration board flying, with the campsite owner
flailing on top like a just-landed fish. Throughout this
extraordinary display of inadequate tussling, Brenda stood,
hands on head, saying things like, 'What are you DOING?'
and 'Not the chairs! Not the chairs!' while grabbing me and
shoving me behind the windbreak in the pointless hope that
I would somehow be spared this woeful scene. The fight
couldn't have lasted more than a minute but it felt like an
eternity. Caught up between the collapsed table and one
folding chair, my father scrabbled on the floor as the campsite owner, who'd managed to upend himself off his back,
leapt to his feet and, picking up his squashed hat, strode off
while proclaiming that he HAD unzipped our tent and it
was a victory for anti-establishment supporters everywhere.
My mother, staring down at the shattered remnants of our
evening, was livid.

'What the hell do you think you were doing?' she yelled,
casting a despairing arm over the devastated scene. 'Look at

this!' she added, picking up a crushed game piece. 'Kevin Keegan's broken!'

'He broke my glasses, Brenda!' my dad yelled back, still trying to get his leg out of a camping chair. 'Bloody mad man! Broke my glasses! And they're my good ones! What was I supposed to do? Let him get away with it?'

The man with the ice cream was still staring. I caught his eye. He raised his eyebrows at me. I sighed and looked at the floor. Sometimes, I thought to myself, death could not come quick enough.

My parents were in rancid moods. I was trapped in a tent with two people not speaking to each other and a stinking bucket. This was some holiday. We had woken to a thin yet persistent drizzle and, because no one was speaking, I was sitting on a now wonky camping chair with the collars of my coat upturned so I didn't have to breathe in the toxic bucket fumes. It was like being trapped in a jam jar with two wasps that couldn't quite be bothered to go for the kill and have done with it. Instead, my parents slunk and moped, occasionally mumbling barbed comments under their breath and using me as a pointless conduit for communication. 'Could you ask your father,' began Brenda, 'if he knows where my poncho is.'

'Tell your mother,' replied Dad, who was only five feet away, 'that it's in the back of the car.'

And so on.

Argument or no argument, we were still contractually obliged under International Holiday Laws to have a 'day out' which, given the circumstances, meant a grumbling car journey and a lot of standing around in silence with hands firmly in pockets. Everyone was so determined to be in a thick sulk that not even the unbridled joy of bacon sandwiches could improve the atmosphere. We had gone to Blackgang Chine, a coastal ravine to the south of the island that laid claim to being the oldest amusement park in Britain. The immediate attraction was what seemed to be a job lot of fibreglass dinosaurs which, even to my increasingly cynical eye, were genuinely impressive. Other children were running up to them, climbing up tails and swinging on the Tyrannosaurus Rex, but I did not. Somehow, I felt slightly too old, a little self-conscious. My childhood was slipping away unnoticed, quietly and without a fuss.

That said, the last remnants of my childhood fire were not completely extinguished. Adolescence may have been creeping towards me like malevolent ivy but I wasn't quite ready to be pinned down yet. We had wandered past a triceratops in a clearing that, as I turned into it, caused the breath to catch in my throat. There, in front of me, was a full-sized Wild West town. I had never seen anything like it. Just like a scene from the black-and-white movies I so loved watching on Saturday afternoons, it was a street lined with wooden buildings; there was a saloon, a general store, a sheriff's office, everything you'd expect to see if you fell through a wormhole into turn-of-the-century California. I was amazed by it, all cynicism evaporated. Unfettered joy coursed through me, an explosion of excitement and wonder. Even my parents, who had barely spoken up till this point, were startled out of their apathy. Sometimes the greatest joy can be found in the most unexpected places and, as I ran back and forth through the swing doors of the old-time saloon and my parents pretended to be Butch and Sundance, I felt a last glow of uncomplicated delight and a happiness I would not experience again until I climbed out of the revolting pit of my teenage years.

We needed to be careful. Things had taken a turn for the better. Everyone's mood had improved and we'd enjoyed a round of ice creams. If we stuck to our present course we had a fighting chance of getting through the day without a further skirmish. Even the weather had cleared: blue skies had pierced the clouds and a delicious warm breeze had led to a peeling off of layers. We had perched ourselves at the edge of the chine, a dramatic ravine at the mercy of the elements. We weren't to know it, but where we were standing would be gone in the next twenty years, washed away by the rain. 'Wasn't that brilliant?' said my mother, faith restored.

I nodded. 'I loved it,' I said. 'That's the best thing we've ever seen on any holiday ever.'

'Told you the Isle of Wight would be good,' said Dad, chucking a lump of chocolate into his mouth.

'And the day's turned out lovely,' added Brenda, taking a deep breath of sea air. 'What shall we do next?'

'How's about,' started my dad, sticking his chest out a little, 'a spot of orienteering? It's like a walk. But a bit more advanced and exciting.'

'Well, hang on,' said my mother, 'isn't that where you don't know where you're going and you need a compass?'

'Yes,' said my dad, sucking on his chocolate.

'But we haven't got a compass,' pointed out my mother.

'Ahhh, we'll be all right,' said dad with a dismissive shrug. 'Just follow the sun or something. It's only a walk. How hard can it be? We'll follow the coastal path, go inland a bit, come back out again. Easy. And you can pick which way we go, Em,' he added, tapping me lightly on the shoulder. 'Shall we go left or right?'

Delighted to have been given a decision of such magnitude, I spun round on the spot with my eyes closed. 'That way!' I shouted, as I came to a halt. I was pointing in the direction of a long, thin path that led off to the east of the chine.

'Great!' said my dad, tucking the remains of his chocolate bar into his pocket. 'Then let's head off!'

'Hang on a minute. Don't you have to split up to do orienteering properly?' asked Brenda, as we meandered off. 'And run. Isn't that what it is? Running around trying to find things? With maps?'

'We can split up if you like,' said Dad, grabbing at a long piece of grass. 'Make it a competition. Perhaps we can do that when we're into the thick of it. Find a bit of wood. And run round it.'

'Yeah!' I shouted, because that sounded thrilling.

'I don't know if I'm that good at running,' mumbled my mother, raising a hand to shield her eyes from the sun. 'Hasn't it got hot? Lovely.'

The walk was easy enough: all gently dipping slopes and well-trodden paths. The views out across the sea were arresting and an air of relaxation had descended. Tiny pink flowers clustered in messy heaps along the pathway and butterflies seemed to be everywhere, flitting awkwardly as if they found themselves surprised to have wings. We had clambered over broken walls, negotiated our way past discarded canoes and upturned rowing boats and then climbed again to find an extraordinary rock that, from the side, looked like a man's face in profile with a jaunty cap on his head. The most noticeable feature was the cliffs that seemed to be on the verge of giving up, melting away into soft landslides so that the line between land and sea was a gradual blurring rather than a dramatic descent. We had seen plenty of wildlife: a small field mouse hanging on to a stray ear of corn, a red squirrel, flourishing on the island and yet to be eradicated by their more aggressive cousins and, alarming yet electrifying, a snake that had slithered across our path with unexpected nerve. All in all, this advanced walk was proving to be a great success.

'Right then,' said Dad, stopping and putting his hands on his hips. 'Let's have that orienteering competition. See that lighthouse? We'll start there. And then we have to go off in staggered starts and the end will be that point in the distance. See it?' We looked past him towards an almost indistinguishable spot. 'Right. I've got a watch so I'll go first and then you go second, Emma, and Brenda sets off last. And leave thirty seconds before you start because it has to be staggered. That's the rules. And you can get there any way you want. Your route is up to you. You just have to get there as quick as you can.'

Perhaps it was because the sun was out, perhaps it was because we'd enjoyed a full hour of uninterrupted holiday bliss. But for whatever reason, my mother, whose antenna for trouble was usually so acutely attuned was, contrary to every grain in her body, oblivious to the very obvious set of disasters that could possibly strike. 'Wish I didn't have to carry this poncho,' she said, tying it round her waist.

Tony, who could never enter into family competitive sport without pretending to be a TV commentator, was now fake-limbering up on the spot while interviewing himself with the long blade of grass he'd been carrying for much of the walk. 'I'm confident,' he said, leaning to speak into the cluster of grass seeds. 'Training's been going well and the competition is rubbish.'

'Daaaaad!' I protested, thumping him on the arm. If it was the last thing I did, I was going to beat him and beat him good.

'And so here we are,' Dad battled on, shrugging me off, 'at the Isle of Wight All-Comers World Orienteering Championships. Three runners and riders, of which I am the best, who have to get from here to there. We're moments from the start. He checks his watch. He notes the time. He reminds the rest of the field that they have to wait thirty seconds before they start. Aaaaaaand...he's off!'

As he dashed away through bracken and long grass, I was itching to get going. Mum was counting down from thirty and had a hand on my shoulder to stop me running off before I was allowed. 'Five, four, three,' she counted down, patting each second with her hand, 'two, one! Off you go. And be careful!'

Her words were already forgotten. The mist of battle had descended. Ahead of me, Dad had disappeared. The path curved away from the cliff edge and began to wind inland preventing a clear line of vision as to where he might be. I had kicked off at quite a pelt but was hampered by an uneven terrain that had me leaping, careering and stumbling with every footfall: tall ferns clattered against my thighs, the occasional thistle whipped at my arms. The path I had taken was rising and, as I reached higher ground, I found myself in a clearing with open views on both sides. I looked back and was able to pick out my mother ambling through the grass. She was out of it. It was now a two-horse race. Catching my breath, I strained to look ahead of me. Nothing. But then, suddenly, from behind a stone wall, up popped Dad. He'd taken off his shirt and had tied the arms about his neck, making it look as if he was wearing a cape. He was still running but there was something slower and more deliberate about him that spurred me with determination. Onwards I ran, my breathing sharp, punctuated by the sounds of a kick of dust, a scrape over rock, the lash of sharp grass. I still wasn't entirely sure where I was supposed to be heading, but with Dad's flapping shirt as a marker, I was the fox chasing the hare.

I had been running for no more than five minutes when I came to the fork in the path. One way led inland, the other, down towards the sea. In front of me the ground seemed to be crumbling away and as I got closer I could see that I had arrived at a small yet significant ravine that meant a large detour to get round it. Looking up, I could see Dad, pacing away to the left. Perhaps, I thought, I could find a way to cross the ravine without having to take the long way round.

I ran forward to see if there was a way down. But as I skidded towards the edge, I caught my foot in a hollow to my right, twisted my ankle, stumbled and found myself falling forwards. I was going over the edge. I was going to fall off the cliff and there was absolutely nothing I could do about it. Thankfully, I didn't have time to contemplate my own life or enjoy those fleeting moments of lucidity that people who are about to pass out of the land of the living claim to enjoy. Instead, I found myself sliding head-first down a steep but not sheer chalk bank, arms outstretched and screaming. Chalk dust was flying up into my mouth and eyes so that when I came to rest I was disorientated and spluttering. My heart was thumping like the clappers and I was so shocked by my sudden tumble that I was momentarily unaware of the sharp, searing pain radiating up from my ankle. I had landed on a ledge about twenty feet from where I had fallen and, having wiped the chalky dust from my eyes, I was able to ascertain that, actually, things were not as bad as they looked. I was in no immediate danger of falling further and, having taken a peep over the rim of the ledge, I could see there was another heaped sludge of crumbled landslide. The meaning of which was that, if I was so inclined, I could happily slide down to reach the small beach at the bottom. The problem was how to get back up. There were no steps or pathways climbing up out from the bay. If I left the ledge, I'd be trapped. My next problem was how to get back up to the cliff top. Given that I had slid more than fallen, it wasn't inconceivable that I could claw my way back up. I came up on to my knees and tried to stand. The pain in my ankle was excruciating and, as I tried to put weight on it, I let out a small, wounded yelp. The situation was now obvious: I was in trouble and I needed help.

I looked up. The sun, beating down with a mid-afternoon intensity, was bouncing back off the chalk ridges, making it difficult to stare upwards without squinting. My only chance would be to catch Dad as he went round the edge of the ravine. At the moment I had fallen he had been going away, along the length of the near side, but in a matter of moments he would have to reappear to come back up the far side. I didn't have long to wait. Out from a haze of sunlight he came, shirt flapping behind him, trotting along the ridge above me. 'Daaaaaaaaaaaaaaaaaad!' I yelled. 'Daaaaaaaaaaaaaaaaaaaaaad! Hellllllp!'

Hearing me, he slowed and looked behind him. He couldn't work out where the shouting was coming from. 'Daaaaaaaaaaaaad!' I yelled again, waving with both arms. 'Down here! Down here!'

And then he saw me. His hands slapped themselves to his head. He couldn't believe what he was looking at. Surely this was a father's living nightmare. Without even stopping to say anything, he turned round and started running back. In a matter of minutes, his head had appeared directly above me. 'Oh God! Em! Are you hurt? Are you all right?'

'My ankle hurts,' I shouted back up to him. 'But other than that I'm all right. I just slid down.'

'Right!' said Dad, sitting on the edge of the cliff top. 'Wait there. I'm coming down.'

'No!' I shouted. 'Dad! No! Wait! You can't...' but it was too late. He had launched himself downwards and was clattering towards me, on his back and at some speed.

Landing with a thump, he scrabbled himself over to me and, spitting chalk out of his mouth, said, 'Which ankle is it?'

'Right one,' I said, grimacing as I moved. 'But Dad,' I added, 'we're both stuck now. How are we going to get back up?'

'Well can't we slide down on to the beach and then come back up?' he asked, having a look at my ankle.

'No. There isn't a path back up from the beach.'

He stopped what he was doing and looked up at me. 'You're joking,' he said, leaning forwards to have a look over the ledge.

'No. I'm not joking. Now we're both stuck.'

My father, his shirt flapping horizontally behind him, froze with the realisation of what he had just done. He only had one thing to say: 'Your mother's going to kill me.'

It was five minutes before we saw her. Dad had tried, with some effort, to scramble back up the cliff face, but to no avail. The chalk was too crumbly, too fragile, and so we sat, both staring upwards in a resigned, doom-laden silence. My ankle, badly twisted but not broken, was already swollen and bruised but, as long as I didn't move it, was bearable. In the grand scheme of things we'd had a lucky escape. Now we just had to face my mother. As she hove into view, Dad stood up and started yelling, waving his arms in wide sweeps through the air. My mother, seeing him almost immediately, stopped in her tracks and stared. It was the long, hard stare of a woman trying to comprehend exactly what she was seeing. Her hands moved to her hips. 'We're in SUCH trouble,' I noted in the quiet hush.

'I know,' my dad whispered back. 'Sometimes, where your mother's concerned, death would actually be preferable.'

There is nothing more chilling than a calm yet livid mother and when her face appeared above us, granite-set and questioning, we just stared back up at her, waiting for the storm. 'What do you think you're doing, Tony?' she asked in a tone as cold as ice. 'Is this your idea of a joke?'

'She slid down,' said my dad, pointing an accusatory finger in my direction. 'So I came down to help her. And I thought we could go down on to the beach but then I didn't realise there's no way up from the beach so I tried climbing back up this bit but...'

'Stop speaking, please,' said my mother, clamping her eyes shut. 'I don't want to hear another word. Emma, are you all right?' I nodded. 'Right. Well I suppose I'll go and find someone with a ladder.'

She disappeared from view but then popped back again. 'Oh, and Tony,' she added. 'Don't think I'm going to let you forget this. "Let's go to the Isle of Wight," you said. "Let's go for a boat trip." We're all nearly drowned. Then you have a fight with a hippy. Who fights hippies? Who? And now this. Never again, Tony. Never. Again.'

'I am in such shit,' muttered my father.

'Yeah,' I said, agreeing. 'You are.'

Salvation came in the form of a man in soft sandals. He had a long, extendable ladder, which was lowered down so that Dad could piggyback me up and off the ledge. As we came over the rim and on to solid land, my mother was standing with her arms folded, her face like thunder. After thanking the gentleman with the ladder, who for some reason was keen to get away as quickly as possible, my father made a feeble attempt to gloss over the entire incident. 'Well,' he said, untying the shirt from around his neck, 'I suppose this means you win the orienteering.' A comment that was met with a glare so frozen, it was a miracle the sun didn't set for ever.

My sprained ankle had done for us. The following morning, with me unable to walk, we had been forced to pack up and head for home. 'Another great holiday,' Brenda commented as we drove on to the ferry to the mainland.

'Are you being sarcastic?' asked my father, a question that required no answer whatsoever. How my parents remained married after this holiday, I will never know.

Chapter Ten

The Final Blow

By 1979, everything had changed. A dark, miserable cloud of adolescence had descended and I was engulfed by it. I was thirteen, delighted by nothing, awkward and moody. My resting state, once inquisitive and alert, was now the rounded shoulders of indifference. Like a slug, I would creep round the edges of rooms, longing to go unnoticed. My bedroom became my bolt-hole, where I would be locked away for hours, listening to the same records over and over as I lay on my back, staring at the ceiling and wondering why everything felt so painful and despairing. My parents, once my friends and playmates, were now the scratching posts for my misery. I couldn't bear them.

Just as the decade was coming to an end, so were our summers spent camping. We didn't know it yet, but that year's holiday would be our last inside a tent. My mother, disgusted that Britain had turned Tory, was determined to return to France. 'At least they believe in equality!' she railed. My father, who was still carrying the disgrace of the previous year's fiasco heavy on his shoulders, was in no position to argue. In a way, it seemed fitting that my final challenge would be back in the country that had provided such a multitude of woes. It felt like a dare and I was ready for it.

We would be returning to Aix en Provence, the town in the South of France where we had spent an inauspicious twenty-four hours three years previously. There was a vague recollection that the campsite had been wonderful and so, because my mother was determined to play it safe, it was decided that a return trip would be just the ticket. Despite a decade of disasters, there was still a tiny scrap of hope that this year, perhaps, we would finally have a trouble-free holiday.

At first sight my mother was right: in the blazing sunshine, Aix was a platter of delights. From the sweeping avenue of the Cours Mirabeau, lined with fountains and plane trees, to the brooding presence of the Montagne Sainte-Victoire to the east, Aix felt classy. The campsite, where we had so briefly stayed, was just as impressive. It felt spacious, with a picnic area at its base and a steep road that wound up towards the *patron*'s office. Our pitch was at the top end of a slope, providing us with beautiful views to the north and south, surrounded by the smell of herbs: rosemary and thyme that grew wild all about us. The mountain, which had so inspired Cézanne, was our immediate backdrop and we sat on that first evening, watching in silence as the limestone rock changed in a symphony of subtle colours, all pinks and reds, as the sun made its westward decent. Amazing cloudless skies, where the stars assumed an incredible depth and meteorites delighted, were our evening's entertainment. We needed nothing more.

It felt dangerous to even be contemplating it, but as we got up the next morning, there was an air of calm. One we weren't used to. Even I, consumed with self-conscious discomfort, felt relaxed and, dare I say it, verging on happy. The sun was radiating a lazy glow, one that offered nothing but respite from our immediate troubles, and the camp seemed packed with Dutch families, all of whom were extremely friendly. Our immediate neighbours were from just outside Amsterdam, spoke perfect English and were so beautiful, they looked as if they'd been popped out of moulds. There were two children, a boy of my age and a girl a few years younger. They were bronzed, blonde and bubbly. I was instantly drawn towards them.

Juriaan, the boy, was confident beyond his years and did a lot of standing around, hands on hips, with a towel tossed over one shoulder. The girl, Miah, was a scrap of a thing, full of energy, and seemed to be greatly enamoured with bouncing up and down on the spot as if she were attached to a spring. Both of them were fascinated by our Land Rover, Bessy, still a relatively rare sight on mainland Europe, and so Dad let them go inside it, stand on the side plates and sit up on the bonnet. It brought me instant kudos. Suddenly and against all odds, I found myself being regarded as 'cool'. I was thrilled. My parents, palpably relieved that I had found some playmates, had heaved a collective sigh of relief: I hadn't scowled at them in over twenty-four hours. This really *was* a holiday.

The facilities at the campsite were excellent. There was a massive pool, an area for playing badminton, a covered table tennis hut and, in addition to the usual onsite camp shop, a small but none the less breathtaking takeaway van that did frites and crêpes. I was obsessed with it. I had never watched crêpes being made before and found the whole thing wondrous as if I was witnessing the birth of high art. I was used to British pancakes, all lumpy bits of flour served in a collapsed heap. But in France, crêpes were an art form, from the first ladle of batter, to the spreading thin over the hot round plate, to the delicate flip with the spatula through to the intricate folding that left you with a fan of glory stuffed with a whole host of delights. I thought you could only have sugar and lemon with a pancake. The fact that you could spice things up with chocolate, blueberries, ice cream, chantilly cream, strawberries, toffee and nuts or – and this totally blew my mind – cheese and ham was like being transported to a fairyland of miracles. I couldn't get over it.

I had been enjoying a crêpe dripping with chocolate. Miah had been on hand to oversee the proceedings and, in between bounces, was taking large bites that left her face smothered and sticky. We were wandering over to the pool where Juriaan was hanging out with some other Dutch boys and conducting a small but none the less competitive diving experiment that involved bombing and jumping in backwards. I could only look on in awe. I had never been taught to dive and was still going through a phase of swimming that involved wearing my snorkel at all times. Confidence and water was a combination I was yet to enjoy. Food wasn't allowed inside the pool area so Miah and I leant up against the mesh fence that surrounded it. Miah was still bobbing and had decided to launch herself into an impromptu rendition of the Abba song 'Dancing Queen', which I was enjoying but praying I wouldn't be expected to join in. I may have been enjoying a brief return to form but the talons of adolescent mortification were never quite off my shoulders.

In front of us there was a large ditch that ran along the length of the track and, as I stood, watching Miah leaping and twirling, I noticed a car lumbering slowly towards us. There was a woman at the wheel, hair heaped up like spaghetti, a lit cigarette pierced between two blood-red-painted fingernails. She was wearing a heavy pout and had the look of someone who couldn't quite be bothered. She also had the look of someone who wasn't that good at driving and, as she saw Miah dancing at the edge of the track, she veered to the left in an unnecessary attempt not to crush her soft legs under the wheels of her car. As she swerved, the front right wheel hit a small but solid decorative rock, sending the front end of the car upwards, only to come smashing down, seconds later, into the ditch. The car crunched to a halt. The woman, refusing to accept her current predicament, pumped her foot on the accelerator, puffed something in French and kept throwing one arm into the air as if by so doing it would somehow extricate the car from the ditch. It did not.

Everyone had stopped what they were doing. In the lazy and rarefied atmosphere of the Aix sunshine, a car tipping into a ditch was as major an event as they came. It had all happened so suddenly and in such horrible slow motion that there wasn't time to feel anything approaching alarm. Instead I just stood, half-eaten crêpe in hand, and stared, incredulous. A small crowd had gathered and I muscled in with them to peer in through the woman's open window. She was wearing a lime-green bikini and, although I couldn't understand a word she was saying, was hitting the steering wheel with her hand enough times to make it pretty clear that she was livid. A man in some dangerously tight trunks was flip-flopping round the front end of the car, inspecting the damage. The car was wedged in at an awkward angle and after a few attempts to reverse it out, accompanied by a cacophony of encouragements in various languages, it was obvious that it was going nowhere. It was a fascinating experience to watch someone else have a disaster. I was so used to being at the receiving end of miserable episodes that I was unmoved. This was nothing. I'd fallen into a toilet. Beat that.

The man in the crushing trunks seemed to have formulated a plan and, having spent a loud five minutes calming down the female driver who was now determinedly finishing her cigarette in a plume of defiance, he marched off. Sensing that there was more to be seen, Miah and I wandered off after him, along with the rest of the small gang of children that had now gathered. To my surprise, he marched in the direction of my mother, who was sitting, hat on head, reading *Catcher in the Rye* underneath a plane tree. 'Excuse me,' he said in a thick

French accent. 'But would you ask your father if he could help us?' I blinked hard. Had I heard that correctly?

My mother looked up, her head falling to one side. 'Sorry?' she said. 'My father?'

'Yes,' nodded the man, pointing towards Bessy. 'Your father. We need his Land Rover to help pull a car out from the ditch.'

It was very rare that my mother would laugh out loud but she found the thought that Tony had been mistaken for her father a concept so hilarious that it was a good few minutes before she could even speak. With tears rolling down her cheeks, she pointed in the direction of my father, who was walking towards the tent with a plastic bag in his hand. He'd been to the shop to buy peaches. 'Tony!' she called out, waving her book in the direction of the man. 'He thinks I'm your daughter!'

My father, seeing the small crowd gathered in front of our tent, was rightly puzzled as to what was going on. 'What's all this?' he asked, glancing about.

The man in the trunks stepped forward. 'There is a car,' he explained with a jerk of his head back down the hill. 'And she has got stuck in the ditch. Can you help to pull it out with your car?'

My dad gave the bloke a thorough once over. 'Yeah, all right,' he said eventually. 'But that's my wife, she's not my daughter. That's my daughter.'

Everyone turned and looked at me. I took a bite of my crêpe.

'But that's my wife. Understand? I mean, I know I'm going a bit grey but...come on.'

Bessy was proving to be a star turn. Not only did the man in the tight trunks want my dad to drive down to the bottom of the ditch but he also wanted to ride in the Land Rover with him. Not only that, but everyone wanted to have a go. The car was crammed. There were children stuffed into the back, teenagers standing on the side plates and various scantily clad gentlemen squeezed into the second row. It was like a scene from the last days of Saigon but without the sense of panic. The woman in the ditch was still sitting, head in one hand, and pouting, as Dad, with the help of the man in the trunks, attached a rope to the back of her car. As Bessy pulled the car up and out, there was a loud cheer and applause. My dad was a hero. For the first time in twelve months, I looked at my father and actually liked him. This holiday was verging on miraculous.

'Do you know,' said Tony, nudging me, 'that woman didn't even say thank you. Bloody French.'

'Yeah,' I said, beaming back at him. 'Bloody French.'

There was no need for further words. We were both too happy to speak.

Aix market was a fairground of treats. Used to the scrappy, half-arsed English equivalent where, if you were lucky, someone might be selling some maggot-eaten apples or some low-grade knock-off Soda Stream machines, I was blown away by the sheer quantity of goods on offer. A maze of stalls was spread wide, striped canopies rippling in the breeze, and each one was packed, not only with fresh, ripe produce but with things I had never seen before: huge, purple-veined bulbs of garlic hanging on the stem, bunches of bound dried flowers heavy with scent, barrels of exotic nuts and fruits, peaches the size of a boxer's fists, cheeses in their whole state with plates of free samples to taste, iced-fish stalls with fish I'd never even heard of, heaped and hanging *saucissons* that gave off the most wonderful, deep bouquet and, best of all, an extraordinary mobile rotisserie that had at least a hundred birds –

chickens, geese, duck, guinea fowl, partridge – all slowly turning as they roasted and again, giving off the most delicious aroma that filled the air so thickly, you could taste it. There was an air of the barbaric too: poultry stalls where the heads were still on the chickens sent chills through me, as did the cages of live poultry from which birds were dragged out, wings flapping, only to be tied together by their feet and tossed into panniers or hung over the back wheel of a bicycle, squawking with protest as they went.

Mum was in her element, wafting about in a floor-length, white cotton Laura Ashley skirt with huge milkmaid pockets. 'I feel well posh in this,' she had said, putting it on in the cramped confines of the tent. As far as my mother was concerned, the trip to the market was a treat on a par with a night out at the theatre and, ever mindful that French women were in a permanent state of immaculate presentation, she was keen to blend in. Her appearance, however, rather than melting her into the crowd, was having the opposite effect. She was drawing attention. She had clearly overdone it and, as we walked, it was noticeable how many heads were turning.

Over to the left of the market there was a small gathering of people, circled around something that, as yet, we were unable to see. A swarthy man, dressed in a Romany-style waistcoat and trousers, had peeled out from the crowd and, spotting my mother, made a beeline for her and grabbed her by the arm. He was dancing on the spot, like a jester, and had a parrot on one shoulder that kept bobbing up and down and squawking, '*Bonjour! Bonjour!*' My father, not believing what he was hearing, found the whole thing hilarious.

'The parrot's speaking in FRENCH!' he yelled, shaking his head.

Behind the man, in the circle around which everyone was gathered, there was another man, similarly dressed and playing a flute, as well as a llama, a chimpanzee and a goat. The goat, which had enormous curved horns, was wearing a jacket embroidered with images of what appeared to be people dying in horrible circumstances: there was a man having his head chopped off, a legless woman and someone of indiscernible sex being hung by the neck. In front of the goat there was a steep flight of steps leading up to a tiny circular platform. As the flautist played a strange, haunting tune, the goat ascended the steps while the llama, which was holding its head at the oddest angle as if contemplating the world sideways, stood and stared. The chimp, held on a chain, was sitting on an upturned bucket, picking its nose. The goat, having climbed the steps, then crammed all four hooves on to the tiny circular platform and simply stood, gazing out, as the parrot screeched, '*Bravo! Bravo!*' and then, inexplicably, '*Comment ça va?*' It was, without a doubt, one of the most unnerving spectacles I had ever witnessed.

'Bit primitive, isn't it?' whispered Tony, shaking his shoulders a little. 'You know, sort of spooky.'

The man with the parrot on his shoulder had started creeping round the circumference of the circle with a hat out, asking for money. Spotting him and also feeling unsettled by what she'd seen, my mother gave us both a nudge and said, 'Come on, let's go.' We turned to leave but, noticing that we were making a dash for it, the man scuttled over, like a crab, and, hunched in front of my mother, held out the hat while gesturing towards her outfit.

'You see, he thinks you're rich or something,' said Dad in something of a whine. 'I told you not to dress up. I haven't got any change either. I've only got a twenty-franc note. We can't give him anything.'

My mother, shooting my father a short but none the less

withering glance, turned to the man and, holding her hands out, said, '*Pardon monsieur. Rien. Rien.*'

'*Pas de l'argent!*' added my dad with a wag of his finger. '*Non! Pardon! Au revoir!*'

The man, who had been grinning and bowing, stopped what he was doing. His face, which had up till that point seemed jovial, clouded over, and a scowl as deep as the seas set in. Reaching into his pocket, he pulled out what seemed to be a jewelled chicken's foot. Lifting it into the air, he waved it three times and then tapped me on the forehead with it while emitting a disturbing hissing noise. Recoiling from having been touched by a dead chicken's foot, I let out a small noise to register my disgust, only to have the parrot, fixing me with its beady eyes, bob up and down in my direction and say, '*Tu es morte! Morte! Morte!*'

I stared back. 'Did that parrot just tell me I was dead?' I asked, turning to look at my father.

'Oh my God,' said my mother, clutching at my shoulder. 'They've just cursed Emma. Tony! Do something!'

But it was too late. They had gone, swallowed into the crowd. So that was that. I was going to die.

'I'm sure the parrot didn't mean it literally,' said my mother, chewing her lip. 'And besides, it's all just silly nonsense anyway. Don't give it a second thought.'

But it was hard not to give it any sort of thought. I had grown up in the clutches of the capricious Holiday Gods and now I had been given a top-up curse by a green, evil-eyed cockatoo. I had been thrown storms, sickness and a multitude of close encounters with bodily fluids, but death was something else entirely. I needed to be on my toes.

We had returned to the campsite to find our tent floating on a pool of water. The heat wave had brought with it the risk of fires and the camp owners, mindful that the site was set among dense, but dry-as-a-bone, vegetation, had made the decision to flood the area using hoses. Because the ground was so arid and the hosing so intense, the water was settling into small lakes that were lifting the tents up from their awnings, making them look as if they were gently shifting in the sunlight. My father, who had never been a great fan of soaked canvas, went slightly bananas. 'What the hell?' he squealed, tapping at the moving ground sheet with the end of his foot. 'Everything's sopping wet! What are they thinking of?'

'But it's so hot, Tony,' reasoned my mother. 'It'll all be dry again in a few hours.'

She was right, of course, but it was decided, given that hosing was still ongoing, that we would get back into Bessy and head off again, this time to Marseille, about twenty miles away on the coast. France's second largest city was a melting pot of cultures, the port a magnet for an influx of immigrants, many from Algeria, which gave the city an exotic, African feel. It was also, in 1979, in the grips of an economic downturn and unemployment and poverty were rife. Organised crime had slithered in and had the city tightly coiled. It felt dangerous and unnerving from the off.

We were heading for the Old Port area of the city and had needed to negotiate a swarm of traffic that, after enjoying the open roads of the French countryside, we weren't quite used to. It was blisteringly hot and even with all of Bessy's windows open we were still wilting in the heat. We had crawled in bumper-to-bumper traffic down the main city boulevard, sweating and fractious. The hot air was stifling and Dad, seeing a small sign for the Old Port, decided to 'take the off-road route' and at least get us moving. Instantly we were into a spider's web of back alleys, a dark and narrow maze of sharp turns. The Land Rover, squeezing through the tight lanes, was an imposing presence.

We didn't quite know where we were going. Dad, who used to swear by 'following his nose', was basing decisions on which way to go just by what seemed to feel right. The truth was, we were lost. As we slowed down to a crawl, I became aware that men in long tunics were gesturing towards us and yelling as we passed. We were driving through a residential area and there was an air of hostility that was palpable. My mother, like a bat for sensing trouble, turned to me and said, 'Shut up your windows, Emma. Do it now.' I did what I was told. Dad, finding himself at a dead end, had been forced to turn right into a lane that was barely wide enough to accommodate the Land Rover. We were squeaking through but ahead of us there was a group of ten to fifteen men blocking our path. Seeing us, they began to gesture angrily in our direction.

'Oh God, Tony,' whispered my mother, turning sideways to include me. 'This is dangerous. What are we going to do? Can we back up?'

I turned and looked behind us. To my alarm, there was another group of men striding down towards us. We were hemmed in. Realising that we were in a genuinely precarious situation, my mind turned to the parrot. Was this, I wondered, to be my glorious end: murdered in a shadowy alley by agitated men in dresses? My heart thumping, I grabbed my dad by the shoulder. 'Get us out, Dad,' I said with a sense of some urgency. 'Get us out now.'

My father, spurred on by a Neolithic urge to protect his womenfolk, shoved Bessy into a higher gear. The surge forward created a ripple of resentment and someone, appearing from the side, thumped the back of the Land Rover with a fist. My mother let out a startled cry and I turned to see that three men were trying to grab on to Bessy's roof and get on to the side plates. As we pressed forwards towards the oncoming group, Dad blared the horn, the low, deep klaxon bouncing off the walls. The men in front of us were all shouting, arms raised, while most of the group behind had managed to clamber on to the car. Angry faces appeared at the windows, fists banging on the glass. My mother had reached an arm over the back of her seat to grab hold of my hand. We were terrified. We had no idea why we were being attacked. All Dad could do was edge forward and try not to hit anyone. The road widened a little at the bottom of the street and with more space to manoeuvre, Dad managed to swerve the car a little so as to shake off the men on the side plates. As the last one fell off and with a gap in front of him, he slammed his foot down on the accelerator and off we sped, careering round a corner and screeching off until, realising that we had left them behind, Dad pulled over and we all sat, panting.

'Jesus Christ,' said my father, his head hanging on the back of his seat.

At that precise moment two faces appeared at his window. They were two Germans carrying backpacks. One of them tapped on the glass. 'You will take us to the station. Yes. Now.'

We all stared at him in disbelief. My father, lifting his head, took one look at him, sat up, slammed Bessy into first and shouted, 'Fuck off!'

'This place is AWFUL!' wailed my mother, shaking her head as we drove on again.

I was just glad I hadn't died. All the same, that parrot had clearly meant business. I'd been warned.

Given that we had come to the conclusion that Marseille was a shit heap, we had left it at speed and driven on to the small seaside town of Le Ciotat. The beach was relatively tiny and was nestled at the foot of some cliffs. It was just past noon and the weather was sweltering, even with the relief of a sea breeze. My father, after carrying all our stuff down to the beach, left us to find a shop and bring back some lunch. He was wearing a brown vest top with white trim around the neck and arms and a pair of light blue shorts. As he left, he gazed up at the sky and said, 'It's so hot. I'll put cream on when I get back', and with that, wandered off up the steep cliff steps. He was right, it was blazing. I had stripped off down to my patchwork bikini and could already feel my skin tightening in the midday sun. Getting a suntan on holiday had, in previous years, been a by-product of the experience rather than the *raison d'être* but now I had turned thirteen, it was all change. I wanted a tan and I wanted it bad.

'Have you put cream on, Emma?' asked my mother, who was busying herself behind me with the windbreak and some towels.

'Yes,' I said, lying. I hadn't put on one drop. Not one. I wanted to lie very still for a period of many hours and quietly bake until I had an angry red line that ran all the way across my bikini bottoms. Only then would I be happy. Not only that, but my best friend at school, Sarah Biggerstaff, had told me that if you're in water you get a better tan so my next plan, as soon as my initial roasting was underway, was to lie in the sea for as long as was humanly possible.

The sea was barely moving. There were hardly any waves and those that were there were half-hearted as if even the water was too hot to bother. There was also a strange metallic sheen glistening across the bay and a smell that was verging on the industrial. My mother had wandered down to the shoreline to dip a toe in and had looked at me, wading out, and then looked down at her foot which was now smeared with a strange oily effluent. 'Emma!' she called out, lifting her leg and pointing at it. 'The water's very dirty. Don't swallow any!' Not that I was paying any attention: I had basting to do. Because public information films of the 1970s were quite specific about not being allowed to swim for at least one and a half hours after eating (if you did, drowning was inevitable), I knew that I had to cram in as much water-based tanning as I could before Dad returned with our lunch. To this end, I pulled on my snorkel and just lay on top of the water, arms and legs spreadeagled so that I could achieve the greatest skin-to-sun ratio possible. The water was very murky, the sand beneath me dark and dirty. Over to the left I could see a dead fish bobbing miserably. I didn't care. I wanted to get brown.

Dad was gone for about forty minutes and, because my fingertips had turned that nasty shade of grey that meant you'd been in the water for too long, I decided to weave my way back up the beach. As I did, I quickly checked the top of my bikini, straining to look over my shoulder and down my back. I had a result. There was a definite line of difference between uncovered and covered skin. This day would be mine before it was out. I threw myself down on my beach towel to carry on the good work and noticed, with not one jot of alarm, that my hair smelt like the bottom of a festering bin. Oh well. No matter. Dad, I noticed, was making his way back down the cliff steps, bags in hand. He had bought baguettes, tomatoes, a *saucisson* and a couple of cheeses. Not only that, but we had peaches, ripe and fit to burst. He was sweating profusely and wearing a frown that was deep and pained. My father was very fair-skinned and his shoulders, exposed to the sun, had burnt and blistered in the short time he'd been walking.

My mother was appalled. 'Tony!' she declared with a gasp. 'Look at your back! It's bright red! And you've got blisters! Already! Oh! Cover up! For goodness' sake, cover up!'

Unfortunately, there was nothing to cover up with. So my poor father was dispatched back up the cliff steps to the car to fetch a small, black umbrella. He then sat on the beach, crunched into the paltry shade it provided. French people were openly laughing at him. One man just stood, pointing at him and guffawing. It was official: my father was the object of ridicule.

My father's blistered back had created a convenient diversion. I wasn't just burning, I was cooking. My mother, who'd had her nose buried in a book, hadn't looked up since lunch but when she did, she let out a small yelp of concern. 'Emma!' she cried. 'Please tell me you put some cream on after your swim? Please tell me you did that?'

I didn't reply. I had entered into a woozy netherworld of confusion; one where the heady brew of too much sun and toxic waste was taking its toll. I may have muttered something incomprehensible. The fact was I was burnt to a crisp. My mother, taking off her sunglasses to take a better look at me, prodded at my shoulder, only for a bright white fingerprint to appear for a fleeting second. It was her touch test for sunburn and I had passed with flying colours. My skin was a livid crimson and was giving off pulsing, radioactive heat. I hadn't moved in about two hours and so, as my mother insisted that we all leave and return to the campsite, I was unaware of the full extent of the agony to come. My skin, racked tight by the sun, screamed with pain at every bend and step and, when it came to sitting back in the Land Rover, I was so sore and sensitive that all I could do was perch on the edge of the seat, trying desperately not to touch any surface.

Brenda was livid with the pair of us. Dad's shoulders were a mass of bubbling blisters while I looked as if I'd been submerged in a vat of red paint. 'Don't expect any sympathy from me!' she declared, waving a hand in our direction.

'What did I say? Put some cream on. You've only got yourself to blame.'

The only immediate relief I could hope for was water followed by a tip-to-toe sponging in camomile lotion, a gaudy pink liquid that dried on the skin and would provide a brief respite from the appalling pain. Before I could have that applied, my mother dispatched me to the shower unit where I was instructed to stand under cold water for at least ten minutes. It was agony to walk. With every step, it felt as if my legs were going to burst open like exploding tomatoes. I felt disorientated and peculiar, as if my brain had been slowly steamed inside my skull. I had almost made it to the shower block when I heard a familiar voice. It was Juriaan, waving at me from inside the pool area. He was gesturing for me to go in and, because I didn't quite know where I was or what I was doing, I obliged. 'I am teaching diving!' he announced, hands on hips. 'Come. Now I teach you!'

I just stared at him. All I could think about was trying not to spontaneously combust. 'I have to have a shower,' I mumbled, attempting a feeble point towards the wash block.

'Later, later,' said Juriaan, grabbing me by the forearm.

'Aaaaaaaaaaaaaaaagh!' I winced.

'Now,' he said, ignoring me. 'You stand with your toes here. At the edge. And you put your arms up. Like this.'

'Owwwwwwwwwww!'

'And then in you go! Like this!' Juriaan, keen to display his diving prowess, glided into the water, disappeared and popped up again, tossing the hair out of his eyes in one deft shake of the head. 'So now you dive!' he yelled, gesturing at me to join him.

I was so wracked with pain and so addled with confusion that I didn't have the strength to say no. I stared down at the water. It did look cooling. Maybe, I reasoned with myself, diving in would help ease the endless smouldering distress that I found myself in. Perhaps one leap would be the answer to my prayers. I curled my toes over the edge of the pool. Just one dive. That was all I had to do. Juriaan was flapping his hand from the middle of the pool and shouting encouragement. A group of younger children were to my left, treading water and watching. The pressure was on. It was hard to find a gap between the swimmers and so, as I committed to my dive, I skewed right, pushing myself off the edge with an upwards bounce. I had made a dreadful error: not only was I now diving into the shallow end, but I had made such a leap upwards that there was no hope of a graceful glide across the top of the water. I was going down and I was going down hard. At first, it was almost pleasant. The water on my skin provided an instantaneous release from my flaming hell but then came the scrunching of my arms followed by a muffled but significant impact as my forehead bounced along the bottom of the pool. Stunned but not unconscious, I floated back up to the surface. Water had gone up my nose and I was now streaming with snot while scrabbling for the side of the pool, where I clung on for dear life, coughing and spluttering. If ever I had wanted to look cool in front of strangers, this was not the time. I looked like a choking, drowning rat. Juriaan just stared at me and said nothing. Even he was embarrassed. To top off my misery nicely, my bikini top had come loose and what tiny burgeoning breasts I had were now on display for the world to see. Somehow I crawled out from the pool, lay panting on my side for five minutes and then pulled myself up. I couldn't look at anyone. So I didn't. Instead, I stumbled off back in the direction of our tent.

'Good,' said my mother, looking at me. 'You've had a shower. Right. Let's get the camomile lotion.'

My sunburn was so extensive that my mother wasn't

quite sure as to the best method of application. Normally she would have had me sitting or lying, but my torment was so total and the area of coverage required so extensive that she got me to stand, arms out, so that she could pour rather than dab the cold, pink lotion down my front and back. Dad, who was so hot that he was lying under the Land Rover, peered up at me from behind the front wheel. 'You've missed a bit,' he said, pointing out a small un-smothered spot on the back of my thigh. I was a bright, prawn-pink from head to toe. The lotion, although providing some relief, dried very quickly, becoming chalky and cracked, so that I had the look of a mud-covered warrior who had inadvertently stumbled into an icing shop. I couldn't sit, and I couldn't lie. All I could do was stand inside the tent and whimper.

'And the silly thing,' chided my mother, tossing the now empty bottle of camomile lotion into a bin bag, 'is that you'll peel. So it will all be for nothing. And let that be a lesson to you.'

I was starting to feel properly ill. I was dizzy and boiling. My forehead was pounding and the world around me seemed to be gently spinning. I had to lie down but getting into a horizontal position was easier said than done. Sharp twinges of hot, acid pain sliced through me with every movement, each millimetre of exposed flesh raw to the touch. I didn't know what to do with myself. I was in so much pain and my brain was so melted that all I could do was stare up at the tent roof, occasionally emitting small, pitiful whimpers. I had extreme sunburn, had swum in a toxic sea and given myself a dull, but nevertheless significant, blow to the head: was this, as the parrot predicted, the beginning of my end?

The fever took hold in the middle of the night. I was delirious. Faces swirled in and out of vision, sounds came and went. I was drenched in sweat, my throat tight and dry. At one point, hallucinating, I thought I could see a large leather beanbag rotating slowly in the upper left-hand corner of the inner tent. It had long metallic spikes protruding from it and every now and then, it would stop rotating and descend, at considerable speed, in the direction of my face, swerve away at the last moment and then return to its original position, where it would continue spinning, like a large malevolent bee. I was vaguely aware of my mother, who spent most of the night trying to cool me down with cold flannels to the forehead and cool water washes for my hands and feet but, other than those brief moments of consciousness, I was rambling and lifeless.

The heat inside the tent was unbearable: it was like being in a pressure cooker, the hot, dead air stifling. As soon as first light was up, my parents, stricken with worry, carried me outside and lay me down in the shade of the Land Rover. I had improved slightly after several rounds of dissolvable aspirin but was still feverish and disorientated. Because the shaded area in front of our tent was only going to last till mid-morning, Dad was busying himself trying to arrange the windbreak so that I could be shifted alongside it and moved when necessary. I was lying on the floor on an air bed and Miah and Juriaan had wandered over to stare at me, as had several of the campsite children, drawn by the attraction of the small unfolding drama.

'Are you sick?' Miah had asked, twirling in a circle.

'Yes, she is,' interjected my mother. 'Don't stand too close, please. Give her some room.'

Everyone shifted backwards a few steps, but I was too interesting a spectacle to be left entirely alone. The crowd was going nowhere. Miah's mother, a solid woman with a face like a bulldog, flip-flopped over. She was wearing an orange bikini and stood, hand on one hip, giving me the once over. 'Back in Holland,' she began, speaking to my mother, 'I am a nurse. Would you like me to take a look at her for you?'

My mother, delighted to be in the hands of a professional, readily agreed. Our Dutch neighbours, who seemed to be vastly better at camping than we were, had proper camp beds in their tent and one was brought out so that I could be made more comfortable. As I lay on it, Miah's mother peered into my eyes, felt under my chin and asked me to stick out my tongue. She had a slightly rough touch as if she was handling a large and unwieldy joint of meat and I felt a little pummelled. Not that I was in any fit state to complain: I was so weak and incoherent that someone could have delivered a sharp blow to the back of my head with a wooden club and I wouldn't have batted an eyelid. 'I think we should take her temperature,' I heard Miah's mother saying. 'This way we know how bad the fever is. I will fetch my things.'

There was a lull in the proceedings. I let my head flop to one side and caught the eye of a small boy in the crowd. His legs were crossed as if he was desperate to go to the toilet but he was so determined to see what would happen next, he was hanging on for dear life. There were at least fifteen people now gathered at the base of our pitch, all of them staring at me, some of them with their arms crossed, others holding towels and wash bags, but all of them fascinated. Miah's mother returned. She was holding a small, green plastic box in one hand. As she unhooked the catch, she said, 'So I take the temperature now.' With one deft manoeuvre, she shook the thermometer in one hand and flipped me on to my belly with the other. I didn't quite understand what was happening but, suddenly, my bikini bottoms were being pulled off me and something cold and solid had been shoved up my arsehole.

She was taking my temperature rectally. In front of strangers.

The words of the parrot rang in my ears. '*Tu es morte!*' it had squawked. '*Tu es morte!*' As I lay, thermometer sticking up out of my anus for all to enjoy, a calm descended. This was it. This was my final moment. Death was now only moments away. I was a thirteen-year-old girl with a thermometer in my bum hole. I didn't want to go on living. I could never face the world again. I was beaten. Finally, the Holiday Gods had won. It was time to put up my hands and admit defeat.

'Yes,' said Miah's mother, slipping out the offending instrument and reading it. 'She is very hot.'

What did I care? I knew I was hot. I could have told her that without having to endure the humiliation of a rectal probe in public. As it was, everyone in the immediate vicinity had witnessed a foreign object being rammed up my back passage. Someone towards the back of the group had actually applauded. I looked up and, again, caught the eye of the boy who needed the toilet. His mouth was hanging open, his eyes as huge as saucers. He would probably remember this moment for the rest of his life. But not as much as I would remember it, branded into my memory banks with a flame-red poker.

'Yes,' added the woman with a nod. 'She needs to see a doctor.'

'Thank you so much,' said my mother, touching the woman lightly on the forearm.

Thank you? Thank you for what? Destroying my life as I knew it? Maybe some other holidaymakers could roll up and stick some other things up my anus for everyone's amusement? Perhaps they could form a queue? I wasn't going anywhere. And neither was the crowd. Maybe my mother could charge ten francs a shove? Only my father, my dear, sweet father, understood what had just happened. Quietly and without making a fuss, he crept up and pulled my bikini bottoms back to where they should have been. 'I can't believe she just did that,' he whispered, patting me on the hand. I looked into his eyes. I had the gaze of a stuck pig. Any life that had been left in me was extinguished. *Bon voyage*, cruel world.

The doctor was very good-looking: all floppy black hair and lazy brown eyes. He was wearing jeans, brown loafers with no socks and a short-sleeved white shirt that was undone to his mid-chest. My mother, who had kept out of my way since the incident with the thermometer, took one look at him and came over a bit giggly and unnecessary. My father, wearing red swimming trunks, a T-shirt with a picture of Mork and Mindy on it and grey socks to cover up his own sunburn, did his best to hold his own but it was no contest.

'When did this begin?' asked the doctor, accent like silk. He had perched himself on the edge of the camp bed and had a distinct smell about him that was part cigarette, part musky cologne.

'Yesterday,' explained my mother, flicking her hair over one shoulder. 'She had a bit too much sun. And she swam in the sea at Le Ciotat.'

'*Boufff*,' puffed the doctor, raising his eyebrows. 'You swim in the sea? This is not such a good idea. So. Now I take your temperature.'

'Noooooo!' I yelled, managing to sit up. I even put my hands underneath me. There was no way I was being penetrated twice in one day.

'The doctor will take your temperature the normal way, Em,' said my dad, taking a step towards me and folding his arms. He looked ridiculous but, at that moment, he was my only hope. 'Can you take her temperature in the mouth, please,' he added, fixing the doctor with a manly stare. 'Only in the mouth.'

I was running a temperature of 102 degrees. The doctor, who had diagnosed me as having something that sounded like 'La Greeeeep', had handed my parents a prescription as long as your arm. Six medicines had been recommended: a cream for my sunburn, an anti-inflammatory for my sunburn, a post-blister ointment for my sunburn, pills for the fever, an anti-emetic pill in case I felt nauseous and a mysterious bonus pill that we couldn't quite recognise. 'This last thing,' asked my father. 'What is it?'

'A suppository,' said the doctor. 'You administer it into the anus.'

My father shot me a quick look. No chance. No chance whatsoever.

And so the Holiday Gods had had their final laugh. On the one holiday that had promised to be so enjoyable, I spent the remainder of our time in the shade and sleeping. Hours were meaningless, days indistinguishable. My childhood holidays weren't going out with a bang, they were drifting quietly away to a dry and deadened end. Every last scrap of joy had been sucked out of me: I was ready to be a teenager.

But there was one final and awful twist to the tale. I was not the only casualty that summer. Bessy, our faithful Land Rover, the car that had been everywhere with us, through thick and thin, through gales and sickness, was on her last legs. There was something tired about her, like an old lion that's lost the thrill of the hunt. The long journey back to Hitchin was a struggle: her back springs had broken and her chassis was covered in rust. She was like a first-time marathon runner, plodding to make the distance and hating every step. When we arrived home, my broken-hearted father took her for a once over to see if anything could be done. The news was not good: the work needed was so extensive that, from a financial point of view, she was worth more to us as scrap. The dreadful decision was made. Bessy would be leaving us, sold to a car dealer who would break her up for parts.

On the day she was being sent away, all three of us got into her and sat for one last time. We were all in tears. I lay on the long seat in the back, holding on to the edge as if in one, long, final embrace. I loved that car; we all did. She had kept us safe and been our port in every storm. It felt like a terrible betrayal, as if we were sending a family member to die.

'Do you remember all the holiday songs we used to sing?' asked my mother, sniffling. '"Here Comes the Sun". Do you remember that one?'

My father nodded. 'We should sing Bessy one last song. Before she goes. Send her off proper.'

And so the three of us sat, my parents in the front and me, having moved up, in my usual seat just behind them, and sang 'The Long and Winding Road' by the Beatles. We were in bits. It was, without a doubt, the most pitiful, sob-wracked singing anyone could ever hear. At one point my father, voice catching in his throat, just slumped forward and rested his head on the steering wheel. My mother, as the last line was gulped out, threw her head back and wailed, 'Please forgive us! Please!' and I, forehead in the crook of my elbow, tormented and distraught, blubbered thick, heartfelt tears all over the handrail. I had never experienced such grief. My heart had been ripped from my chest.

Mum and I couldn't face going to the dealer, so Dad was left to take Bessy on her last journey alone. We stood and watched as she rumbled away, clinging on to each other for comfort, tears running down our cheeks. A cavernous hole shot through our family. And nothing would ever fill it.

My father had returned, forty-five minutes later, with a lime-green Citroën Dyane which he had bought on part exchange for Bessy. We stood and stared at this new cuckoo in our nest and I felt my heart harden against it. I would never love it. Never. Even the fact that it had an inbuilt radio and cassette player meant nothing to me. It was all flashing lights and baubles, a plastic insignificance. Bessy had been an honest car with no frills. You knew where you were with her; she was solid and true. But now she was gone. It was the end of an era.

Our decade of holidaymaking had been an unmitigated disaster. At every turn we had been thwarted and pummelled but, to our credit, we had never given up. We had battled on year after year, hope in our hearts, but now, with Bessy gone and the 1970s crawling to an exhausted end, the jaded cynicism that would define the 1980s was creeping towards us. My father, convinced that all our bad luck was tied up with the tent, wanted nothing more to do with it.

It was a warm late-summer evening. I was about to go back to school and had been lying in a hammock at the bottom of the orchard, staring up at the apple trees. The sunlight had softened and was casting a dappled glow through the leaves. Hoverflies hung in the air and there was a smell of wood burning over the hedges. Someone over to the right was having a bonfire. Mum was weeding to my left, on her knees and in a big floppy hat. Neither of us had spoken, both of us lost in our own worlds. Dad, who had been up at the top end of the garden reading the paper, wandered down to see what we were both up to. He emerged from behind a bush and was wearing a cap to cover the bald patch that seemed to have appeared overnight. He kicked his way through the longer grass, hands in pockets, and came over, leaning against the apple tree towards my feet. 'I'm thinking of having a bonfire,' he said, giving the hammock a gentle swing.

'What for?' asked Mum, looking up and squinting towards the low sun. 'We haven't got anything to burn.'

'Yes,' said Dad, picking up a long blade of grass and twisting it round his finger. 'We have. I want to burn the tent.'

'*Burn the tent?*' said Brenda, a little shocked. 'Don't be mad. You can't burn the tent.'

'Why not?' asked Tony with a shrug. 'We all hate it. It's brought us nothing but misery. Let's burn the bastard.'

I sat up. 'Please, Mum,' I said, shocked but excited at the same time. 'Let Dad burn it. It's evil.'

'Don't be silly,' replied Mum, getting up off her knees. 'Tents aren't evil. We can't burn it. I never heard of anyone burning a tent. That's nuts.'

'I want to burn it, Brenda,' said my dad with a sense of steely resolve. 'It's bad luck and I want it gone.'

'But what about next year?' asked my mother, walking towards us. 'What will we do?'

'Something different,' declared my dad, defiant. 'Emma, get up. I need you to gather some sticks.'

It felt as if I'd been asked to gather diamonds: every stick was a means to our desired end. The tent was going to go up in flames and that would be the end of it. I would never have to sleep in it, sit in it or shit in it again. I ran round the garden with a wheelbarrow, ferreting under trees and breaking off dead branches, until it was full to bursting with dry, flammable material. Dad had broken up a few old planks he'd found in the garage and was making a pyre-like structure on a disused vegetable patch. I heaved the wheelbarrow over and tilted it upwards until the sticks and dead foliage I'd gathered tumbled out. Dad moved the lighter, driest stuff to the bottom so that it was packed under the tiered planks and made a platform with two other broken bits of wood for the tent to rest on. The tent, still in its blue canvas bag, was placed on top of the unlit bonfire. I was glad it was being destroyed. We had been dogged with ill fortune and disaster. Only a sacrifice would appease the Gods. The tent had to die. Dad, wanting to make sure it burnt, got a can of lighter fluid and tipped the whole lot over it until the air was filled with fumes. 'Right,' he said, pulling out a box of matches from his pocket. 'That should do it.'

'Are you sure about this?' piped up my mother, standing behind me with her arms folded.

My dad looked back at her over his shoulder. 'I have never been more sure of anything in my life,' he said and, with that, he lit the match and threw it on to the bonfire.

There was an instant explosion of blue and orange as the lighter fluid sucked up the flame and boomed upwards, engulfing the tent in fire. Smoke funnelled into the air, black and vicious, while wood spat and crackled with the shock. As I watched the fire take hold of the tent, its surface blackened from the off, I felt a release as if we had finally managed to step off an interminable treadmill. The three of us stood and watched in silence as the bonfire settled into a slow burn, flames licking up, embers spitting against the darkening sky. And then I remembered. 'Wait!' I shouted. 'We've forgotten something!'

I ran off to the garage. I knew what I had to do. It was in there somewhere and I was determined to find it and bring it to justice. 'There you are,' I hissed, discovering it behind some gardening tools. 'You're coming with me.' I picked it up, triumphant. I was moments from redemption.

'The bucket!' I yelled, clattering back, with the pink, plastic devil tucked under my arm. 'We've got to burn the bucket!'

With one toss, the bucket rotated high into the air and then fell, landing squarely on top of the blazing tent. The destruction was immediate. The bucket, overwhelmed by heat and flames, imploded, contorted plastic shapes collapsing in on themselves until solid form gave way to liquid. The bucket was gone.

'That was good,' said my dad, impressed. We all nodded. A terrible burden had been lifted. We were never going to go camping again. The tent poles would be used to grow peas, the ground sheet cut up to cover the compost. It was as if we'd been tethered to a pole, forced to go round in circles, but now found ourselves free.

'Next year,' I said, as we all walked back up the garden, 'can I bring a friend on holiday?'

'If you want,' said my mother, putting an arm about my shoulders. 'Mind you,' she added, looking back at the still burning tent, 'what are we going to do now?'

'Anything we want,' said my dad. And do you know what? I believed him.

Acknowledgements

There are, of course, a host of people without whom this book would have been impossible: Jake Lingwood, my lovely editor at Ebury, who has been a sparkly-eyed joy from start to finish; my agent, the graceful Camilla Hornby, whom I am so lucky to have it's verging on the ridiculous; Alison Macaulay, without whom the French bits would have been entirely wrong; and my friends, who all helped in tiny, imperceptible ways, but special mention must go to Perks and Kate, who let me write at their farm in Cornwall, and to the Fizzbomb, whose afternoon email sessions kept me amused whenever I was stuck on a sentence. But the greatest thanks must be reserved for my parents, Brenda and Tony, who are the beginning, the middle and the end of what you have just read. Without them, there would be nothing.